GATE OF REBIRTH

GATE OF REBIRTH

ASTROLOGY REGENERATION AND 8TH HOUSE MYSTERIES

Haydn Paul

SAMUEL WEISER, INC.

York Beach, Maine

First published in 1993 by
Samuel Weiser, Inc.
Box 612
York Beach, ME 03910

Library of Congress Cataloging-in-Publication Data

Paul, Haydn.
    Gate of rebirth: astrology, regeneration, and 8th house
mysteries / by Haydn Paul.
        p. cm.
    1. Eighth house (Astrology) 2. Astrology and psychology.
    I. Title.
    BF1716.28.P38   1993
    133.5'3—dc20   92-45557
                                                        CIP
ISBN 0-87728-761-9
EB

Cover art copyright © 1993 Chamnan. Used by kind permission from the Visual Dhamma Gallery, Bangkok, Thailand.

Typeset in 11 point Palatino

Printed in the United States of America.

The paper used in this publication meets the minimum
requirements of the American National Standard for Perma-
nence of Paper for Printed Library Materials Z39.48-1984.

Contents

To Alan Moore, in appreciation of a renewed creative and inspirational friendship. May the power of your imaginative storytelling never fade. And to all other members of the Fellowship of Scorpio, let those eagle wings soar!

"The important thing is not to stop questioning. Curiosity has its own reason for existing. One cannot help but be in awe when he contemplates the mysteries of eternity, of life, of the marvelous structure of reality. It is enough if one tries merely to comprehend a little of this mystery every day. Never lose a holy curiosity."

—Albert Einstein

1 The Underworld of the 8th House

LEGENDS TELL OF HIDDEN treasures and riches lying beneath the surface in the underworld's dark caves, protected by guardian dragons and monsters, and sought for by heroes, gods, and saviors. After great adventures, trials and tribulations, these mythic figures return with secrets of regeneration, renewal, and rebirth to reveal to the world. Yet how many recognize that we can emulate their journey by an astrological inner exploration that parallels mythic and archetypal paths, and in which we become the hero or heroine intent on stealing away the mystery from its dark guardians?

The 8th house of the horoscope has traditionally been described as the house of sex, death, regeneration, occultism, secrets, crisis, or emotional and sexual union, and is associated with the sign Scorpio and the planet Pluto as overshadowing rulers and prime influences on this sphere of human experience. These can be terse labels to ascribe to this specific house, but many of the 8th house mysteries still remain unfocused and unexplored in respect to their implications for individual and social transformation.

Despite the fact that all astrologers use the natal chart and the 8th house when interpreting planetary influence, there remain profound depths that have evaded greater insight and understanding and which are often superficially considered without sufficient awareness of how 8th house influences operate within the psyche and personality. The consequence is that this house becomes one of the least understood of the twelve houses. A concentrated investigation reveals the significance of this transformative gateway because it symbolizes several

important issues of existence. By willingly submitting ourselves to the 8th house adventure, we can contact regenerative possibilities that society and individuals need for
evolutionary growth; especially as we are now poised at the
brink of a new millennium and the prophesied Age of
Aquarius, where the realization of interdependence is crucial
for planetary survival.

The Gate of Rebirth explores the major themes of the 8th
house, perceiving this sphere of the natal chart as a gate, a door-
way, or a passage to enter the Underworld existing within the
individual and collective psyche. Through this house, we
can pass beyond the gate to investigate a personal underworld
and encounter the domain of Pluto-Hades, a realm of shifting shadows, darkness, and unconscious depths, where we
may fall victim to fearful avoidance of our unredeemed and
disowned self. It is here that the hidden treasure of rebirth can
be found by those courageous enough to seek the veiled
spiritual mystery.

Emanations from the 8th house awaken us to recognize
that something other than our separate self influences and shapes
our experiences, development, and destiny. We can observe
a need to expand by identifying with something greater than
the singular, limited self; this is the root impulse inspiring religion, nationality, politics, and society as the extension of human
relationship slowly brings civilizational and cultural progress.
Individually, we develop by discovering and asserting our separate identity, exploiting personal talents and resources, learning effective communication with others, building upon
family lineage and collective heritage, displaying procre-
ative and creative gifts, taking our place in socially productive work, and acknowledging our need for adult partnerships.

All these maturation stages reflect the first seven houses
in the horoscope, indicating a growing self-awareness and interaction with others. Then comes the 8th house crisis prior
to opening into a higher level of consciousness, insight, and
human activity as suggested by the 9th through the 12th

houses, which incorporate the god image, the aspirational and meaningful life, the creatively beneficial social influence, the social conscience of group awareness, self-transcendence, or the sacrificial life for collective healing.

The issues of the 8th house cannot be avoided by anyone engaged in self-development paths and spiritual searches, for progress in this area of life can be tainted by repression, which results in an imbalanced personality. This in turn causes distorted perceptions and often the individual unconsciously projects various rejected and disowned aspects of self.

Historically, the unease that many religious teachings display toward human sexuality, feminine energies, and a preoccupation with constructing compensatory fantasies of a heavenly paradise for believers, or threats of hell and karmic retribution, are symptomatic of an unintegrated 8th house. There are many examples of reputed Christian saints and yogic ascetics who repress sexuality, practice physical flagellation or distorting static body postures, imposing an often uncomfortable and unnatural celibacy on themselves by believing that this somehow makes them pure and holy. Their psychological stress and body-rejection spills out into imagining Satan's seductive succubae and the temptations of sexual fantasies, or into vicious diatribes portraying the vile torments and tortures awaiting nonbelievers in eternal hellfire and damnation.

Unfortunately, sexuality remains a controversial subject in Western cultures, and still teeters precariously on the razor-edge of taboo and acceptability; indeed, sexual content in the mass-media often provokes greater condemnation and attention than do real obscenities in the world—wars, genocide, unnecessary starvation, eradicable diseases and abuses of human rights. Our collective priorities and values are distorted, and this is derived from a collective failure to comprehend the mystery guarded by the 8th gate.

The 8th house is often described as the battlefield of physical and emotional crises prior to reaching various turn-

ing points in life, and it is interesting to note that after the traumatic anguish of World War II, a new phase of social upheaval
commenced in the late 1950s. Emerging from the post-war decade
of peace and reconstruction came an energy of Dionysian rebirth in the West—the formation of a youth culture and more
liberated attitudes challenged the stagnant conservatism that
still dominated society, seeking to dispel and dismantle
restrictive cultural structures.

The birth of rock n'roll and the assertive voice of idealistic and hedonistic youth generated worldwide repercussions
as the emphasis in the 1960's on utopianism, sex, drugs, and
rock music posed difficult moral and political questions, and
the appeal of glamorous Eastern religions attracted the attention
of many who were unimpressed with familiar Christian
rigidity. Many felt enlivened and empowered by the mixture
of Dionysiac and Orphic elements and the hippie and alternative counterculture movement began to proliferate, offering an intoxicating vision of exciting personal liberation and
freedom. Timothy Leary's high priest message of "Turn on,
Tune in, Drop Out" had resonance even beyond those experimenting with psychedelic drugs, as a need for social regeneration started to become increasingly apparent.

This period saw the explosion of major 8th house issues
in a social awareness that could no longer be ignored, evaded,
or repressed; issues that were inexorably rising from the unconscious. The less conditioned young were the first to feel
the liberating effects, welcoming the prospect of sexual discovery, lifestyle experimentation, and the new mental worlds
promised by the stimulation of cannabis, marijuana, and
LSD. Parallel to this, came increasing demands for self-autonomy
and civil rights, as individuals grouped together to assert political
empowerment against perceptions of dehumanizing gov-
ernments. The battlefield included the need for greater self-
understanding and freedom, so people could realize how
the interaction between self and society operated, and how
contemporary society could regenerate and reshape itself by
mastery through crisis.

Government exploitation of "power over" citizens was questioned and challenged in the 1960s. Civil rights and liberation movements multiplied, and the independence of both nations and individuals to choose their own destiny clashed with the power blocs of the established status quo. Radicalism faced conservatism as the relationship between self and society was examined and redefined.

As traditional social certainties broke down, new pressure groups emerged as representatives of a collective shift, voicing the needs and demands of those willing to take a new look at previously evaded important spheres of human life. Feminism and the international women's movement evoked a latent assertive power skeptical of male domination rights, and insisted on the necessity of social transformation to change patriarchal attitudes and cultural supremacy. The embryonic ecology movement cast a doubtful eye on the value of unrestrained economic exploitation and the visible results of technological impact polluting the environment, with a consequent danger to the survival of natural habitat and animal and plant life species; a message that is now receiving worldwide attention, support and approval, although only a decade ago green supporters were still suspiciously dismissed as cranks. A revival of new spirituality spoke to people desperately in search of life meaning and purpose; imported Eastern mysticism initially assuaged this thirst, which eventually combined with the insights of psychoanalysis, self-help therapeutic techniques, the restoration of older Western occult and mystical paths (magic, Qabalah, alchemy, and spiritualism). This search led to the broad church of the New Age and the human potential movement. Through this channel ventured the resurgence of contemporary astrology and a psychological perspective devoted to holistic integration.

With these positive contributions to society came a darker side as repressed collective tendencies also found release. The nature of city environment and individual personality caused polarized responses to the Dionysian tune; either a gift of liberation or a degenerate descent were the most apparent options. The rush of new life was too heady a mixture for many whose own nature proved ill-prepared to deal with "the madness of freedom." Drugs were transformed from an initially liberating high into a deadly and dangerous low, as physically addictive drugs such as cocaine, heroin, and crack replaced the sensual stimulants on the streets, and drug abuse became socially endemic, warping and destroying many unsuspecting and innocent lives—especially those from the underside of society and the disadvantaged ethnic minorities.

Pornography ran rampant, visually exposing aspects of human sexuality—which had previously been private or taboo—with an explicit glee and provocative intent; most of this degraded and exploited women and devalued sexuality by fermenting lustful obsession, and in some cases became the trigger for sexually violent offenses. Sexuality broke free from the bedroom and was openly displayed in society, proving liberating to some who accepted their sexual preferences, while threatening many more who were unable to integrate their sexual nature and those who retained older, cultural attitudes and morals. Some found the newly discovered sexual demands and appetites disturbing, feeling pressured to conform to performance expectations. Some developed an insecure and inferior body-image, with beliefs of inadequacy. There were constant references to an insatiable need for effective diets and cosmetic body-surgery.

Homosexuality came out into the open, even though it was present in all societies for centuries, and a common—if minority—human sexual inclination. Gay Rights groups formed for mutual protection and fellowship, and society was faced with a conflict between minority assertions of alternative sexual preferences and prevalent homophobia and disregard for human rights, revealed by those who felt threatened by homosexual political activity, books, films, and photographs. And then the specter of AIDs appeared, a disease often transmitted by certain sexual practices. For many, this provided an opportunity to reinforce existing social disapproval and condemnation of the consequences of homosexuality, promiscuity and liberated sexuality, despite the fact that contracting AIDs is not exclusive to either homosexuality or promiscuity, and can also be transmitted through contaminated blood or needle drug use. The problem of AIDs is like an ironic postscript from the gods, suggesting that another look at sexuality is still needed.

Death still remains a preeminent social taboo zone, where the mention of serious ill-health, or the death of a friend or family member is guaranteed to stop conversation and make everyone feel uncomfortable, as if reminded of something that should be ignored as long as possible or kept at a distance in case it is contagious. Yet there is a noticeable collective transformation occurring in regard to the value of human life. Previously, human life has been fairly expendable, recognizing that old age and the inevitability of natural disasters, war, disease, and starvation is a continual culling of a population. Different attitudes to human death are now appearing, partly due to the medical ability to prolong health by treating disease, and the ability to direct international aid to countries whose population suffers from famine, thus saving many lives that otherwise would have been prematurely lost. This growth in world compassion and a publicly driven demand that aid be given—such as helping the Kurdish people trapped in the mountains of Iraq, or the starving Ethiopians, or earthquake victims—displays an intensifying awareness of others and a dawning sense of world responsibility to diminish unnecessary pain.

Human life is currently being revalued, and the potency of television's global eye is important to the unfolding compassionate spirit, which emerges as an 8th house awareness of the crucial relationship between self and other. The growth of hospices and death education, such as the work pioneered by Dr. Elisabeth Kübler-Ross, shows a need for a dignified ending to life, and a realization of its implications to how we live now. An alternative reaction is cryogenics—the long-term freezing of dead individuals hoping for a later rebirth and resurrection by future medical advances. But old age and the obvious encroachment of impending death remains an uneasy taboo subject that most prefer to avoid, and in our consumer-dominated culture, those on pensions with less money and less need are often marginalized and socially disempowered.

Contemporary music has become a channel for greater awareness, especially for the young, through lyrics expressing political and ecological concerns. We now see a greater artistic honesty and depth that exposes a broader range of emotional experience and insight which is valuable to many seeking solace by musical identification. The rhythmic power of music crosses international boundaries and transforms attitudes and values. Modern concerts can become a substitute for a collective ritualized rite, with rock and pop stars serving as icons and semi-divine hero-figures. The Dionysiac and Orphic revival still continues and its echoes can deify stars as legends in their own lifetimes. Or deaths—as in the case of the tragic Jim Morrison—who was consumed by his Dionysiac license and inebriation, rent apart by inner demons and his personal and public expectations of the role he was to perform. Many are fascinated by tormented, creative, and famous personalities—such as Morrison, Lennon, Monroe, Van Gogh—attracted by a vicarious thrill to their lust for life intensity, yet secretly glad they are not driven like that.

Somehow, humanity has opened the 8th house Pandora's box, perhaps through a hesitant recognition that for genuine advances to be made these issues need to be encountered and reconciled for individual and planetary health. Perhaps our evolutionary timekeepers have decided that the time has come to leave our adolescence and approach maturity; unless we discover how to deal with the unconscious demons we have unleashed, we may be consumed by our ignorance, and even the Phoenix may struggle to rise again from the ashes of planetary pollution, or nuclear, chemical, and biological war with which we threaten our existence.

We may be an experiment in consciousness, tested to determine the suitability of our species for a more universal awareness; created to experience the cyclic process of involution-evolution through the interplay of spirit and matter. We descend into form and slowly struggle to ascend and return to spirit, striving to embody the innate peak and ideal level of consciousness that the encoded human program can attain. Now, our test is about the attitudes we collectively hold regarding the primal forces of life, and how we integrate these and shape our society, civilization and culture. How this is collectively answered and demonstrated reveals our ability for regeneration and offers a transformation of universal perception and identification.

The Regenerative Force of the 8th House

The underlying purpose of the 8th house is to provide the opportunity to expand limitations by a process of identification, primarily through relationships and social interaction. We can no longer afford the luxury of a self-centered perspective that is isolated from the needs of the whole. By expanding our worldview as a result of social participation, and by identifying our connection and responsibility to the collective, the option emerges for an individual-social exchange, transmuting and regenerating vital primal energies. Until we can achieve a healthier understanding of 8th house issues, key spheres of society will remain distorted and limited.

This central encounter is with the life-principles and energies symbolized by Pluto and Scorpio, wielders of the innate regenerative force in our reality. Many find it difficult to handle these powerful psychic energies, either as the "incurable wound" that resists healing, or by self-injury through abrasive relationships, inner conflicts, and frustrations. Yet, these can also assist our development by presenting a liberating force that subverts and breaks down personal and social obstacles that inhibit growth. Pluto's natal position is a major area requiring transformation, and as Pluto and Scorpio overshadow the 8th house, this also becomes a collective gateway to potential regeneration. Outworn old forms, psychological patterns and lifestyles are destroyed by Pluto's erosive force, prior to enabling freed energy to restore opportunities. This process is often experienced as life crises and turning points, where options are presented to alter our destiny by choice and decision, and normally occurs after a period of searching for release from increased frustration and stress.

Feelings of psychological discomfort, pressure, and a fear of everything collapsing often accompany Pluto's activity, perhaps marked by progressions, transiting aspects or movement into a new house. An intuition of impending, irresistible change and the "death" of something important and valued hovers disturbingly at the edge of awareness. Many feel instinctively threatened by what is subtly occurring, preferring to resist and reject rather than submit to the inevitable. Radical changes in a valued sphere of life pervades the whole inner life, as if decay and death is experienced on every level. Anguish, anger, doubt, grief, despair, rage, feelings of losing power and helplessness can all combine to deepen the sensation of darkness, doom, and depression. An apprehension of loss as a spark of life is extinguished, a fear that nothing will ever change or improve extends pain, frustration, confusion, and loss of direction and confidence. Life turns a more harsh face as conflict resists the unfairness of existence. God changes into the Devil, laughing at our struggle, and we may realize that we have created an imbalanced picture of light, failing to conceive and include an ambiguous Janus-faced deity.

Yet as darkness slowly fills us from within, obscuring our clarity, faith, and direction, we can register the nature of the opportunity that is being offered. For something new to be born within us something has to die, or be removed, and Pluto only demands the sacrifice of what we have outgrown, exchanging regenerative potential for the transaction. Our apparent loss becomes our gain; and if we are wise, we realize that the process of relinquishment is a bargain and for our benefit.

Pluto is falsely vilified and defamed by those who require greater insight. We are only able to cooperate with Pluto and Scorpio energies when we trust our fate and destiny; then the reversal occurs, and the Devil is transformed into the light-bearing God. Our denial of life's renewal process brings pain, while the acceptance of change brings meaningful regeneration. Discounting Pluto's presence in the chart or ignoring the influence of the 8th house is futile and foolish. Rightly approached, Pluto becomes a generous friend, revealing inner treasures, potential, and resources that may have previously remained latent. Instead of the bitter fruit that was tasted during the inner descent, the returning ascent is sweet-tasting, laden with gifts and an expanded, integrated perspective that renews life and instills purpose, meaning, and direction. Encountering Pluto is like a touch of the Self, dying to the old and being revitalized as the new—becoming one of the twice-born.

It is worth noting that the 8th house is 150 degrees from the first house, a quincunx aspect, implying that what can regenerate the separate self may be discovered in the 8th house. Part of the quincunx influence is to clarify the divisive concepts of self and others by indicating the existence of universal relationship, and this is the 8th house's focal issue. The quincunx suggests the potential therapeutic rebirth through the mystery of inner and outer relationship. By exploring the 8th house, we may discover how to be self-regenerative and use these potent energies with consciousness, purpose, and productivity.

Through regeneration we become invested with an enlivening spiritual power enhancing integrity, autonomy, and capacity to revitalize wonder and appreciation of existence. The universe is seen as overflowing with invigorating light, consciousness and life, and any separative illusory barriers disperse with insight. We are renewed and redirected toward our original state of being; we are reborn again with a new vision. These may appear enigmatic and mystical statements, but such are the effects of tasting the fruit which grows in the dark underworld and whose healing nature is sought for by religion and all on quests of self-exploration.

ASTROLOGY AND THE 8TH HOUSE JOURNEY

The value of modern astrology is the emphasis on self-awareness, becoming conscious of our inner psyche and the quality of interaction with the outer world, so that conflicts are diminished and fulfillment increased. This requires effort to refine and understand those directing psychic patterns that influence physical, emotional, mental, and spiritual actions, desires, and needs. Through evocative symbolic imagery, astrology attempts to examine and interpret the interplay of innate universal relationship, summarized by the Hermetic axiom, "As above, so below."

Astrology uses various techniques to mirror the hidden psyche. The initial intellectual natal analysis can be augmented by a higher intuitional reperception, where the synthesized importance of the whole being supersedes personality parts and provides a growing realization of life's unity. Emerging from this are paths to self-realization, transformation, and actualization that satisfy the impulse to "become oneself," informed by an astrological vision that requires holistic thinking for a more creative interpretation of the chart.

The approach of holistic astrology is that while personality parts and specific chart factors can be initially isolated (planets, houses, aspects, elements, etc.), for deeper investigation, the intention is that each of these can lead the inquirer toward the personal holistic center or Self.

As the variety of astrological reflections indicate, personality is extremely complex and each level of expression exists within a psychic matrix of mutual reciprocity, influence, and interaction. While various subpersonalities (different planets) may tend to act independently or convey contradictory messages, the individual task is to integrate these into a coherent whole so that inner cooperative harmony rules. This becomes the essence of the spiritual path, the aim of Jung's *individuation* or Assagioli's *psychosynthesis*, where the parts are adjusted, and molded by a new internal pattern of holistic order.

The role of the transpersonal astrologer is to assist this process by providing an interpretation that identifies probable fragmented and unintegrated personality aspects, while also indicating possible routes toward holistic self-understanding, healing, and reintegration. The astrologer can highlight areas of the psyche which may be repressed, disowned, or imbalanced , in addition to indicating latent resources, talents, and potentials that can form a meaningful life direction; the astrologer can help to empower others into taking a more creative role in shaping their future.

The 8th house journey passes through the gate of rebirth, emphasizing the need for both astrologer and client to recognize the pivotal, redemptive experience offered by this psychological descent into the unconscious. This journey can become a conscious, transformative awakening, healing by a participatory rite of passage of the fundamental cyclic pattern of life-death-rebirth. This may not be an easy passage, as this gate offers only mastery through crisis whenever periodic individual and collective pressures accumulate within the unconscious and demand release. The question is whether this can be achieved with constructive creativity or with explosive destruction?

The reward for success is higher consciousness even when inner struggle and traumatic experiences may be met. Initially this does not appear a journey to the light, and instead leads us into realms of our hidden self that many prefer to ignore or evade those areas of obsession, compulsion, repression, and selfishness that comprise our Shadow-Self and Dark-Side. The cost of entrance is facing personal and social taboos, releasing rigidity and conformist or conventional boundaries that restrict freedom and awareness. We experience inner demons only to eventually recognize that by holistic recognition and acceptance, they are transformed into guiding and inspiring angels at our journey's culmination.

Examining how this can be achieved and installing a few signposts along the way is the intent of *The Gate of Rebirth*, by focusing attention on the elusive and intrinsic mysteries guarded by this house and asking how we can reclaim our personal power, become regenerated and live from an understanding of universal relationship.

This passage takes us down into the Earth's womb to explore the individual and collective unconscious psyche, creatively responding to a fate that operates as an inner director who demands obedience. Rejecting these hints tends to introduce pain and frustration as obstacles inexplicably prevent fulfilling aims and desires. By shifting our reactions and surrendering to inevitability and necessity, we can open a new direction, and relate to an unfolding purpose that fate wishes us to reveal. Collaborating with our fate is possible when we are willing to accept this indicated path, sensing a deep meaningful resonance within our being.

It is a strange way; part of us says "yes" and part says "no." As Jung observed, the unconscious operates in an ambivalent and paradoxical manner, where one tendency strives to become conscious—to break free from bondage—and another remains repressive and cautious, stirring fears and whispered threats whenever we stand at boundary-lines and consider whether to cross beyond normal limits and barriers. Yet if we avoid the psyche's needs and remain trapped by our fears, the repressed energy retaliates by taking possession through compulsive or obsessive traits, those self-consuming mental-emotional inner voices demanding repetitive actions, seeking to direct us into certain experiences which ensure that we eventually pay attention to their message.

One point worth remembering is that while Pluto-Hades is the nominal Lord of the Underworld, especially established in the patriarchal cultures of Greece and Rome, more ancient wisdom associates the Great Place Below as the domain of the Dark Mother, the chthonic Earth Mother, the Serpent Mother, the Goddess and Feminine principle. Pluto represents this universal power, as a son, servant, executor, and symbol of the hidden, life-bearing goddess-womb. Earlier Goddess images from matriarchal cultures emphasized a self-fertilizing deity, a phallic Mother who receded deeper into her own depths and dark mysteries, leaving her phallic potency to be invested in her God-son. The seed of rebirth can only be discovered and reclaimed from within the womb of our psyche, hidden from sight.

We enter the Great Place Below via caves, fissures, and the mouths of volcanoes that symbolize the eruptive emergence of unconscious energies through psychological splits and conflicts. When we wait to cross the River Styx, Charon, the ferryman for the dead, demands a coin in exchange, signifying the need to relinquish all accumulated possessions no longer needed. Until this transaction is made, there is no further progress. Only the souls of the dead can pass Charon's scrutiny, either those leaving physical form, or those seekers enduring death during life and brave enough to search for renewal and answers.

The Underworld quest is one which Joseph Campbell described as a monomyth, those heroic adventures so prevalent in world mythology and legends. One key myth is the Sumerian tale of Ereshkigal, the Lady of the Great Place Below, and Inanna, the Queen of Heaven. Inanna descended into Ereshkigal's world, and was "brought naked and bowed low" according to the accepted laws and initiatory rites for all those wishing to enter the secret kingdom. Inanna's fine clothing and regalia, the signs of her power and status, were ritually stripped away as she progressed gradually losing her dignity, pride, identity, and certainties in deference to her accepted surrender to something greater than herself. This divestment was enacted at each of the Seven Gates to the Underworld where sat Ereshkigal at the center of her Mystery, attended by her servants, the Fates.

The Mystery of the 8th house concerns the reconciliation of self and others. Misunderstanding this relationship has caused

Western and Eastern dissociation and divisive tendencies within individuals, creating similar—if greater—social difficulties. The 8th house Mystery refutes the gnostic and Eastern belief that freedom from the wheel of rebirth and karmic bondage can be found by separative techniques. When mind and spirit are deliberately divorced from physical instincts and emotional needs, this results in the fallacious splitting of spirit and form, with inevitable dualistic concepts of higher and lower natures that have characterized the structure of human thinking that was historically influenced by exclusive Platonic, Christian and ascetic self-denying attitudes. The intrinsic presence of these conditioning attitudes and worldviews in our culture means that even holistic perspectives have to be communicated in dualistic language.

The 8th house becomes the battlefield of dualism and unity, fought between self and other across various types of relationship. Learning how to move beyond the dualistic mind to the unified mind is the gift of this journey, and this involves the renewal of individual reality, as self dissolves into the other and the other dissolves into the self. The purpose of our difficult endeavors is to realize a unified conception of the Self as a totality, a wholeness that included and integrated both the apparent opposites of "light and darkness," which the Eastern symbol of Tao and the interacting yin and yang represents as the way of wisdom. Joseph Campbell states in *Hero With a Thousand Faces*: "The two—hero and his ultimate god, the seeker and the found—are thus understood as the outside and inside of a single self-mirrored mystery, which is identical with the mystery of the manifest world. The great deed of the supreme hero is to come to the knowledge of this unity in multiplicity and then to make it known."[1]

Quite simply, this is the adventure that the 8th house invites us to join, and waits to open the gate for our passage. From the conflict of the unresolved two to the unity of the one is

[1] Joseph Campbell, *Hero with a Thousand Faces* (Princeton, NJ: Princeton University Press, 1990; London: Paladin, 1988), p. 40.

our journey. And as Inanna experienced descending toward Ereshkigal's mystery, we, too, can follow in her footsteps as each of the following chapters can introduce us to one aspect of this teaching until, mission completed, we may return reborn as the wounded healer to serve all.

8TH HOUSE ASTROLOGY

On the wheel of life, the first six houses are concerned with innate individuality and actualizing potential during life. The upper hemisphere houses (7th to 12th) are more concerned with the quality of individual and social interaction, the experience of relationship that so characterizes human existence. Separate individuality has to come to terms with communal living by discovering how to create satisfying intimate partnerships, productive and purposeful relationships, and contribute to collective progress. These requirements are not easily met, and our failure to comprehend properly the nature of personal and planetary relationships has consequences in increased individual and social suffering.

The upper hemisphere houses focus on issues of relationship, social participation, and ideologies which interpret and order reality; through these involvements we can participate in producing personal and social change. These changes are stimulated by varied self-other interactions with groups, partners, ideals, and ideologies being important. Our experiences of contacting such collective expressions can be profound—transforming our worldviews, self-images, future life-direction and generating new social innovation. For instance, falling in love and having an adult relationship is one major crisis-point; discovering spiritual teachings, new age visions and the human potential movement is equally crucial for many. Both are crises which can redefine individuality and relatedness at a conjunction of inner and outer realities.

Through the presence of the "other" we are inexorably drawn into the collective life, where potential can be released by social participation, marriage, and family life. The shift from self-centeredness to awareness of the equal value of others is a lesson requiring understanding; maturity arises when this relationship is grasped and applied in daily life. This changing emphasis reflects the biblical allusion to loving your neighbor as yourself and being your brother's keeper, and we see signs of this recognition dawning in humanity as the fact of the world family becomes increasingly apparent, and individual compassion extends in a concept of shared global responsibility.

Dane Rudhyar comments that "the eighth house is a very important house, but one that is hard to interpret in an individual chart."[2] This is because its realm of influence spans unconscious and conscious levels and is an interface between individual and collective; it is this relatedness which is explored, and this is continually shifting in each person and society.

The 8th house represents universal change, renewal, and regeneration, a source for potential rebirth that ensures that any stagnation is only temporary. In the natural zodiac, this corresponds to Pluto and Scorpio, "one of the least understood signs of the zodiac and the most unintelligently maligned,"[3] states Rudhyar in *The Astrological Houses*. In the solar year's nature cycle, Scorpio stands at mid-autumn, the gate to winter. Vegetation and fruiting abundance has declined, reaching a cyclic disintegration and death prior to new seeds entering the earth's dark womb, to await spring renewal.

As a correspondence to this 8th house regenerative quality, Gnostic Christianity assigns the symbolic number of 888 to Christ, indicating essential beliefs centered on the mystery of crucifixion and resurrection. Each eight represents a level of rebirth; the instincts and sensory feelings (biological-physical-emotional), the intellectual mind, and the spiritual level, known as the the triple death and rebirth process of spiritual

---

[2] Dane Rudhyar, *The Astrological Houses* (New York: Doubleday, 1972), p. 110.
[3] Dane Rudhyar, *The Astrological Houses* (New York: Doubleday, 1972), p. 105.

liberation. This is the *Gate of Rebirth* theme approached from various perspectives. The 8th house gift is self-knowledge, acquired through the regenerative journey, and this awakens us to the fact of universal relationship.

Rudhyar provides an incisive perception of the 8th house's importance: "It is in terms of eighth house types of experience that a person has to make perhaps his or her deepest and most vital choices. These choices will affect not only the individual but society as a whole. In that sense, the Existential philosophers are right in saying that every man is responsible for the whole of mankind."[4] Attempting to investigate this challenging statement is this book's ambition. This is not an exhaustive or definitive effort; such complex issues cannot be compressed so easily, but it is offered as an aid to stimulate greater attention and thought to a house whose depths are so often avoided.

8TH HOUSE PLANETS

The 8th house is a meeting place of "I and Thou," "Us and We," and focuses on individual interaction with others, both as an intimate one-to-one experience and extended to include humanity, the world and the universe. An 8th house planet indicates that a particular planetary principle, function, and activity can be most effectively manifested in terms of 8th house issues. This planet (or planets) will represent key psychological needs, desires, and actions that are both self-assertive and self-revealing. By evaluating an 8th house planet, we may gain insight into specific areas of our potential, direction, and life-lessons, discovering how we may be self-limiting or how purpose can be gained. The planet asks us to inquire about what is happening as a consequence of personality tendencies, and the 8th house reveals where these tendencies are expressed and what results are probably experienced in daily life.

---

[4] Dane Rudhyar, *The Astrological Houses*, p. 110.

Each planetary nature suggests a predisposition to interpret 8th house issues in a particular way; the planetary principle biases our needs so we may experience only what we expect to find, for reality is shaped and reflected by our creative unconscious mind and primary attitudes. If we accept this worldview of a "self-created universe," then responsibility is highlighted, and attention needs to be directed toward redefining formative attitudes, values, and beliefs. Creative power is returned to us by how we interpret experiences, choosing whether these are seen as either positive or negative. Positive values can be found in whatever experience life presents to us; our reactions determine how we handle these. For instance, Viktor Frankl's incarceration in a Jewish concentration camp was obviously extremely painful and harrowing, a shock to any faith in human goodness. Yet out of this came *Man's Search for Meaning,*[5] an affirmation of man's ability to discover an uplifting deeper meaning in the midst of any experience, and a sharing that has proven inspirational to many readers.

There can be a natural attractive preoccupation to the planetary principle that dominates the 8th house; this can operate almost compulsively and obsessively, or be a major factor within relationships. The impulse to act in certain ways or to satisfy certain needs should be easy to recognize, although becoming more aware of how this planetary presence creatively influences perceptions of 8th house issues can be very beneficial. This planet may form a filter or veil that colors a worldview; greater planetary insight into how this indicates psychological traits may suggest alternative options of expression and direction that previously were unavailable.

In astrological attempts to uncover individual life-plans, we have to ask: what purpose does this 8th house planet suggest? What meaning does it convey? What direction does it indicate? How can this planet serve us more effectively? How

---

[5] Viktor Frankel, *Man's Search for Meaning* (New York: Pocket Books, 1984; London: Hodder, 1987).

can we integrate this principle into our consciousness, and learn how to use it as a cohesive, transforming and motivating impulse? How can we constructively manifest its power and potential? How does this energy operate in our psyche and society? What role does it play in our destiny? How does this planet shape our experience and reality? What lesson, challenge or opportunity does this planet offer us? Do we cooperate with this planet's nature or do we resist its promptings and messages? Does this planet act positively or negatively in our lives? These are questions that can be directed at any planet in any house; through such a process, self-understanding and astrological insight is increased in proportion to the effort made.

If the 8th house has several planets, distinguishing between planetary principles and "voices" becomes more complex, often appearing as a combination of contradictory messages, demands, needs, and impulses. Psychological stress may be intensified and 8th house issues may assume a significant overshadowing of individual concerns. If these planets remain unconscious, then any compulsive and obsessive behavior has stronger roots. For inner health and balance, insight into these planets is necessary through acceptance and integration of their messages.

Each planet requires some degree of deliberate transformation and renewal; it is rare for any individual to comprehend and positively express an 8th house planet without first experiencing the consequences of misapplication. For many, these planets remain problematic, a source of difficulty, a point of vulnerability or a seeping wound that evades easy healing. When many planetary voices are simultaneously raised, it is hard to distinguish separate needs; confusion and struggles between dissimilar needs dispels clarity. The initial step to cure this is to hear each planet's independent message prior to attempting to satisfy all at once.

If the 8th house is untenanted, these issues do not simply disappear, as they provide a context for an unavoidable experience of relationship. Lacking a focal planet to channel energies, the cuspal sign assumes greater importance and should be considered for insight. The planetary ruler of this sign and its house can be interpreted as connected to 8th house matters, as this may refer to the type of energies which are most needed to encounter successfully 8th house experiences. This lack of planetary representation may suggest a diminished individual emphasis with 8th house concerns, especially if another house is heavily tenanted, suggesting a higher priority with other life-lessons. However, another implication may be that these issues remain unconscious and that awareness should be directed to that sphere for greater integration. Moon's Nodes, Part of Fortune, focal point of a t-square or other planetary configurations may include an 8th house dimension, and should be additionally noted.

If planets are retrograde, then introspective activity is increased and given priority over external activity. Attention is redirected inward and the planet is experienced by the observant personality as reflective. The attraction toward the unconscious may be stronger, perhaps with a motivation to explore the psyche and evoke inner resources rather than be assertive in the world. Inhibitive barriers preventing self-expression can restrict outer impact, and a struggle to release potential is likely. Thought-loops may easily form around compulsive and obsessive tendencies, as repetitive mental patterns and emotional fixations circle in the unconscious and echo in the conscious mind.

Retrogrades may be used positively for an inner search, examining psychological processes and pursuing the labyrinthine thread into the self. Penetration into depth and insight is possible, and despite the complexity encountered, this journey may reveal new paths of individual potential that were previously closed.

Personal choice dictates whether retrogrades are experienced positively or negatively. If their constructive quality is energized then the planet can assist meditative practices, opening doors to profound depths and enabling a regenerative process to unfold inner strength, self-understanding, power, and extend universal relatedness. If their destructive quality predominates, then barriers are maintained, obstacles and blockages appear insuperable, and withdrawal tendencies prove inhibitive. Repressive evasion is likely and regressive thought-loops more common. Personal power is diminished while self-absorption dissipates connectedness. Social integration and partnership adjustment is also decreased.

Cuspal Signs

The 8th house cuspal sign indicates the type of experience, attitude, and activity that can most effectively channel personal potential through 8th house issues. The sign's level (symbolized by the element) and type of natural expression is the most suitable approach to explore these issues and gain self-knowledge. We find self-expression easier to achieve through these cuspal sign characteristics and particular context, as this sign symbolizes underlying motivations which determine our choices and action.

The twelve zodiac signs are twelve primary energy patterns, often considered as archetypes or universal formative principles which construct our reality. Astrology utilizes these as the twelve personality imprints, with each sign reflected by a worldwide group of individuals displaying those specific qualities through their lives and interacting with the other eleven sign-groups. Ancient wisdom termed the whole zodiac the soul of nature, and astrology has developed as a symbolic system to comprehend the microcosm-macrocosm relationship. Each sign symbolizes a specific type of universal and archetypal energy release which becomes an archetypal human type of experience and activity.

Dane Rudhyar considers the zodiac in terms of the biblical Holy City: "It *is* an abstraction and a symbol, just as the

Holy City with its twelve gates—in the Biblical allegory—is an abstraction and a symbol. The zodiac is the Wall that separates all inhabitants of the Earth-surface from the universe. Symbolically, this Wall has twelve gates, twelve signs of the zodiac, twelve channels through which universal energies flow."[6] Rudhyar also develops the concept of Four Portals, the midpoints of Taurus, Leo, Scorpio, and Aquarius, those fixed signs through which archetypal power is released. Scorpio, the natural ruler of the 8th house "represents the power released toward the formation of the universal being"[7] which implies a journey to integrate our whole nature.

The cuspal sign is generally considered more important than any other sign which bridges the 8th house. However, if the cuspal sign covers only a few degrees, then its influence may be diminished in terms of effect and resonance within the psyche. The other sign may then display greater personality relevance and activity, and assessing both signs may provide valuable indications of personality predisposition of the type of archetypal energies and qualities expected, and which will color their perceptions of reality and 8th house issues. Even contemplating the important characteristics of 8th house signs can be a useful exercise in understanding personal responses to this house and on which level they are most active and effective (element of signs). This is a simple procedure that can be applied to every house as a technique for insight, and can often be overlooked in a mass of astrological data.

The element of the 8th house sign suggests the level of primary response to the themes and energies of this gate. When two signs are prominent—the cuspal and another bridging the 8th house—both elemental responses can be observed, and

---

[6] Dane Rudhyar, *The Astrology of Personality* (Santa Fe, NM: Aurora Press, 1991), p. 250.

[7] Michael Meyer, *A Handbook for the Humanistic Astrologer* (New York: Anchor Press, Doubleday, 1974), p. 53.

these may stimulate either complementary or contradictory psychological pulls.

Earth can respond cautiously, almost resistant to changes, and tries to impose stability through concentrating on security needs. It is a physical reaction, with priority placed on practical application—how these issues can be manifested in life—and tends to favor the release of will and power in pursuit of tangible achievements.

Water responds with emotional yearnings stirred by unconscious needs, and can be highly sensitized and vulnerable due to empathic receptivity. Emotional reactions can either harness emotional power for self-assertion or form defensive barriers. Psychism and intuition is likely.

Air responds with intellect and mental activity, either as free thinking capable of detached objectivity and conceptual inquiry, or as thoughts manipulated by unconscious compulsions. Self-assertion comes through ideas, mental perception, and articulation. The main 8th house impact on air evokes mental interest, curiosity, and investigation of these themes.

Fire responds with enthusiasm to 8th house changes, welcoming the intensity and aspirational adventure that this house offers. Fire's optimism is to live more fully, and can see this gate's promise as an answer to beliefs and hopes, providing a purpose to pursue. However, the impulse to act before thinking may be detrimental to steady progress. Fire initially reacts the most enthusiastically to certain 8th house issues, especially those involving power and sexuality, yet can shrink from the implicit "death" and sharing of resources these indicate a decrease in personal pleasure.

A Water House

The 8th house is one of the water group (the trinity of soul) connected to the 4th and 12th houses. These correspond to a deeper level of emotions and feelings that may exist beneath conscious awareness, submerged in the unconscious mind, and often accumulated during the past. Childhood experiences and conditioning leave their mark on instincts and inbred responses, perhaps negatively by fears, damaged self-images, doubts, and unexpressed emotions. Sensitivity and openness to life are often shocked by the recognition of painful vulnerability, and various levels of armor are erected as a protective shield. Where issues of sexuality, death, and power over people are concerned, many wounds occur through these encounters.

The 8th house emotional experience includes moving beyond self-preoccupation by meeting the other; within that exchange is the comprehension that "hell is the other, heaven is the other." Individual feelings are awakened, provoked, and excited by relationship, and the cumulative effects of these responses increase from birth. Few reach maturity without needing some healing of this level, and few reach old age without enduring emotional stress. One essential 8th house message is the ongoing requirement for emotional regeneration, so that feelings can flow in inner and outer harmony and do not become rigidly locked through repression, as this is self-wounding and inhibits prospects of wholeness.

8TH HOUSE ASPECTS

Aspects between an 8th house planet and another in the chart highlight particular individual desires and motivations that have relevance to 8th house issues. Aspects relate two planetary principles together for the experience of the characteristics of those planets. Ideally these principles can cooperate, producing psychological harmony and positive results in life. Yet many aspects reveal a disparity of principles—the square or opposition—and demand effort to discover how these can effectively operate together instead of being abrasive and negative. For instance, a Mars-Saturn aspect implies the issue of controlled use of energies, and whether this is constructive or destructive depends on personal reactions to the type of aspect involved.

Aspects contribute to the weaving and structuring of the personality, connecting numerous tendencies into a coherent pattern, and indicating opportunities for self-expression. The challenging aspects of squares and oppositions may point out blocks and obstacles hindering ambition and progress. They can reveal where planetary and psychological principles are unintegrated, unconscious, or relatively inactive and unexploited. In these areas, growth can be attained through effort and self-searching, and the struggle with unreconciled planetary energies is often a stimulus for development, even if initially inspired by a need to diminish inner discomfort and frustration. Harmonious aspects—most conjunctions, sextiles, and trines—suggest motivations and potential that should be more easily manifested, and these aspects increase self-confidence and enthusiasm, alerting us to recognize opportunities for growth.

Conjunctions intensify planetary characteristics, striving to blend and merge two distinct energies. Both planets feel compelled to be pulled together, as if forced into a dynamic relationship and told that they have to work together. The conjunction produces a personal need to unite two principles so they function productively and harmoniously. Conjunctions reflect definite personality impulses, and often indicate a psychological blindspot due to their subjective intensity and lack of objectivity. The individual tends to closely identify with the conjunction's planets, and the need to synthesize these forces may enhance planetary cohesion or pose difficulties in reconciling conflicting functions, such as a Jupiter-Saturn conjunction.

Sextiles emphasize the potential application of mind, intelligence, and inventiveness. They act as catalysts for explorative curiosity, opening us to learning and education as a basis for external creative and productive activity. Sextiles have a mentally stimulating effect, and as they bridge different elements, they introduce complementary principles together. Effort may be needed to make full use of sextile potential, and some may fail to fully respond to the opportunities offered by life. Ideally we can activate our sextiles and insure that motivations are consciously pursued and not left passive and latent. Conscious use of sextiles can assist in resolving various personality challenges, as well as helping the expression of individual talents.

Trines signify potential creative and positive attitudes, where both planets coexist in relative peace and harmony, providing self-confidence, contentment, and pleasure. The trine is supportive and stabilizing, capable of absorbing and dealing with conflicts, operating as a stress-reducer. However, this relaxing effect can sink into passivity, and attention is necessary to activate the trine's creative function. Trines rarely initiate change; their potency emerges when we apply individual gifts or talents. Trines assist ease of expression; they can connect us to our inner life, especially those higher states where harmony, synthesis and imaginative creativity are found. Working with the trine's planetary principles can feel energizing or inspiring as they enable a higher attunement. We may also have "lazy trines"—a personality preference to avoid effort and struggle or to take the easy route—not living up to potential. Many people mismanage trines. Trines should be actively used as resources, but if they are not regularly expressed, then they may become inactive or nonproductive.

Squares suggest the presence of internalized stress between the two planets involved in the square aspect. They are often experienced as inner friction or psychological conflict related to the issues and principles of those particular planetary characteristics. Each planet involved has a tendency to obstruct and inhibit the others' intention and expression. The value of the square is to force us toward an inner transformation and resolution of unintegrated issues, mainly through the unavoidable inner discomfort that occurs, which is symbolized by the square's planets. The square demands our attention and requires that we reconcile imbalances and conflicting psychological traits. Clarifying these inner voices is essential, and working with squares can become an important source for personal growth.

Planets in opposition symbolize a psychological state where two different motivations or aims create inner confusion and a dissipation of energies. The two planets have different "intentions and needs", and both "speak with loud voices," demanding our commitment to their objectives to the exclusion of the other. A tension develops from the pulling apart of these two planets, and one consequence may be the favoring of one and the denial of the other. A new balance needs to be established between these planetary principles; we need to discover how to equally integrate and respect both—perhaps by consciously allowing each planet its own opportunity to fulfill its needs and intentions, while not regularly relegating either to a secondary role. When oppositions begin to be rebalanced, then unconscious projection onto people and the world is lessened, perception is more clear; and our disowned shadow no longer distorts clarity.

I have included descriptive interpretations of 8th house influences by planet, sign, and aspect. They are viewed through the focused perspective of each chapter's theme, and these interpretations are intended to be suggestive and provocative, drawing attention to how these may operate in specific natal positions. Interpretations are not meant to be definitive or conclusive; no astrological interpretation or analysis can ever match that elusive ideal, and they are obviously liable to adjustment in respect of the whole chart configuration. These interpretations are concerned with increasing our awareness of the 8th house mysteries and how these issues shape individual and collective reality.

Astrologers evolve their own approach to the starlore tradition, reflecting their interests, priorities, and purposes. While my experience confirms the relevancy of holistic astrology with the clients I attract, I acknowledge that other approaches can be equally valid with a different clientele, and that mine may be less suitable due to its emphasis on individual transformation. Working from a spiritual perspective and being committed to paths of inner development, I believe that contemporary astrology can provide one of the most profound and insightful sources into individual and collective psychology that is currently available, and is additionally quite accessible. A holistic chart interpretation can give a basis for self-inquiry that lasts a lifetime, and can be valuable to all engaged in the quest for self-understanding. It is in this spirit that *The Gate of Rebirth* is offered to the worldwide constellation of astrologers.

2 Myths of Rebirth, Renewal, and Regeneration

THE NATURE OF THE 8TH HOUSE mystery path is indicated by myths, legends, symbols, and imagery associated with Pluto and Scorpio; considering these can aid our understanding of the psychological processes involved in exploring unconscious realms. For people with a prominent 8th house, these mythic encounters have a deep inner resonance and are inspirational when identity foundations are being undermined. Mythic encounters are also signposts on the path that has to be traveled. The eighth way demands endurance and courage, and is a solitary path where certainty is only discovered when the hidden gift is received. The Underworld Treasure is of great significance, and the wheel of life's eighth gift is the transformative mystical rebirth, the aim of all genuine religious, mystical, and occult quests. While given freely to successful seekers, and indicated as the culmination of their efforts, the nature of the journey ensures that none are able to receive unless they have completed the process of renewal.

These key myths of rebirth, resurrection, and renewal are the heart of ancient mystery schools and reoccur in various complementary forms within diverse cultures, having been created by adepts to point toward evolutionary development. The new age and human potential movements all partake of this mythic process by emphasizing self-transformation, life-renewal, and the manifestation of latent potential. Collectively, our utopian visions of a millennial new world order and the transition from the Piscean Age to that of

Aquarius alerts attention to regenerative needs. These are inspirational, drawing individuals and society ever-onward, searching for the Christian promise of life more abundantly, an attribute of spiritual reconnection. Working with the 8th house is one of the Gates to personally verify this promise, and the mythic tales reveal the probable types of inner experience that may result when this Gate is opened.

In this house of Scorpio, we meet conflicts, tests, and crises. No life is free from these, and even if we have an untenanted 8th house, its influence still pervades our experiences. An energy of renewing change is represented, inherent in existence whether we choose to accept this or not. Scorpio has been described as the sign of magic, whose purpose is to release the soul within form; white magic is applying the higher soul energy through the cleansed personality to uplift and evolve the collective human spirit. The individual and collective test is "which will triumph, spirit or matter?"

The battlefield is the realm of opposites and dualistic attraction, where truth and illusion are so closely interwoven in human perception and our self-ignorance so great that many fail to understand their real nature. The key challenge focuses on personal desire: is it self-centered or devoted to the good of all? In the constellation of Scorpio lies Antares, the Red Star, an apt reflection of the color of human desire and passion for material life, and the main 8th house issues involve the metamorphosis of our desires and relationships, so that self-preoccupation shifts to an awareness of the higher value of "us."

An esoteric keynote to this House of Crises is, "Warrior I am, and from the battle I emerge triumphant."[1] If we assume this attitude, it can be regenerative and may serve as both shield and inspiration as we explore this difficult path.

---

[1] Alice A. Bailey, *The Labours of Hercules: An Astrological Interpretation* (New York & London: Lucis Press, 1977), p. 102.

PLUTO, DEMETER, PERSEPHONE
AND THE ELEUSINIAN MYSTERIES

The mythic abduction of Demeter's daughter Kore by Pluto, the God of the Underworld, reveals important 8th house themes due to the association with planetary Pluto, ruler of Scorpio. In Greek and Roman religious myths there were three levels to existence—the Underworld, our level of the Middle Earth, and the Overworld of Olympus, the heavenly domain of Gods and Goddesses. Pluto (the Greek Hades) was a son of Kronos and Rhea, brother to Poseidon who ruled the oceans and dark twin to Zeus, the Heavenly Father-God. Pluto is often depicted as an intense, brooding, dark-haired and bearded god, who has an outsider function within mythic teachings. He is rarely a major character and acts primarily as a presence, although his Underworld and realm of the dead is important.

Pluto is lord of the depths, whose teaching is of death and regeneration. Once the boundary line of the River Styx has been crossed, his influence is the transformer, destroying all that is outgrown and outworn and bringing deep, intense experiences. He confronts his subjects with the mirrored reflection of hidden things, the revelation of their secret personality exposed in a world prohibiting escape, except for possible rebirth in certain cases. In his dark, stygian caverns, serpents gathered as his companions: here, dragon myths proliferated, ancient symbols for occult wisdom and knowledge, healers, and sharers of enlightenment. Pluto comes from the word *plouton* meaning riches, wealth, treasures and gifts, and as in many later derivative traditions, the underworld became the repository for treasures guarded by dragons.

For Pluto-Hades, there are no earthly physical altars and temples, unlike those where other gods and goddesses received sacrifices and worship and who had priests and priestesses mediating divine oracular guidance. In our world

Pluto is ever-present, hidden by his helmet of invisibility because death is everywhere, the constant uninvited companion of life, ready to appear when the innate seed of death has
ripened.

The Goddess Aphrodite/Venus thought that Pluto needed
the transformation of love, and she sent Eros to strike him with
an arrow of passion. Inflamed by an urgent need for a partner to be Queen of the Underworld, Pluto fell in love with
Demeter's young daughter Kore, abducting her as she picked
flowers. Pluto claimed her for his bride and returned to his dark
kingdom. Aphrodite's intention had been fulfilled, as she had
also felt that Kore was too innocent and virginal, considering
this an interference with her development. Aphrodite's wisdom saw that she needed an intimate and loving union for maturation. Pluto became the perpetrator of a "phallic penetration
into a virginal psyche," violating Kore yet simultaneously
awakening her to an unresistible fate governed by the necessity of her evolutionary growth to the next stage of being.

Demeter (or Ceres) was an Earth Goddess, one of the lineage of Earth Mothers from Gaea and Rhea, matriarchal symbols of fertile life. She is portrayed as golden-haired, mature,
beautiful and grave, crowned by ears of corn and ribbons, holding either a scepter, torch or ears of corn. Demeter's main role
is her maternal guise as the sacrificial mother who acknowl-
edges and accepts the natural cycles of existence, from birth
to death and regeneration. From Demeter springs maternal
images of love and care for children, and despairing at Kore's
disappearance, she searched the world in her pursuit. Due to
Demeter's preoccupation to discover news of her daughter,
her energies of growth, fertility, and renewal were withdrawn from Earth, and eventually nothing new was growing. Men petitioned the Gods to restore fertility and Demeter
was led to the Gate of the Underworld, declaring that until
she reclaimed her daughter again, the energy of growth
would still be withheld. Zeus/Jupiter sent Hermes/Mercury
to persuade Pluto to release Kore, and reluctantly he complied,

secretly offering Kore pomegranate seeds to eat which symbolized marriage and cunningly sealed their union, binding
her to the Underworld.

A compromise was agreed between Pluto and Demeter;
if Kore—now renamed Persephone—was to return with her
mother, then she had to spend six months annually with
Pluto in his chthonic world. Demeter agreed to this and on
returning to the sunlight restored Earth's verdant fertility again.
The change of name from Kore to Persephone implies an
initiation, as the hierophant often gives the aspirant a new name,
symbolizing the rebirth of the twice-born. Kore represents an
outgrown level of personality which needed rebirth through
inner transformation, and in the depths of change discovered
an inclusive wisdom and mature self-insight. The virgin
innocent is no more, now that she has opened and been pen-
etrated by another; her life is expanded and enriched, and she
passes into adulthood ready to integrate her womanhood. An
important step toward wholeness is taken, and Persephone
becomes the periodic Dark Queen, Source of Renewal, the one
who destroys the lesser light only to reveal the greater light,
and who as Daughter of Earth connects the triple mystery, bridging Olympus-Earth-Underworld.

As part of this triple mystery, Demeter released her Earth
magic teachings to humanity, inaugurating initiation into
her sacred mysteries at Eleusis, an Earth cult which often had
forest temples where secret rites and ceremonies were undertaken. The Demeter-inspired Eleusinian mysteries were a
Greek cult with correspondences to the Egyptian Goddess Isis,
focused on the archetypal birth-death-rebirth mythic pattern and the importance of life-giving harvests of earth's
food and fruits. Demeter was the mistress of magic and plen-
itude, manifesting the generative principle on both mundane and higher levels. Through becoming an initiate of
Eleusis, a greater force was recognized, acknowledged, and
respected, and aspiration sought to embody that power as a
holy channel. As initiates stretch toward the higher nature and

fulfillment of evolutionary potential, they discover that the
path weaves downward and into the dark.

The Eleusis Mysteries reenacted the primary myth of universal and personal creation, revealing the generative origins
of life from procreation and birth, life's journey and the
preparation for the soul's descent into the Underworld,
repeating Demeter's example in search of Kore. There are indications that classical initiation rites included a mysterious
and frightening passage through a black chamber, which aspirants had to survive prior to being allowed entrance into
a second chamber where brilliant light symbolized rebirth.
The initiate process was designed as a transforming psychological crisis, possibly involving hallucinatory stimulants
to activate an "inner death" prior to experiencing greater
life. By passing the Eleusinian trials, the seeker was reborn
as an initiate.

Persephone is encountered in dual guise, as both maiden
(Kore, representing the first guide of innocence) and as the
Wise Woman, the Crone or Chthonic Hag, the source of feminine wisdom and insight into nature's secrets. She befriends
the successful initiate and shares her knowledge, offering
seeds as emblems of life's rebirth, symbolized by the seed-
filled pomegranate fruit. Her teaching is that the "death of
the seeker" is demanded in exchange for rebirth. Neophytes
in pursuit of the bright light of wisdom are led ever-deeper
into the darker regions of their unconscious being in order
to unearth the hidden treasure and spiritual seed unrecognized
and forgotten since birth.

Fragments of a Rite of Isis state this clearly: "There is also
a death in life and this leadeth on to rebirth. From death we
arise reborn, by the embraces of Persephone are men made
powerful."[2] The blessings of Heaven shower down on to
Earth and into the Underworld as rain, which Eleusis perceived

---

[2] Cited in Carl G. Jung, *Man and His Symbols* (New York: Dell, 1968; London:
Picador, 1978), p. 337.

as a sign of loving communion between the triple-level world. Eleusis used purification by water as symbolic of this inner union, which perhaps later inspired the Essene and Christian rite of baptism. Heaven's response was evoked by calls of "Let it rain," and the fruits of the Earth's Underworld by "Be fruitful."

Through submission and acceptance of spirit-matter fused within their own natures, the Eleusinian initiates were given an opportunity to enter the way of wholeness. If their dark side was not acknowledged or rejected, the gates remain firmly closed and initiation prospects are aborted. This same situation remains today, and one purpose of *The Gate of Rebirth* is to reaffirm potential wholeness, while indicating that this particular path still enters Pluto's dark haunts.

THE UNDERWORLD QUEST OF DIONYSUS, ORPHEUS, AND CHRIST

These are three mythic and religious teachers who embody images of the dying and resurrected-regenerated god, whose material forms are destroyed yet reappear transformed as liberated spirits. They display the universal cycle of creation, death, and re-creation—the continual natural process.The Underworld quest is the seeker's search for spirit, and if successful, their return to our world is a symbolic guarantee of our faith and hope of the spiritual life.

In most ancient pagan cultures, the path of descent is more prevalent than an ascending path to the spirit, and images of caves, caverns, tombs, barrows, crypts, and catacombs are common. Legendary heroes like Herakles and Theseus also descended into adventures; Theseus into the Minotaur's black labyrinth, Herakles actually into Hell, and the healer Asklepius also ventured there to heal his own wounds ("Physician, heal thyself" for self-integration) and to administer to imprisoned souls, a task that Christ later duplicated, resulting in their

ascension on the third day. All of these reenacted the initiatory rites of entombment and resurrection in glory.

The cult of Dionysus emerged from the Eleusis mysteries, with a connection indicated by some versions giving
Demeter as his mother after being raped by Zeus, or sired by
Pluto and Persephone. The most common legend has Dionysus
as the son of Zeus' affair with the human Semele, who became
the victim of Hera's rage and jealousy at Zeus' infidelity.
Hera waited until Dionysus reached the brink of manhood
before divinely driving him mad; thrusting him down into
human depths, filling him with human passions and desires
until he lost and forgot his semi-divine nature, falling deeper
into the power of his unconscious mind and compulsive tendencies. Dionysus symbolized unredeemed humans, drunk,
hedonistic, selfish, ignorant, and blind to their foolish behavior.
His own lack of self-insight and negative actions needed
transforming as all he could perceive was darkness, negativity,
and feeling lost, before his senses could be reclaimed and sobered
by an inner light.

As companions to Dionysus on his mad wanderings
were Silenus, the satyr, and a band of maenads, inebriated
hedonists, and seekers of physical gratification. Yet Silenus
was also his tutor, watching over him in his sufferings, and
attempting to mirror both his false and true nature back to
Dionysus, hoping to reawaken him to his real status. Silenus
was half man and half beast, a satyr who saw that Dionysus
was lost within his lower nature and had broken contact
with his higher human potential. Dionysus was a god in the
making, and eventually his realization of this returned through
encountering his own madness.

Like the Biblical Prodigal Son, he resolved to return to
his father's house, purified his nature, and cast off the shackles of madness and misidentification that had imprisoned him
for so long. He had explored his Underworld so thoroughly
that he released the treasure of his hidden light, and reawakening, enabled his return to Olympus as a reward for his initiatory trials.

Dionysus is also one of the dismembered gods; reputedly the Titans first fragmented him during childhood, which later resulted in Hera's spell sending him insane. An alternative version has the renewed and recreated Dionysus torn apart by his Maenad followers for his abandonment of their path, in an earlier parallel to the later Orpheus mythic experience. Athene, Goddess of Wisdom, rescued his heart, and Dionysus was reborn, rising again as a God of Renewal and forerunner of the resurrected Christ.

Both Dionysus and Christ were exemplars of a similar message, the relinquishment of the lesser, separative self, substituted by a redemptive union with the higher spirit. The Dionysiac Mysteries reenacted his adventure of wandering and suffering prior to experiencing his *gnosis*, which shattered his previous abandonment to the material world and physical pleasures. Dionysus implies that the transformation of human frailty can result in self-understanding and mastery, freeing the hidden god-seed. He becomes a symbol of rebirth, a figure of hope and eventual salvation, and a representative of the twice-born, those children of the double door (who awaken both human and divine seeds) and the birth of physical form and rebirth of initiation.

The Dionysiac Rites often exalted excess and loss of control by frenzies of inebriation, ecstatic practices and orgiastic sexuality, in an attempt to heighten senses to divine perceptions and by a physical affirmation of the wildness of life energies. The lower human nature was unlocked and exploited to be fertilized by the chthonic Earth Mother, where wine as a fruit of the earth, the phallus, and the opening into darkness were hailed as sacred mysteries. They believed that by indulging in extreme ritual hedonism a divine contact could be made.

The Mysteries of Dionysus were celebrated with wine and bread, broth produced by the fruits and corn of the earth and "offspring" of the Earth-Mother, Demeter. Wine was shared as the sacred cup of communion, and as repeated in later Christianity, the vine was held as sacred. It was an image of

the union between God and human. Christ declared: "I am
the true vine. I am the vine and ye are the branches," and
instituted the Eucharist communion for his disciples.

For the Dionysiacs, wine was the stimulant or symbol for
the transition from lower consciousness to the receptive
intuitive state, where they were able to receive the Mysteries'
guarded secrets. Senses were heightened further by sensual
and sexual acts, often repeating the "sacred marriage ceremony"
of Dionysus and his consort Ariadne, in preparation for their
divinely inebriated inspiration. Through these rites, they
hoped the soul would be liberated from the prison of flesh
and redeemed by the ecstasy of sensual, sexual and sacred
eroticism. They anticipated that the Dionysiac Hierophant would
reveal the transformative Mystery to them during the ritualized ingestion of wine and bread containing the spirit of
Dionysus into their own bodies. The Christian Eucharist conveys the same teaching today and Sufi mystical imagery
often employs words of inebriation to ecstatic bliss and being
"drunk on God's love."

The Orphic Mysteries succeeded those of Dionysus, and
represented an intermediate stage prior to the appearance of
Christ. These myths were a development of Dionysus risen,
and Orpheus was the Master of the Muses, Harmony and
Rhythm, the possessor of the seven-stringed lyre of universal knowledge and the seven creative rays of the spectrum
which revealed the seven-fold mystery of initiation. The
beauty and musical power of Orpheus enchanted all who lis-
tened, and he was especially attuned to the cycle of Nature.
His teachings and Mysteries displayed a higher morality,
preaching a severe asceticism in distinction to the libidinous
license of Dionysus. The Orphic vision sublimated the lower
nature to a higher conception of the spiritual quest, by creating a path through beauty, art, gentleness, compassion and
fidelity, evoking more elevated human qualities when aspiring
to divine contacts.

Orpheus also descended into the Underworld in search of his wife, Eurydice, who had been fatally wounded by a snake. He wanted his lover returned to life, charming Pluto and Persephone by his musical skills to agree that Eurydice could return with him on the condition that Orpheus did not turn to look at her. On the journey back, Eurydice pleaded with him to look at her, fearing that his love had faded; his heart touched by her entreaties, Orpheus turned and Eurydice disappeared into the Underworld.

One implication of this may be the requirement for *trust* while passing through the Underworld's darkness or else all will be lost. As most inner explorers recognize who have traveled this way, there may be a narrow dividing line between emerging with inspiring insight or suffering a psychological collapse.

For his failure, Orpheus was torn apart by the Thracian Bacchantes angered at the loss of Eurydice. This breaking into pieces inflicted on Orpheus can also be interpreted as symbolizing the results of personality repression, when aspects of the self are disowned and rejected, causing fragmentation, and personality splits. To some degree this happens to all of us, and an essential task of the Underworld quest is to rediscover these missing vital fragments, returning with them as treasures to the surface and this time "re-piece ourselves together again" from a holistic perspective.

Both Dionysus and Orpheus are prototypes of Christ, who encapsulated many older mysteries in his own living legend. All are mediators and divine men, teaching a religious path that includes many ancient agricultural patterns incorporating elements of fertility gods of rebirth, resurrection, and renewal, seasonal or cyclic returns, and the stages of birth-growth-maturity-decay and eternal recurrence. In the context of nature, all reflect Mysteries of the Green Ray; inner and outer harmony, control of the elements, and nature mysticism and oneness. They are teachers of the Triple

Mystery relationship between Nature-Man-God which lies at the root of 8th house issues.

THE HERO QUEST

The Hero Quest is an archetypal pattern found in many culture's myths and legends, where an inspirational, courageous adventurer endures multiple trials and tests on the journey through the world. The hero represents individual potential, the strengths and higher qualities released through challenging encounters with monsters, demons and death-defying risks. In many of these tales, the hero is destined to experience the Underworld, implying a descent into the psyche to confront secret demons and to release those imprisoned spirits. The hero encounters a shadowy presence guarding the downward passage, yet recognizes that the only way forward to pass this test lies through darkness. The hero's options are either to defeat the guard; make friends with the presence and so pass onward into the black kingdom; or fail this test by being defeated and descend only by physical death.

Beyond this guardian of the threshold, the hero can experience a reality that is both strangely familiar and unfamiliar, where tests continue and helpers may be met. Ordeals are undergone, and if successful, the hero may claim his or her reward, the reason for the quest. Part of this process is transcending fears by integrating and redeeming the hidden dark-side. For the male, traditional rewards include the sacred marriage, where the hero receives "sexual union" with the Earth Mother-Goddess; the atonement with God the Father, a recognition of Son-ship; or his own apotheosis, transformation into an idealized deification. Treasures, too, can be discovered in this Underworld, and for some heroes the trial is choosing either material riches or spiritual riches, testing their response to matter or spirit and can be a trap for the unwary. The results of a successful mission are expanded consciousness (more life) and a free liberated spirit, returning to the surface world with gifts of restoration, those elixirs of life to be shared with others, perhaps in the form of mystery teachings. It is in the darkness that an understanding of W. B. Yeats' Golden Dawn name can be comprehended: "Daemon est Deus Inversus."

One of the Twelve Labors of Herakles has particular affinity to the 8th house mystery path and lesson. This is the slaying of the dangerous Lernean Hydra, which was a serpent-dragon beast with nine snake heads dripping poison from their fangs, lurking in a dark cave surrounded by a swamp, preying on local people for food. The problem dealing with the Hydra was whenever a head was cut off two more appeared. As Herakles prepared for the eighth Gate experience, his teacher said, "One word of counsel only I may give. We rise by kneeling, we conquer by surrendering, we gain by giving up."[3]

Similar to all creations of the darkness, the Hydra cannot bear light, and in his battle with the monster, Herakles remembers his teacher's advice, drops to his knees and raises the Hydra high over his head toward the sunlight, breaking its connection with the chthonic powers and exposing it fully to the sun's rays, where it begins to shrivel and die. Only one head remains, and this is immortal with an embedded jewel; Herakles cuts this off, carefully burying both in the earth under a rock. The teacher acknowledged the hero saying, "The victory is won. The light that shines at Gate the eighth is now blended with your own."[4]

The Hydra symbolizes our basic, lower nature, sometimes repressed into unlit caverns of the psyche, denied as failing to fit our self-image. Here disowned energies remain unpu-

[3] Alice A. Bailey, *The Labours of Hercules: An Astrological Interpretation* (New York & London: Lucis Press, 1977), p. 67.
[4] Alice A. Bailey, *The Labours of Hercules: An Astrological Interpretation*, p. 68.

rified, unredeemed, yet act by casting subtle poisons into our personality, causing us to live in separative and wounding ways to ourself and others. Here lie the Hydras of jealousy, lust, revenge, anger, frustration, violence, envy, deceit. The Hydra's nine heads were said to represent sex, comfort, money, passion, fears, hatred, power-desires, pride, separation, which—individually and collectively—we need to transmute by discovering right use of our creative, generative, and sexual energies to move beyond selfishness into serving the whole.

Encountering our personal Hydra and major "heads" of this are related to 8th house lessons, in that we need to realize and accept its hidden presence; few exist who have no secret Hydra within them. We all have many desires which need understanding not repression, and may require raising to the light for insights, acknowledgement, and healing as we transform our difficulties by translating the issue to a higher resolving perspective. We have to accept our whole nature in order to walk the holistic path; self-denial and evasion only lead in the opposite direction. Exploring this Underworld of human nature has been the work of psychoanalysis since Freud, and an integral part of all sincere religious and spiritual endeavors for centuries. Each of us has to experience the battle of Herakles and the Hydra for ourselves.

EROS AND THANATOS

The Greek gods Eros and Thanatos relate to the primal urges of sex and death within the human being, those poles of existence that are profound, obsessive, and yet remain socially taboo subjects in many cultures, associated with collective evasion, hypocrisy, ambivalent feelings. These primal forces which underlie 8th house energies many find disturbing, and were reinterpreted by Sigmund Freud, the pioneer of modern psychoanalysis, whose theories are often preoccupied with examining these issues active in the personality.

Freud had Scorpio rising, with Saturn and Moon in a Gemini 8th house. For Freud, the sexual impulse was the key to understanding human nature and psychological reactions, and the subconscious was the source of primal instincts, repressions, chaotic compulsions, obsessions, sex drives, and hidden motivations, all of which have astrological correspondences to the 8th house. Freud reintroduced Eros and Thanatos as components of the psyche, often deeply connected to the *Id*, which he conceived as archetypal forces of sexuality and destruction, involving violent, bloodthirsty, primitive, and volatile instincts that still existed beneath the controlling facade of culture and civilized humanity.

For the Greeks, Eros operated on dual levels. On the highest he was a primal creator-god whose passion engendered the material universe, a cosmic force creating order from chaos and a great cosmological concept of divine love inspiring and attracting universal relationship. On the lower, he was a minor god of human love and polarized sexual attraction, where sacred and profane love met in human union. Eros was a child of Aphrodite/Venus, and one of her constant companions with the Three Graces, having the role of coordinating the ordered harmony of the elements which composed the universe. He was associated with erotic love and fecundity, and like his later, weakened derivative Cupid, his bow and arrows sparked obsessive passions in the hearts of all struck by love; even Pluto was not immune.

The story of Eros and Psyche is an early version of Beauty and the Beast. Psyche was a mortal daughter of a king and had no suitors despite her great beauty. In desperation, the king consulted a sacred oracle which instructed him to sacrifice her; she was to be prepared as a bride and left chained on a mountain peak, where she would be claimed by a monster.

This unusual command had been sent by Aphrodite, jealous of Psyche's beauty, who also ordered Eros to cause Psyche to fall irrationally in love with the monster. However, Eros failed to direct his arrow properly, and nicked himself with his dart of love, falling obsessively in love with the beautiful Psyche.

He took her to his palace, and Psyche still believed that she had been taken by a monster.

Eros only visited her during night's darkness, fearing that exposure to his divine light would blind her. Psyche was forbidden to look at her captor, and planned to kill him and escape. Her curiosity grew, and she concealed a lamp so that in the still of night she could see and kill him. As Psyche stared at her god-lover and abductor, droplets of oil fell on Eros, and he woke and disappeared. In that moment, Psyche fell in love and wanted him as her beloved, pleading with Aphrodite and the gods to return him to her. Aphrodite agreed on the condition that Psyche descended into the Underworld, where she would bring back the treasure of a precious ointment from Pluto and Persephone. As this was a gift between the gods, Psyche was forbidden to open the ointment box; yet her curiosity again was stronger than the divine fiat, and she opened the box releasing the ointment's perfumed vapor, which cast Psyche again into the Underworld and her unconscious mind. Eros took pity on Psyche's plight and gained permission to reawaken her and both returned from the Underworld to enter Olympus, where Zeus allowed their reconciliation and marriage.

In this myth, several themes are interwoven; the injunction to follow or submit to divine directions, or endure the consequences; the inevitable descent into the Underworld as a rite of transformative passage; the power of love; the fact of human curiosity, which can lead in dual directions with positive or negative results; and the union of the sacred and the profane, god and humanity with the merging of beauty and the beast.

The brother of Eros was Thanatos, the son of the Goddess Night and a God of Death, who served Pluto and his Underworld by continually sending new subjects for his dark kingdom. At some point in life, everyone touches the presence of these holy brothers, love and death. Thanatos was a dispenser of fate, where all face the consequences of their actions and attitudes by choosing a path at every crossroads of life. Thanatos has been rediscovered by Freud as the latent death-urge within the psyche, an ambivalence to material existence and an impulse for renewal which invariably means the death of the old, limiting pattern.

James Hillman, in *The Dream and the Underworld*, describes this as: "The innate urge to go below appearances to the "invisible connection" and hidden constitution leads to the world interior to whatever is given... The autochthonous urge of the psyche, its native desire to understand psychologically, would seem akin to what Freud calls the death drive and what Plato presented as the desire for Hades.... It works through destruction, the dissolving, decomposing, detaching and disintegrating process necessary both to alchemical psychologizing and modern psychoanalyzing."[5]

In the 8th house, this impulse is often activated and released through sexual, intimate and ecstatic surrender during the little death of the orgasm; by the pain of rejected or frustrated emotions and sexual needs, causing relationship's catalytic and cathartic effects; the attraction of self-transcendence, initiation and rebirth; and literally by self-destruction when resisting necessary changes and deaths of an outworn self. Self-destruction may be physical, emotional or mental, and can result from severe repressions; psychological disturbances when sinking into the Underworld; a lack of self-acceptance and knowledge which creates unwise choices; or by negative attitudes which devitalize and atrophy life enjoyment.

There are many walking around who are effectively already dead, and these are not the twice-born initiates! In the 12th house, this impulse to dissolve or transcend a separated individuality which acutely feels alienation from the universe is often expressed through acts of self-sacrifice, perhaps by idealistic service to others. As Carl Jung observed: "That the highest summit of life can be expressed through the symbolism of death is a well-known fact, for any growing beyond

---

[5] James Hillman, *The Dream and the Underworld* (New York: Harper & Row, 1979), p. 27.

oneself means death."[6] In this context, all who seek inner growth
will encounter Eros and Thanatos at crucial stages in their life.

THE PHOENIX, EAGLE, SCORPION
DOVE, AND SERPENT SYMBOLISM

These are key symbols associated with the 8th house rulers,
Scorpio and Pluto, whose themes and messages reoccur in the
mythic Phoenix, Scorpion, Eagle, Dove and Serpent. These are
archaic images present in many legends and which are often
representative of initiated mystery teachings.

The Phoenix is the archetypal bird of resurrection and rebirth, a symbol of inner regeneration and soul immortality. This
is connected to the heroic Underworld descent and endurance
of a secret initiation cycle of rebirth, by kindling an inner
flame to consume the old self and release the new spirit. It is
a motif of perpetual renewal, and an image that can valuably
be contemplated by all engaged in self-discovery, as it holds
a key to the 8th house and unlocks hidden treasures.

The Phoenix is a symbol for Pluto and Persephone, and
reminds us of our innate capacity for revitalizing change
and that we are not as fixed as we may foolishly believe. We
are as malleable as we can imagine, able to withstand many
major, radical life-changes as we strive to unfold our potential. Many life barriers are self-created and imposed through
fear. The Phoenix power is available to all who open themselves to its renewing nature, yet it has an inexorable effect,
as in the truth that a real initiation never ends. In Hermeticism,
the phoenix often symbolizes the accomplished alchemical transmutation of human regeneration, The Magnum Opus, the Great
Work, and indicates a secret alchemical formula for this
process. Initiates have been termed "phoenix," emblematic
of renewal and spiritual birth.

---

[6] Carl G. Jung, *Psychological Reflections* (Bollingen Series, Vol. 31. Princeton, NJ:
Princeton University Press, 1970; London: Routledge & Kegan Paul, 1974), p. 324.

Scorpio's animal symbolism is more complex than other signs, having the Scorpion, Eagle, Dove and Serpent as attributions. The Scorpion is a later correspondence, probably introduced because few could attain the higher levels of the Scorpio path, due to failing or ignoring a transformative quest and resorting to displaying lower qualities. Scorpio's repressive tendency is demonstrated by an effective defense mechanism, an implacable, impassive mask that veils their intensity and stormy passions from view.

The Scorpion threatens with its deadly sting, but only in self-defense, and this provides the trait of self-destructive, vindictive revenge associated with Scorpio. Generally, the scorpion's threat is sufficient protection to dissuade predators. Its ability to survive in extremes of climactic conditions and environments is reflected by Scorpio's tenacious, willful, and determined personality, where resilience is paralleled by a tendency to create periodic radical life-changes, like a snake shedding an outworn skin. Many people can take a literal or psychological "step back" when dealing with a powerful Scorpio personality, sensing a disturbing, transformative and dangerous energy in their aura, either felt as extremely attractive or repellent.

Scorpios can be solitary figures, reasonably content with their own company, retaining pride and integrity, and refusing to easily submit to external authority and control. Scorpios appear to thrive on generating periodic crises through challenging others by confrontation or championing social causes; through such testing and transformative encounters, Scorpio can grow wiser and stronger, releasing repressed emotional energy and enabling deeper integration. However, if individual Scorpios fail to be self-transformative, their energy can become redirected and sting their own well-being and life-enjoyment, perhaps by projecting an adversarial stance on to others through paranoia and relationship conflicts, and where selfish desires are paramount, they tend to build their success at the expense of others.

In Sumeria, Babylon, and Egypt, the scorpion was often sent by the gods to punish the sin of hubris, man's egocentric pride and insolence which offended against their fated circumscribed limits allowed by the gods. One legend tells of the egotistical Orion, the Hunter, who was killed by a scorpion sent from the bowels of the earth by Hekate, mistress of the night and world of the dead; this was the fate of the Underworld for those who transgressed and became bound to their lower nature.

The Scorpio challenge involves the right use of their potential and scope, which can range from a base, degraded expression when their lowest, separative human characteristics dominate, to a truly elevated height of the advanced human. This is the Eagle symbol, an aspiration to soar high above mundane desires and emotional demands to liberate spirit from the prison of matter. The Eagle has a higher vision, looking down on the world from its vantage point in the sky; yet it cannot remain there and the Eagle has to return closer to earth.

In the Bible, the four cosmic animals of Ezekiel's vision had the faces of a human, lion, bull and eagle, representing the signs of Aquarius, Leo, Taurus and Scorpio. The Scorpio dilemma and question for humanity is: am I angel or animal? What is my true nature? How should I respond to my separate desires and needs? Why am I attracted to explore the darkness while longing to discover the light? Why am I torn between the axis of light-darkness, on the cross of spirit-matter? Why am I given the bittersweet cup to drink to the dregs? Why is mine the Phoenix Path? The evangelist St. John, author of the esoteric allusive biblical vision of Revelations, is associated with Eagle symbolism, and he terms this higher self perspective "those who have gotten the victory over the beast,"[7] indicating the scorpion which was not considered a product of a healthy evolution.

The individual process through Scorpio and the 8th house mirrors the natural cycle of death and rebirth, as observed in the West during the months of late October-November,

---

[7] Revelations: 15: 2.

when summer's fruits and productive fertility have been har-vested, and nature reverts back into decay and passivity prior to winter cold; the seeds hide in the wet, dark earth in prepa-ration for new germination and cyclic growth next spring.

The identification of Scorpio as a serpent is extremely revealing, pointing to the 8th house depths ruled in con-junction with Pluto. Since medieval times, the serpent-snake has been linked with evil and the devil, as a misinterpreta-tion of the biblical Genesis where the serpent-tempter, the Father of Lies, persuaded Eve to eat the fruit of the tree of knowl-edge, giving consciousness of good and evil. This is the Prince of the World, Lucifer, whose name was derived from "light-bringer," and is a notorious fallen angel whose gaze tra-verses the range from light to darkness, for the sinful attitude of "Better to reign in hell than to serve in heaven," as Milton portrayed his character in *Paradise Lost*.[8] This is the Scorpionic struggle against submission to others or to inner gods, and in that painful process striving to assert to thine own self be true.

Serpent imagery is found in numerous ancient cultures—Indian, Egyptian, Chaldean, Mayan, Chinese, Judaic and Christian. The serpent was an ideal symbol for immortality and self-renewal, representing the potential for consecutive rejuvenation, either within the current life, or as serial rein-carnation, cyclically shedding its skin as if a metaphor for life divided into separate chapters of experience, passing through phases of birth to death and beginning again. Ouruboros en-circled the world, continually devouring its own tail, an image of eternal recurrence and action. The association of ser-pent with the male phallus is common, reflecting the creative energy of God, as in the Scorpio glyph referring to the erect phallus and organ of reproduction. It was the serpent that made Adam and Eve conscious of their duality and knowledge of sexual shame, covering their sexual nature by fig leaves. The serpent symbolized the manifestation of regenerative force at every universal level, as an eternal perpetuation of life.

---

[8] John Milton, "Paradise Lost" as cited in *The Poems of John Milton* (New York & London: Oxford University Press, 1958), p. 12.

Serpent, dragon, and snake symbolism was adopted as the imagery of sacred initiates, adepts, hierophants, and masters of the wisdom. These were the guardians of Earth's secrets and "the great mystery in the mysteries," those inner paths for "reclothing and rebirth in the universal mysteries,"[9] into the final phases and higher gnosis which led beyond our material level.

The serpent was perceived as the first beam of light radiated from the Abyss of Divine Mystery, and the serpent-path could return us to the effulgent light. Serpent, Dragon, Snake, or Sons of...were given to the Wise Ones, the adepts, the Serpents of Wisdom, the Naga initiates, the hierophant-priests of Egypt, Babylon and India. The Druids declared, "I am a Serpent, I am a Druid,"[10] and the Mayan winged serpent symbolized All-Wisdom, while the Inca Quetzalcoatl was a plumed serpent, the bestower of arts and civilization to mankind. The Wisdom Dragons represented the Logos, or heavenly, spiritual teachings of ancient religions, whose regenerative force could be individually raised by the chakra ascent of the Kundalini serpent-power to the highest spiritual crown-sahasra center. Across Earth, the Dragon Paths or Leyline system transmitted the planetary energies through the material world. Serpent mysteries were celebrated and taught in crypts, catacombs, and caves of Egypt, Chaldea, Greece, Rome, India, where the lessons of The Unavoidable Cycle and The Circle of Necessity were revealed.

Early Christianity repeats this descent below ground to preserve the teachings, when Christians gathered in Rome's catacombs. In India, Rishis isolated themselves in caves to pursue solitary meditation and enter an undisturbed yogic samadhi, while the legendary cities of Shamballa and Agarthi were reputed to be underground kingdoms guarding sacred teachings—the KalaChakra of the World—and priceless trea-

---

[9] Gerald Massey, *The Natural Genesis*, Vol. 1, cited in H.P. Blavatsky, *The Secret Doctrine*, Vol. 1 (Pasadena, CA: Theosophical University Press, 1970), p. 405.

[10] H.P. Blavatsky, *Isis Unveiled*, Vol. 1 (Pasadena, CA: Theosophical University Press, 1972), p. 340.

sures. In Egypt, the pharaoh-adept and initiate wore the Uraeus, the serpent crown emblem of supreme power. Greece had the Pythonesses and their serpent oracles. The Osiris myth told of his dismemberment by Set/Typhon the serpent, symbolizing fragmentation by his repressed dark side, his black shadow-self, prior to his rebirth and regeneration by the magic of Isis, an allegory of the trials of the adept.

Moses, the Hebrew trained by the Egyptian priesthood, was a descendant of the Levi, a serpent-tribe; his Tau staff was entwined by brazen serpents, representing his understanding of the magical mysteries of generation and the potency of phallic symbolism. Gautama Buddha was also a descendant of the serpent lineage of the Magadha kings. Jesus stated, "Be ye wise as serpents and harmless as doves,"[11] as the right behavior for his disciples. The Four Evangelist's animal emblems were those of Ezekiel's vision; John embodied the eagle/serpent, Luke the bull, Mark the lion, and Matthew the man/angel. Christ has been portrayed as the lamb, the fish, the serpent exalted on the cross, the lion and the unicorn. Templar lore depicts Christ by serpent imagery as does the Alexandrian Gnostics, the Ophites who use the serpent-dragon image as the sigil of resurrection, and the original Teacher who taught primeval man the Mysteries. The Judaic Qabalah and Tree of Life has the Lightning Flash of divine descent from Kether to Malkuth, which is also termed the Serpent Path of Wisdom. China has great reverent Dragon legends; the dragon is the emblem of their Emperor's lineage, replete with his Dragon's Seat.

The caduceus wand has two serpents entwined in intimate embrace, and is a healing symbol of balance and integration on every level. This represents the harmonious union of spirit-matter, mediation between levels and the promise of transcendence by knowledge of the double-path of black and white. Aesculapius, the Greek god of healing, and Hermes/Mercury both possessed this wand, which also denoted the teachings of fertility, protection, and regenera-

---

[11] Matthew: 10: 16.

tion which so preoccupied ancient minds. Hermes was a messenger of the gods, the overseer of the crossroads who guided souls to and from the Underworld; his phallic wand bridged the known and the unknown, transmitting a spiritual message of salvation and healing from rebirth, as the gates to Heaven open when both Underworld and Earth are joined.

Even today, the interwoven serpent pattern is found within the DNA double-helix spiral of our individual and collective genetic code. The current research into mapping the complete human genome is designed to provide information for regenerative medicine hoping to ameliorate genetic sources of illness or minimize latent tendencies to contract certain diseases during life. The DNA structure was realized through a dream, where the unconscious projected the spiral, snake-like image which conveyed the key to scientific realization and productive inquiry.

The Dove, a symbol of a pacified Scorpio, spiritually dedicated master of inner passions, is connected to Demeter and Aphrodite, Earth-Mother and Goddess of Love-Wisdom. The Dove is a higher version of the Eagle, and biblically was one of the sacred animals once dispatched in search of dry land by Noah from his Ark; and descended on to Jesus during John's Jordan baptism, symbolizing in Christian belief his acceptance by the Holy Spirit and Father, even though traditionally, the dove represents the Goddess and Mother.

The Dove is the higher lighted face of divinity (with the shadow-face veiled from sight) and represents wisdom, power, and order, a messenger of divine will and activity in the midst of human life. Often *dove*, or *Ionah*, or *Ionas* were names given to oracles and prophets like Noah, Jonah, John the Baptist, St. John, and the dove emblem indicated one who was overshadowed by the gods, and who represented divine benediction. The bearer of the sacred dove channeled the invisible presence of spirit, serving as a metaphysical healer, capable of transforming negative energies by repolarization and infusing others by transmitting regenerative and spiritual energies.

The Inner Daemon

The presence of an inner daemon has been noted by many throughout history, and this is an inner entity or guardian who guides and inspires the human journey. The *daemon* or *daimon* reflects the cohesive seed of individuality, a force which continually shapes life from within and which unfolds the unique personal destiny. It is this directive pattern that contemporary astrology seeks to understand through interpreting the natal chart. The daemon is both individual and collective, forming a bridge or channel to inspire whatever the individual must do, a force which encourages people to pursue their unique path with a sense of aim or goal; individual reaction to this either allows cooperative development or resists inner promptings. The daemon expects the enactment of an individual role in the human drama, dispensing a specific task or performance to each (their destiny), and driving them to fulfill their purpose and life-pattern.

Zodiacal myths are often associated with daemon types and imagery, where each major planet and sign has specific archetypal resonances, affinities, and disaffinities. Individuals born under one of the twelve collective human personality types tend to reenact their sign's daemon-myth in some way, as if a human vehicle for an enigmatic, dramatic, and sacred performance of divine creativity. With hindsight, insight, and age can come awareness of a life-pattern previously obscured while experiencing its twists and turns. Famous daemons include the one of Socrates, who chose to follow the path indicated by his inner guide, even though speaking out cost him his life; Carl Jung's inner presence, Philemon who was source of wisdom; and Plato considered Eros to be a great daemon, commanding all by love.

The Scorpio-daemon inspires the individual and social encounter with the dark, destructive, and terrifying dark side of existence. Similar to the opposing pulls of the scorpion and the eagle's flight, Scorpio is torn between the downward and upward path, as will be noted in the Faust legend, written by Goethe, whose Scorpio Ascendant was highly energized. If our response to the Scorpio daemon is creative, we may discover how to positively direct our resources and path, generating constructive changes in ourselves and our culture by acknowledging both light and dark faces, and purifying the "monsters" of the lower nature.

Not everyone is cognizant of this daemon-presence or even welcomes its advice; many turn away from the whispers of conscience in pursuit of their own desires. For those intent on self-development, contacting this guide is encouraged by many traditions and various psychotherapy techniques; the emphasis on channeling is a by-product of this need. Like angels, the inner daemon is a psychopompos of the soul, a mouthpiece for divine inspiration and can lead aspirants safely through tangled wooded paths as a familiar helper. There are links between the daemon and the Jungian anima and animus within the psyche. Occultism often refers to the daemon as "inner teachers/guides" or as the "holy guardian angel" which Crowley and others attempted to evoke via the Abra-Melin formula. In chapter 7, the presence of planetary guides through our 8th house will be discussed, and the need to collaborate with our inner daemon to guide us safely through the eighth Gate.

Faust and Mephistopheles

Goethe's tale of Faust and Mephistopheles includes several 8th house themes, blending the hero quest, the shadow-self and dark side. Faust is a study of the medieval legend, where the magus is confronted by the dark double through a traumatic and transformative bargain. Faust had tasted the bitter fruits of life; he was torn by boredom, loneliness, frustration, and wounded emotions, feeling isolated from his fellow men and the world, angered that he had not received sufficient pleasures and recognition in return for his endeavors. Within his nature, dual attractions and desires vied for supremacy; he longed for both worldly pleasures and the heights of ecstatic spiritual communion with God, believing that his choice was either/or, and that he could not experience both paths.

From a dualistic perspective, these contrasting desires can never be reconciled, and Faust became too aware of the disparate demands of his lower, animal nature and his higher, divine spirit. Crucified between sensuality and spirituality, he experienced the pain of his inner division. Should he take the path leading upward, or the path leading downward? Would just the light satisfy, or did his destiny lie with the darkness? At the crossroads of heaven and hell, which was the right path? He faced the extremes of his nature juggling with both sensual and sexual self, confused by conditioned beliefs demanding spiritual purity. Yet his desires and sexuality were powerful and difficult to deny. He felt that his options were to sublimate or repress either his human nature or his higher self, that matter and spirit were irrevocably separated, and that the sexual being could not coexist with the spiritual being.

The pain of this dilemma and his still festering wounds from life began to distort his perception and perspective; his psyche fragmented under the stressful pressure of futile attempts to reconcile the apparently unresolvable opposites of medieval gnostic philosophy. Discontented with the results of his double quests for material success, emotional fulfillment and metaphysical realization, Faust began to see the world as a tempter who never delivered what was seductively promised. His hopes crushed, ambitions collapsed, and certainties scattered, Faust became bitter and cynical in equal measure to his ideals appearing illusory. Divided by inner separation and conflicting messages, he was lost and directionless, disappointed by dreams and goals that failed to materialize.

As his self-obsessed preoccupation deepened, and his dualistic gnostic beliefs polarized his psyche even more, repressive fractures increased. He was ripe for Mephistopheles to emerge, his dark double and serpent-like tempter, who offered the magus power over all and everything that had wounded him or resisted his will and pleasure. Separate ego tendencies became dominant in Faust, creating the stage for Mephistopheles' temptation.

The price of this offer to possess the ability to constantly renew life and ensure revitalized interest was simply Faust's soul. In his desperation, Faust fell victim to repressed frustrations and failures, lusting for the power and pleasures that Mephistopheles promised would be his when he acquired his magical powers. By Faust's previous unconscious denial of valuable aspects of his nature considered lower and impure, he had unbalanced his psyche, failing to live from his whole nature and inadvertently allowed a disowned self to take secret dominance.

Through repression, inner corruption had festered as a consequence of rejecting his own nature and life's challenge to live fully, including both light and dark sides of existence. His own aspiration to the spiritual heights had led him into disempowering illusion due to misunderstanding the sacred path requirements. Mephistopheles is an objectification of his disowned dark self gaining power over Faust when he accepted the bargain; eventually tricking Faust into giving his soul as forfeit, and apparently dooming him to the eternal damnation beloved by hellfire and brimstone religionists, with even the destruction of those pleasures that Faust thought he had gained.

In several ways, Faust embodies a classic Western dilemma of cultural dualism, those beliefs and attitudes that opposites are "absolutely separated." He thought that the stark choice was either materialism or spirit, the world or heaven, life-embracing or renouncing. Yet his own nature instinctively reacted against this intellectual rupture, intuitively recognizing that a union between the two could be attained, and that his own nature could not be split like this without severe damage and dislocation. The result was Mephistopheles, his rejected shadow, confronting Faust with the basic lesson of the hero-quest—that of realizing the shadow exists. Through self-repression it is forced into the unconscious but it is still manipulating actions and decisions. The hero has to come to terms with the shadow's reality and power, discovering how to assimilate and reintegrate the lost dark side again.

As many individuals experience in their own search, the modern Western challenge is to integrate matter and spirit as one, not to fracture the axis of existence by seeing choices as an either-or dilemma that results in dissatisfaction and self-denial. We may eventually realize that it is our own foolish ignorance and unconsciousness that creates pain and discontent, often arising from an unrecognized dualistic life-perception endemic in this culture, and which elevates the separate ego rather than the unified self.

We join the company of Faust on a quest to balance and integrate our whole nature, otherwise any magical power that we acquire will destroy rather than redeem. Confronting our personal 8th house issues, challenges, potentials, and dilemmas may make us aware of the presence of Faust as an observing companion, monitoring our choices, aware of the tendencies and temptations to which we can fall victim. Yet perhaps we have better guidance today with sufficient recognition of the need for wholeness to replace a dualistic cultural division; although each has to live this teaching rather than giving mere intellectual agreement. In our own way, we will each encounter Mephistopheles, when questioning our self-knowledge and self-other relationships. In our sleep we may have already bargained our soul away, and need now to reclaim our lost self. And then, like Faust, we pursue the redemptive path, descending through the burning purgatory of the Underworld and striving to rediscover the regenerating soul, experiencing for ourselves the transformative mysteries of this alchemical and elemental journey and our destiny to fuse matter and spirit.

3 Personal and Planetary Values— Shared Resources

OUR LIVES ARE STRUCTURED BY THE nature of personal and social values and how these are applied in daily social interaction. Collective values formed from individual choices, attitudes, principles, and beliefs cause a ripple-effect across the world, marking world affairs and determining international relationships, economic stability, and racial harmony. Dominant values create the type of society and culture within which we live, and the fate of humanity is determined by the values that govern collective decisions. Value systems are derived from national religions, political ideology, and inherited cultural traditions that form our primary values, molding us from childhood.

Shared values shape our social "ritual organization," and individuals are expected to conform to collective rules of behavior and lifestyles. This is "programmed" by socialization. Social rituals underlie all levels of relationship—between lovers who agree to marriage, between business partnerships, and between religious or political groupings. The purpose of social ritual is to augment feelings of belonging and unity, and that awareness is extended to include others involved in a common and shared aim. Values become laws of society—rules and regulations—and both intimate partnerships and business endeavors are expected to conform to cultural customs that provide both opportunities and restrictions. The gradual development of value-inspired ritual acts and traditions are social foundations and ones that most people accept without question.

The ritualized nature of our lifestyles may be underestimated, so endemic is it in daily life. We regulate our lives by the ritual of time; we ritualize adulthood at certain ages, allowing sexual activity and marriage; our work ethic ritualizes productive activities; our evening and weekend ritual allows relaxation and personal pleasure; birthdays and anniversaries and state holidays are ritualized remembrances. Such ritual actions can be habitual, and many people go through the motions of enacting them with minimal attention. These rituals can also be positive, creative, and inspirational, increasing meaning and purpose in life.

Our value systems emphasize our life priorities and intrinsic needs—those qualities and actions that we value most highly. Values are more consciously recognized than the attitudes which form them, as we observe and regularly evaluate their context for choices, setting parameters that help decision-making. Value systems affirm our beliefs about how life works and reveal mind-heart attitudes to the universe and the self-society relationship.

Values are self-chosen or culturally absorbed, and when expressing our desires or intentions, we may either bind ourselves to their guidelines in deference to personal moral and religious values, or we may disregard them completely, following more spontaneous impulses and accepting no value-driven imperatives. We may simply reflect collective values, adopting a traditional social perspective and living according to majority lifestyles. We may develop a unique value system derived from personal preferences and which may or may not conform to social convention. We may be conservative in certain attitudes and radical in others, but whatever we adopt, the important recognition is how values shape our immediate experience. In the collective arena, the issue of values is either potentially confrontational when diametrically opposed values clash, or cooperative when a shared, compatible worldview prefers harmony.

Value systems are often dominated by security needs, and in the West most have been imprinted by a consumer and materialist bias, where individual success—and by implication the quality of the individual—is publicly indicated by conspicuous affluence and a high quantity of material possessions. Without the modern technological home, car, satellite dish, super video recorder, compact disc player, or home computer, our lives are not complete according to our consumer-driven culture. We are missing out on a crucial experience that —guaranteed—will bring us total, ecstatic fulfillment and without which we are unsuccessful and socially deprived! Few of us are really immune to being persuaded to exchange our money for such promised bliss, although perhaps the spiritually-minded temptation is toward the weekend workshop that offers us nirvana in forty-eight hours.

These are issues of value decisions; our choices will dictate the degree of planetary exploitation and damage to irreplaceable resources; our values influence purchasing, which in turn can determine what is commercially produced. Fear of stripping away Earth's tree cover has now made recycled paper a wiser choice; slowly, attention is being directed toward our use of oil. A shift of values, environmental awareness, and technological advance could consign gas-powered engines to the museum, replacing them with those powered by electric or solar energy. But this step depends on new public values demanding changes in political and industrial decisions and actions.

The realization that we are not powerless in such matters is gradually increasing as questions are directed at collective attitudes and conditioning values. The questions, "What are we doing? Why are we doing it?" provide scope for a continual process of reassessment, and they need applying to individual and collective desires. Otherwise, we unconsciously repeat old values, attitudes, and directions even when these are outgrown and now causing harmful effects.

We may feel confused and lost when no effective alternative is apparent, but ignorance offers no solution and only increases problems.

PARTNERSHIP VALUES

The experience of intimate partnership is an ongoing adaptation of two value systems, and becomes an immediate and unavoidable exchange of shared values. Compatibility is not limited to sexual and emotional attraction alone, and equal importance should also be given to mental affinity and complementary worldviews and values, or else these may gradually erode the relationship by subjective divisions and objective disputes whenever attitudes and values oppose and contradict.

The 8th house focus on the "self-other relationship" requires greater awareness of how personal values influence and manipulate intimate partnerships and wider social interaction. Issues of joint resources arise when partnerships and marriages are entered into, and many disputes and conflicts result from collapsed marriages and the struggle for ownership of property and shared possessions. Or, during marriage, clarity and agreement may be needed regarding the use of joint money; if selfish actions are taken or different expenditure priorities clash, arguments are likely, and economic stress and disparate values are major causes of marital discord.

A new adult partnership may continue conditioned social values, following a traditional domestic and family oriented lifestyle, conforming to the "ideal marriage" and hoping to ensure an adequate degree of stability and security. Possessions and joint earnings contribute to shared resources, with decisions over their use often taken by a dominant partner, male or female, or preferably by mutual consent and consideration.

Yet, what often fails to be examined is relationship potential—how these shared resources could be utilized to create increased individual and partnership meaning and purpose.

It is easy to become so preoccupied with mundane routines and work that other options fail to be noted. Personal potential remains unrecognized by many; as a concept, it is often socially marginalized, distrusted, and unintegrated as a collective aim and vision. Personal talents and skills can remain unexploited resources that—if released—could offer alternative creative paths for individual and collective benefit. When two people come together, partnership potential can double, if only we were educated to be aware and take advantage of the gifts in our possession. A major contribution of the self-development movement to society is the declaration of human potential and how we can discover latent qualities, talents, and resources by turning within.

The 2nd house experience (overshadowed by Taurus) is concerned with personal resources, and the 8th house experience recapitulates this with the addition of a "collective contribution" and how the self-other relationship can be deepened and improved. This requires applying productive values into social interaction, and is one avenue for expressing the desire to merge stimulated by the 8th house. Our use of resources, finances, possessions, and values have to be balanced by awareness of others, so that we establish a free flow of giving and taking in equal measures, otherwise the process is distorted and imbalanced.

Partnership can be transformed into a productive and purposeful relationship, simply by using resources in ways which introduce a more holistic value system to the world. The process involves taking personal and partnership creative values and participating more effectively in society, so that a unifying vision is disseminated. Our choices in spending money can persuade manufacturers to change their product ranges to be more ecologically friendly; our savings investments can be with companies which are non-exploitative of employees and planetary resources; memberships of holistic groups and international charities can help spread a new planetary vision and assist in world redistribution of money and resources. A transformation of values can transform life; values are powerful, and we need to understand their role in building our world and then consciously assume a cocreative responsibility for its future. The starting place for this is examining our individual and partnership values.

HOLISTIC AND COLLECTIVE VALUES

Since the Second World War, there has been a proliferation of social pressure groups formed to influence society and awaken public attention toward those imminent dangers and abuses that collective ignorance and avoidance can create. Social crises are one result of disparate values in this complex modern world—and within the spheres of ecology, nuclear debate, feminism, and civil rights the relevance of the statement "the personal is the political" is apparent.

Many people in the West have been politicized, radicalized, and awakened to a sense of social responsibility over the last thirty years and, in the process of becoming conscious of collective issues, have redefined their own personal values, transforming their lifestyles and purpose accordingly. What has emerged for people participating in social activism or concern for future planetary well-being has been a heart-driven set of values with a compassionate awareness of planetary relationship comprising their visionary perspective and serving as moral guidelines. In the context of their genuine concerns, they raise provocative questions regarding shared resources and personal and planetary values.

In this period of historic transition and reevaluation of our civilizational tenets, we face a significant world choice. Simply expressed, this is the question of "How do we utilize the energies and resources born of togetherness?" Now that we begin to acknowledge a global identity and shared responsibility, the emphasis of values now asks "How do these assist the general welfare of all? "This is the crux of the division between separatist and materialist values and those which can be characterized as spiritual values.

While narrow, self-interested motives and values can have positive social effects, this is just a byproduct, and their overall influence does little to heal and bridge social divisions, and in many cases amplifies or highlights them. Selfishness is the major obstacle to world progress, and if each society is composed of selfish individuals, then this is reflected by collective attitudes. Selfishness can emerge on various levels, causing dispute and disharmony wherever active.

Spiritual or holistic values suggest an inclusive path for all to benefit—freedom, creative growth, human enlightenment, collective responsibility, concern and commitment, compassionate attitudes, a recognition of human potential, the vision of synthesis and wholeness—all offer an expanded human perspective of a positive, future horizon and inspirational objectives that can dissolve selfish barriers. The key value to realize and apply in our emerging interdependent world involves the relationship of the part to the whole, the individual and the collective, self and other. It is time to merge personal interests to the good of all, and contribute to the development and well-being of the whole. Inclusive ideals and principles can determine new value systems that are so desperately needed for planetary health and survival. In our relationships, a vision of potential guides our steps forward; by recognizing our interdependent oneness, mutual responsibility becomes enshrined in holistic values. These are the foundation stones for the Aquarian cultural revelation of unity, and how new values can build right human relationships and display impersonal "love in action."

The formation of idealistic affinity groups is one response to human challenges, ranging from direct actions—such as disrupting whaling fleets to street theater and mass protest rallies—to internationally coordinated meditational rituals designed to evoke spiritual energies or precipitate a harmonic convergence. What is common to all these varied types of responses is the awareness that "we have but one planet and that we need to learn how to live peacefully in harmony with others and nature." Underlying this crucial shift in collective worldview from one of exploitation and materialist expansion is an 8th house recognition of partnership, relationship, and that "I am my brother's keeper" is the unbreakable connection between self and others. Through this insight comes opportunities for planetary regeneration and rebirth, as the fact of interdependence becomes clearly acknowledged and these implications are understood.

The need for this cannot be overemphasized; the creation of new economic values and ways to share planetary resources are crucial to any emergent Aquarian society. If we are to collectively participate in a rebirth of planetary and ecological awareness, then we start with ourselves and our relationships. By recreating our values in the context of holistic awareness, and intending to release a harmonious, constructive potential, we can share in a planetary endeavor to forge a new vision of shared resources for humanity, and not just for a self-selected few taking more than a fair share by abusing social position and wealth. The alternative to this route is the passive contemplation and abnegation of responsibility as we watch the slow devastation and destruction of our planetary home, continuing to ignore the consequences of tempting excessive consumer and social desires.

This crisis on economic and ecological levels is of our own making. If we collectively act as the self-centered scorpion-type personality, misusing power over others for personal gratification, and satiating our desires at the expense of planetary health, then we are stinging ourselves to death. If we make the forward step to the eagle-type personality, our ability to cooperate and temporarily see from a higher vantage point will enable a renewal to happen. The eagle may use others' resources for personal gain, yet mutual benefits will also accumulate. Currently, the message from those with eagle vision is growing louder in the world; over the last decade, environmental activists have moved from outsiders at the social fringe—perceived as cranks and prophets of doom—to positions of social respectability. Their contribution to our awareness of pollution and ecological damage is now undeniable, and even any reactionary government evasion cannot continue to ignore the green message.

There is still much to do; as is appropriate for 8th house issues, two conflicting worldviews and values stand in opposition and crisis. The old, entrenched values and ideas of exploiting resources and perpetual economic growth as derived from separatist principles still resist the renewing energy of realized planetary interdependence. This is the modern battleground when an outworn path, which is no longer healthy and expansive, and has become restrictive and ultimately defeating, is faced by a new, regenerative path, which uproots previous assumptions, attitudes, and values. If we resist these opportunities for an 8th house transformative rebirth in terms of shared values and resources—by reaffirming a separatist stance—then the impulse for progress and growth is rejected and inevitably will be discovered as detrimental to our personal and collective health.

We cannot stand apart from our collective interaction. Attempting to do so only devalues social cohesion and dissipates energy into unproductive channels. Whether we like it or not, the axis upon which existence manifests itself involves the human experience of self and other. The modern crisis is how we perceive this relationship, in terms of self alone, or of self and other. This choice then determines our later principles, values, and actions. Evolution is the play between the one and the many, and we have collectively arrived at a turning point along this journey. As a Zen koan challenges the seeker: "If the One is reduced into the Many, to what is the Many reduced?"[1] The liberating experience of this, too, is an 8th house awakening.

Even when considering the traditional 8th house connection with inheritances, perhaps of property and money left by parental

---

[1] A contemporary variant of the original koan: "All existences return to One, but where will One itself return to? (The One returns to the Many.)" Yoel Hoffman, *The Sound of the One Hand* (London: Paladin, 1977), p. 111.

deaths, these questions are present: what inheritance will we leave to those who follow us into the world? Are our successors to be victims of our selfish obsession or beneficiaries of our social responsibility? The power of our choice is that we act as "Fate" for future generations, either by healing our wounded planetary ecology and establishing a wiser economic and political system, or by bequeathing a polluted, overexploited world which through selfish ignorance has become a terminal case.

Astrology—Values and Resources

The attitudes that form our values and how we deal with personal and collective resources can be considered through an astrological perspective. As self-insight reveals how we create our lives and experiences, one crucial sphere of this knowledge explores those values that compose our worldview and that direct our choices and actions. Unless we understand the nature of our values, we have no genuine self-knowledge, and our decisions may merely be automatic reactions.

Our attitudes toward money and personal finance may be indicated by an 8th house focus, especially the desire and capacity to receive money from the world through marriage, investments, inherited wealth, knowledge, and business which may offer material and emotional security through prosperity. These can include the consequences of socially sanctioned, legal, contractual agreements binding individuals together. Planets, signs and aspects in the 8th house can imply how we will fare financially in all our social partnerships, or indicate when transit activity offers additional opportunity or restrictions.

A highlighted 8th house can suggest that controlling or investing someone else's money could be a means to accumulate wealth, as has been proven by banks and businesses which use others' resources through stock investments and company growth for their own gain. Aspects to 8th house planets can indicate good money flow or difficulties in producing financial security. Adjusting attitudes and values may provide a key to changing any possible limiting patterns.

Considering astrological influences through the 8th house lens of planets, signs, and aspects can illuminate a reassessment of our values and use of resources beyond purely personal advantage. As a succedent house, the 8th is concerned with how we use the power that is available to us through the angular houses (1st, 4th, 7th and 10th).

We can be questioned as to how we contribute to partnership and collective development. Do we help or hinder progress? Are our values, attitudes and actions part of the solution or part of the problem? Do we squander money, resources and potential? Are we takers or givers? What are our values? How can these be directed and applied for constructive results? How aware are we of our social interaction? Do we acknowledge or deny our personal power and influence?

What does the theme of "we have" mean to you? Are you enriched by others sharing their talents and resources with you? Are you willing to share your talents and resources to enrich others? Do you accept your share of responsibility for what you and your relationships contribute to the world? The following section suggests questions and insights by planet and sign.

SUN (LEO)

Priority is given to personal needs and your value system tends to be very self-referential, with attention focused on meeting personal demands, sometimes excluding a sensitive awareness of others. Your primary values are asserted by living in a way that tries to attract power and influence, although the 8th house tendency for secrecy and manipulation may prefer a behind-the-scenes role. In displaying your talents and personal resources, you expect others' respect and appreciation, even though you are applying resources mainly for self-benefit rather than as a deliberate social contribution; if mutual benefit occurs, then fine, otherwise you favor number one.

Your ambition is to achieve a position of authority and responsibility, where your personal values and convictions receive additional power from prestigious social influence. Hierarchical structures are acceptable provided that you are near or at the top, which you believe is your rightful place. This attitude can become elitist and mold your social perceptions; if egocentric values predominate, then those who are disadvantaged may receive less support and encouragement than Leo generosity can often give.

Alternatively, you may feel inspired to assert your social power, becoming a crusading champion or spokesperson for the needs of the deprived. Taking this path may be very effective, and you could discover how to use innate personality resources and skills to create lasting beneficial change. Persuasion and genuine conviction, commitment, and communication skills may be important, and an enthusiastic sincerity can attract social support for your efforts.

The main challenge for the solar and leonine individual is reconciling a natural egocentric personality with the needs of others. This is the conflict between "I have" and "We have" at the crux of your life-path decision, and this may become a key issue in your relationships and reactions to joint resources. Questions will occur as to how you use personal resources, potential, talents, and how these can be integrated into partnerships and society. Experiences and interaction with others may motivate you to recreate personal and partnership values so that your actions become collectively harmonious, and constructive in effect.

Authoritarian, dominating, and egotistical characteristics may require moderation; disputes over contrasting value systems can become common. A habit of fixed values and attitudes can leave you inflexible when situations change, and more awareness of complex situations and individual needs may allow greater openness and adjustment, or a judgmental attitude can appear uncaring and harsh. Recognizing that the world does not revolve around satisfying your desires or that it doesn't have to conform to your values will be a crucial step in inner adjustment, possibly reshaping your future purpose and direction.

You intend releasing your energies forcefully, although abusing power may be an ongoing temptation and should be avoided. If your emphasis changes from personal gain to collective gain, solar vitality can increase feelings of union with others and relationships can flourish. Clarifying your values and their impact in the world can reveal a new direction toward integration with the group, and this collective dimension can bring more satisfaction than you believe or anticipate. A revised set of values regarding power, resources, and their potential application will be helpful, or egoistic exploitation may distort your effect in the world, making it less creatively significant. Even if you benefit personally and financially, the sense of isolation and alienation may be a heavy price to pay, when instead, by adopting a path of shared values, you can also be successful and appreciate fulfilling relationships.

Care may be necessary to moderate extravagant tastes and spontaneous spending instincts which create imprudent expenses. An urge to expand requires an evaluation of plans and options to determine viability before decisions are taken. Luck and prosperity may be aided by using personal contacts and sharing resources in partnership projects. By shifting your value system to accommodate others' success too, your own potential for life enjoyment can be increased by appreciating inner abundance and the gifts of relationship.

Issues of investments, legacies, and the law can become important, and the quality of family relationships may determine whether these will be favorable or detrimental. If your Sun has challenging aspects, then difficulties may be more apparent—frustrating and restricting you, especially if your attitudes and values have made marital, business, and legal disputes more likely. With harmonious aspects, better fortune may be experienced, and inheritance, business, partnerships, speculation and family finances may be enhanced.

MOON (CANCER)

Lunar value systems and the application of personal resources are dictated by emotional responses to situations and people; these may be strongly conditioned by parental and social attitudes absorbed during an impressionable childhood. Your emphasis is often placed on insuring security and stability, and this creates a cautious, compromising, and predictable approach, where risks are minimized and non-conformity and unconventional acts are rare. You see your role as part of a collective responsibility, and this affects the shape of family life and social interaction by your need for acceptance and approval.

Your mother may have influenced the forming of your value system, self-image, attitudes, and recognition of potential, so looking closely at her impact can be revealing. Observe, too, how your evaluation of options and people is made by emotional and intuitional feelings; attitudes, beliefs, and values are equally connected to emotional biases.

You may tend toward partnership dependency, where your values become secondary to those of a partner on whom you rely. This can result in vulnerability to another's domination and emotional manipulation which should be avoided. Greater self-confidence in your own worldview and potential is necessary, and if this occurs, then progress toward interdependence is possible, adding balance to your partnerships.

Moods and emotional inconsistency are probable and your actions are directed by a compelling need to love and be loved, yet more effort is required to surmount protective and repetitive behavior patterns before a wider social contribution can be made. Tendencies to retreat into a family and domestic shell may limit the release of personal potential, skills, or resources that could be socially constructive.

Understanding your values and attitudes is important, or these may dominate your life by compulsive, unconscious, and automatic decisions. Anxieties about security and stability dictate the nature of relationships and how you use joint resources. You are eager to adopt the "We have" of shared values through cooperation and adaptation. You willingly support a partner to develop his or her potential, even forgetting or limiting your own. Your needs may be surrendered for mutual harmony, and while this can bring peace to the relationship, it may simultaneously repress your own feelings and desires and cause problems later.

For you, partnerships highlight finances, perhaps through joint materialistic progress, inheritances, or business ventures. Harmonious lunar aspects imply that these will be beneficial, and challenging aspects suggest that financial success or struggle depends on the quality of the partnership and your interpretation of emotionally-derived gut-feelings.

With security needs so dominant, risks are few and opportunities often rejected through fear and caution. Yet one personal resource that could be effective is your psychic sensitivity sensing new and future collective trends which will require businesses to service them. The Moon can act like a magic mirror, revealing the activity of intangible forces before their presence is apparent by changing public fashions, interests and needs. If you could ally with a partner who possesses a practical, rational mind, then an effective duo could be formed whose partnership values have a constructive social influence. Moving your attention from a limited personal and family perspective can unlock personal skills and resources that may otherwise be only dimly sensed.

MERCURY (GEMINI, VIRGO)

Mercury's value system and application of resources is dominated by mind and an intellectual worldview which is presented as objective, detached, logical, and analytical, even though it is more personally biased than acknowledged. Often your values are derived from an interpretation and assessment of previous actions and their causes and results, so that a pragmatic system evolves through experience. This may require accumulating information prior to decisions, so your value system may be variable and affected by an evaluation process. However, you may alternatively simply adopt a collective value system as your mental framework and chosen perspective, such as a philosophical doctrine that appeals to your worldview preferences.

Your value-assessment favors objective intellect and may disregard emotions and feelings. Ideas and concepts may interfere with your attitudes and social interaction, possibly diminishing tolerance and patience for the human dimension if under the impression of powerful ideological doctrines. Your scrutiny of options emphasizes practicality rather than sentimentality when confronted by contentious, collective issues. Impersonality and coldness may result from an exaggerated preference for logic, losing sight of simple compassion and human solidarity.

Two possible paths have an intellectual emphasis: one is analysis and division, the other synthesis and relationship. While biased toward analysis, Mercury can operate either way, leading to a detached observation of society or a deeper participation and use of mind for collective advantage. This pragmatic quality may be expressed self-centeredly and dispassionately from an intellectually elitist perspective, or it may serve to inspire a vision of a human community where "divided we fall, together we stand" is the core attitude, and organizational abilities are fused with compassionate logic to build a peaceful and supportive world for all to share.

Values are often influenced by your ethical and religious beliefs, and awareness may be needed to avoid self-righteousness, fixed restrictive convictions, and a separatist worldview. Partnerships will work when basic values are compatible and complementary, and the use of joint resources is most successful when intentions are shared. Intellectual development is the most recognized of your potential; and other talents and qualities may be implicitly devalued by your lacking understanding and appreciation of their relevance in your life. The value of your emotions and intuition is a likely casualty of Mercury's rule.

The retrograde Mercury increases introspective traits and diminishes social integration. Attention is redirected inward, and you may prefer reflective and contemplative thinking, searching for meaning and the connectedness of existence. Thoughts, attitudes, and values can be repetitively reassessed, and your choices and decisions are not lightly taken. You may feel a degree of dissociation from other levels of self and society—an alienation caused by lack of energy when drawn into this focused mental orientation. Disinterest in physical action and emotional involvement is likely, which can minimize social interaction and cause withdrawal. An aura of self-preoccupation is likely, as if detached to allow a slowly occurring deep regeneration of thoughts and values.

A preference for impersonality, theory, or conceptual ideas is likely, and attention may be attracted to studying cultural creations from the past, those which strive to make sense of the complex, contradictory universe through the lens of religion, science, philosophy, art. Any curiosity for the past may need reducing or replacing by a more contemporary focus designed to discover how your social contribution can be made in the present; Mercury's approach to this is to search for a higher, unifying connection, where analysis is superseded by a broader vision of synthesis.

A shift from self-referential values and intellectual activity may be needed, even though this can be difficult to achieve. A new connection between self-partnership-society is required for a new level of integration. When Gemini is the cuspal sign, this may be harder to reach, as dualistic separation is emphasized by the Twins, and the gap between inner and outer may appear less resolvable; with Virgo, the quality of service may be activated, extending awareness of self-other and modifying the inner preoccupation.

With the retrograde Mercury, plans and projects may be continually created and evaluated, yet fail to be manifested. Your potential can remain latent rather than tangibly demonstrated; imagining mental dream-worlds can be more attractive than real life, and these shimmering, glorious castles of mind devour energy that could have been practically utilized. A deliberate effort may be necessary to resist this inward pull, or social disconnectedness can intensify.

VENUS (TAURUS, LIBRA)

Values are naturally aligned with social interaction and tend to emphasize materialism, physical comforts, and pleasures, especially when creating aesthetically appealing environments and feelings of unity. There are intrinsic desires for interpersonal relationships, shared values and resources, partly based on your recognition that mutual assistance is personally beneficial. Security through partnership is highlighted, and most value-decisions reflect your need for definite roots in family and collective affinity. Your values emerge from an instinct for unity, and are derived from awareness and sympathetic feelings for others, although if these are Taurus influenced, then self-centeredness may dominate, or if Libran influenced, manipulative traits may exist.

Venusian values have a passivity and yielding quality, which can unconsciously slide into dependency and submission. You may disguise this in terms of compromise and cooperative behavior. When consciously applied in life, these values can be balancing and harmonious, natural mediators in disputes, and can be reminders that a degree of unified relationship can always be attained if that intention is present. Venus feels related and connected through an instinct to unite opposites, and these values aim to extend and deepen communal sharing and utilize joint resources.

When Taurus influenced, values and resources are evaluated in terms of potential productiveness, and this becomes your criterion for their applicability. What results can be created? What tangible gains can be achieved? Often these duplicate traditional collective values as held by the majority that support the status quo. Psychologically, conservative attitudes dominate and a resistance to change can be observed. Material aims, physical comforts, and luxuries are primary incentives, and possessiveness can sometimes replace sharing as your dominating attitude. Caution and self-preservation characterize choice, as do habitual routines and fixed behavior. There can be a laziness evident in manifesting your potential, an occasional lethargy in motivation.

When Virgo influenced, values and resources are used in a quest for efficient perfection. Wasting energy, assets, talents, and potential is anathema to Virgo, who, despite self-criticism, can display a rigorous intention for self-development and a sustainable partnership. Control and discipline are engrained in these values, where personal and social responsibility is more important than independence and free expression. Virgoan values are practical, discriminative, and conscientious—suggesting a discerning intelligence which veers toward a "purist assessment" of life and people. High value standards and expectations may be set which can result in a judgmental and critical perception, losing touch with the value of feelings and evaluating people from a logical viewpoint. Yet the sense of relatedness remains, and a spirit of assistance to others is genuinely expressed as an inner motivation. Social contribution is often achieved through methodical and conscientious work, and encouraging potential is part of the impulse for personal and social perfection. If talents are present, then Virgo intends that dedicated application can help to release them.

The retrograde Venus may obstruct social interaction, intensifying the importance of personal needs and desires over others. Social trust is diminished and external influences minimized, as less emphasis is placed on social contacts. Conflicts between self-centered values and societal demands may occur, and frustrated resentments can accumulate when your insistent desires meet resistance from others. An immature expectation of fulfillment can disillusion you, distorting idealistic attitudes to life and the world. Perfection is rarely discovered, and unrealistic values may require radical adjustment for inner balance.

The retrograde Venus may aid in developing a unique set of aesthetic values that assume priority in directing choices and decisions. These emerge from a phase of questioning self-worth and breaking free from social impressions. These are often less materialistic, and more aesthetically aware and individually sensitive than the direct Venus values, which—while more socially conscious—are primarily intent on personal pleasures. The retrograde can magnify a search to connect disparate parts of the psyche, assisting self-inquiry and spiritual development; the direct Venus gives priority to external interaction and social cohesion, promoting collective development.

MARS (ARIES)

Values informed by 8th house Mars and Aries influences are shaped by their potential for social assertion, serving as a conduit for enterprising activity intended to satisfy personal desires. Your values embody vitality, initiative, and a pioneering spirit, although they tend toward an aggressive, combative expression fixated on pursuing your destiny rather than making a social contribution. In this context, shared values and resources are less apparent, only activated when personal gain can be guaranteed through cooperative ventures, and then often only temporarily.

The consequences of Mars-influenced values can be either constructive or destructive, depending on your motivations. Uncontrolled desires may direct your values and use of resources from unconscious pressures that are highly self-centered and separative. Or, you could emerge as a force-ful spokesperson and focus for others' needs, serving as a cru-sading spirit in society, perhaps acting for minority causes and those culturally disadvantaged.

Energy may be released impulsively and recklessly, with little thought for its effect on others apart from the opportu-nity to satisfy your desires. Or this energy may inspire and encourage others, forging a united group ready to attain com-mon objectives. The balance between personal desire and the collective good is one of Mars' challenges, and how this is resolved will determine the nature of conditioning values.

When influenced by an 8th cusp Aries, values are dic-tated by a need for urgent and immediate results, so decisions and choices are made by a restless, compulsive impulse of activ-ity and enterprise. The key attitude of Arien values is "Me first," or "I have," and this works against easily developing joint resources and collective responsibility. Competitive instincts are powerful, and compromise and cooperation are qualities that often have to be learned. Insensitivity to oth-ers can be likely, and an argumentative impatience can be dis-played to those with different value systems. Your belief in being right can restrict communication and sharing, and a self-ish commitment to a personal path and exploitation of resources can inhibit partnership development.

The retrograde Mars tends to inhibit this outward thrust, obstructing decisive activity and decreasing initiative and willpower. Inner doubts interfere with self-confidence, and impul-sive risk-taking is not so appealing; pitfalls seem more preva-lent and unavoidable. Frustrations redirect your energies, polarizing the conflict of self-other desires and exaggerating a divisive sense of separation from society. Selfishness becomes self-denial and uncertainty, posing questions of which values, attitudes, and intentions are operative; thought and strategy become delaying steps prior to taking action, and effort may be redirected toward understanding unconscious motivations.

Releasing your potential may prove difficult and demand great struggle, perhaps remaining unrealized. An insight into the paucity of emphasizing material values alone may be discovered, opening a quest in search of inner values that reflect a genuinely individual perspective and that are more suitable for determining decisions. The retrograde may help you distinguish between separatist values and those which can unify, and instead of being a channel for selfish desires, may be transformed into a channel for collective growth.

JUPITER (SAGITTARIUS)

Personal values develop from your need for renewal and to expand potential, serving as a foundation for a more enriched life. Actions and decisions are taken based on their future opportunity prospects, and how they may enable aspirations and aims to be achieved. Your underlying attitude is for growth, which extends either idealistic plans or personal freedom. Social awareness attracts you toward group involvement. One key value is based on a belief that all can benefit by cooperation and draw additional well-being and creative power from a communal spirit. A willingness to assume social responsibility and become a leader or spokesperson may be evident.

Ethical concerns of justice and equality may be motivating factors, perhaps reflecting political, humanist, or religious ideals, and a sense of duty to apply these within society may inspire action. Values are primarily shaped by your need for law, order, morality, and personal convictions. Solidarity is enjoyed when you work within groups, and ritualized activity can be experienced as particularly meaningful. However, you prefer to become a leader rather than remain a follower; any tendency to exploit power over others needs to be guarded against, and you should ensure that empathy and understanding is present in group relationships. If you are a representative of an ideal—political ideology, religion, or humanitarian project—then a distinction between the power of what you represent and your own personal power may be necessary to prevent a distorted and exaggerated self-image. Resources are acknowledged, and you look for opportunities to express and expand skills and talents. As you see life replete with options and a multiplicity of paths, focused discipline and commitment may require learning, or else you may wastefully scatter energies and resources with little definite result or progress. Greater concentration and clarity of purpose is needed for maximum effectiveness. Partnership and joint resources can help define this direction, although you still need to restrict dissipation and ensure that a common objective is mutually agreed. An over-optimistic self-belief may sometimes stretch you too far, and a backward step may be occasionally inevitable to avoid failure; a more realistic assessment of your abilities can help, perhaps provided by others.

The Sagittarian influence increases an idealistic bias and instinct for personal freedom; the search for understanding still dominates and may be less materially interested than Jupiter in the 8th. Exploration and aspiration inspire your value system, which prefers an intellectual worldview and is attracted toward philosophical structures that purport to explain human nature and universal reality. Both values and resources are assessed in terms of enabling expansion into new horizons, and you may be liable to an underlying belief that "the grass is always greener on the other side," which creates a restless, inner agitation that can dispel peace and contentment.

Personal freedom is highly valued, and partnerships need to incorporate this or friction can occur. Directness and honesty in relationship communication is expected, and candor can sometimes be disconcerting and not always welcomed. There can be an ability for deep, profound thought and intellectual resources may be easily accessed, especially in roles of communicator and interpreter of complex ideas and concepts. Life is viewed with optimistic attitudes, perceived as a realm of incredible possibilities and opportunities; focusing multiple options may be difficult until clarity of purpose is reached, but even so, the spirit of adventure is sufficient inspiration and motivation.

The retrograde Jupiter's values inclines you toward inner growth more than materialistic gains, and is based on personal principles and idealistic convictions. You may have a detached mental attitude that precludes compromising and adjusting these principles to account for human nature, preferring them enshrined in purity rather than blemished by any imperfection. Introspection is intensified and time is spent withdrawn in private contemplation. Social value systems and those of others are noted, but your effort concentrates on establishing a personal set of uniquely meaningful values, rather than passively adopting consensus values. Part of this is a rejection of conformity and convention, and a distaste for social conditioning.

Your attitudes may shift between optimism and pessimism; this may depend on previous life experiences and may be reflected by Jupiter's aspects. A tendency for fixed attitudes, high standards, and judging others may affect relationships, making demands on intimate partnerships that could be unrealistic. Righteous attitudes and confidence in your own wisdom may inspire efforts to reform others and society; this may need handling with care and humor or else resistance may be your only reward from an "ungrateful outer world." Resources are considered in terms of prospective inner development with attention turned toward fulfillment instead of accumulating material prosperity. Studying, insight, and intellect are paths for expansion, as you perceive your social contribution to be idealistic and cultural.

SATURN (CAPRICORN)

Values are formed by social tradition, consensus attitudes and beliefs, and can result in a conformist personality, which seeks security by social acceptance. This implies self-limita-

tions and possible repressions of any traits that are culturally denied or condemned—just as establishing a socialized
identity and participating role is considered more important
than asserting your free individuality. Values include discipline and order, as these are perceived as foundations for a
stable community, and your resulting worldview is one that
prefers distinct boundary lines, barriers, and controls as prerequisites for mutual collective security. Abiding by laws, moral
rules, and social codes demands your recognition of collective supremacy.

Caution may increase inhibitions and reluctance to take
risks for growth, and change is often seen as unwelcome
and unnecessary; the value of the past and conservatism are
primary attitudes. A tendency to live with rigidity and a
resistance to assert independent values against predominant
social ones is common.

Yet Saturn values also provide society with effective, practical results, serving as a binding and restraining influence
which ensures a workable degree of collective cohesion.
Saturn insists on productive work for society, where sustained
effort, patience, and duty ensures that social needs are met,
even at the expense of personal freedom. Realistic assessments of human needs are made, serious attitudes to life are
taken, and social responsibility is emphasized. Resources are
applied with constructive logic, and organizational and
planning skills are used to benefit all. Responsible functioning is the key to Saturn's social purpose, and your values reflect this.

The retrograde Saturn amplifies this reliance on traditional
values, and these are absorbed through cultural conditioning
and a socially impressionable personality. Your need for life-
structures as a defensive, and self-defining boundary often
locks in a self-denying instinct. Attitudes can become negative and depressive, perceiving yourself through an inflexible, rigid lens that narrows potential and options, linking you
firmly with the collective worldview. A private, hidden inse-

curity and unease may be felt as an inner pressure, despite the appearance of social acceptability and possible material success. Underneath the surface may lie anxiety, doubt, fear, guilt, shame, repression, rigidity, and self-rejection.

Personal integration can be lost by conformity to "how you should be" according to social belief; this attempt to mold yourself may become painfully uncomfortable—wounding and damaging your psyche. To compensate for such feelings, you may search for positions of control, power, and authority over others, so that inadequacies can be masked by a "superior status." Or alternatively, there may be authority conflicts if you react against the power of traditional values and attitudes when you start striving to create your own.

A fear of change may be noted, preferring routine lifestyles and diminishing spontaneity in exchange for stability and certainty. Your conscience speaks loudly; either the "social conscience" of how you should act according to religious, political, or moral codes, or a genuine inner voice guiding you to break free of imposed shackles to hear the repressed wisdom of your whole nature which requires recognition. The potency of the past needs casting away, and self-esteem and worth can be affirmed as the principle values to live by.

Personal integrity clarifies and strengthens, and as you slowly gain new insight into the restrictive nature of old, repetitive thought patterns, you have an opportunity to be reborn and regenerated by dismantling any imposed conformist value systems that are ill-fitting. By inner inquiry and deep self-contemplation, a renewed personality can emerge, free from unconscious imprisonment and able to liberate skills, talents, and resources to enhance self-development.

When Capricorn dominates the 8th house, values are circumscribed by rational attitudes, prudence, and caution, often expressed as an ordered, disciplined personality and lifestyle. Self-containment and a serious, responsible life-attitude dominates awareness, and conformity to social tradition is viewed as a mature action. Social order, stability, and security are given highest priorities, and a sense of community service may define your purpose. Practicality is emphasized as essential, and a patient, methodical, and conscientious approach conditions efforts. The relevance of organized planning is the bedrock of future success, and rarely will you leap into spontaneous action. Perseverance is another key to applying your values and resources, and a capacity to work long and hard to achieve aims can ensure success.

Rational logic is often chosen instead of emotion and intuition when facing choices, and values are shaped first by your need for self-preservation, rather than by their creative possibilities. A pessimistic bias influences your outlook and a relatively narrow focus may be limiting. Your emotions are often secondary to a purposeful drive, and these may be repressed and denied; discomfort with volatile feelings is likely, and empathy may be lacking.

URANUS (AQUARIUS)

Values are defined by impulses for individuality, independence, and your refusal to passively accept social traditions and consensus thinking; you often see these as detrimental to personal freedom, and losing self into the collective is rejected as akin to death. The importance of change in life is considered an important value to express and experience. Uranian values strive to break away from mass conformity, shaking free of externally imposed controls by asserting the individual right to rebel. This may be disruptive to all concerned, yet may renew limiting routines, habits, and ordering patterns that become unconsciously established in individuals and society. Through changing such patterns can come radical insights, an intuition of better future directions, and an inspiration to expand creative options by shattering inertia.

When Uranian values are encountered, prospects for creative crisis are increased. Your values are determined by their ability to create freedom and independence; unorthodox experimentation appeals, risks are welcomed as adding excitement to life, and an awareness of potential, options, and possibility rejects any acquiesence to an unfulfilling status quo. This instinct for change can easily be misapplied, especially if inspiring a rebellious adversary of society, whose intent is merely to disrupt and destroy, or when social contribution and partnerships are broken by rejecting commitment and participation by asserting an individual freedom which simultaneously denies the relatedness of life.

Uranian values should never be an excuse for irresponsible, evasive behavior. A more mature level of expression is beneficial to all, one which can contribute inventiveness, reformist abilities, positive future visions to society, and an altruistic spirit that can make others enthusiastic about cooperatively creating positive world change. Deviation from the social norm can be either a juvenile, unproductive reaction or a genuine individual step to introduce a new personal and social vision, perhaps by making innovative use of available resources, or by discovering scientific advances. Uranian values can bring a breath of revitalizing fresh air into the world, although this impulse may be difficult to handle consistently and wisely.

The retrograde Uranus can be met in a separatist, destructive manner, inciting the rebellious urge whenever an alienating social rejection is acutely felt. Your values and priorities may be self-centered, losing sight of the equal importance of others or recognizing that their value systems also possess validity and relevance. A sense of "unique superiority" may develop. A wake of dissonance, dissension, and division can be set in motion that affects others' lives as a consequence of insisting upon your personal freedom and liberation.

While intentions may exist to erode social stability there is still confusion as to the relationship—or lack of—between self and other. Part of this social antagonism is derived from feeling isolated and misunderstood, and any radical, unorthodox ideals, or progressive, futurist insights may be dismissed by others as unrealistic fantasies.

Uranian nonconventionality can either spur your development, strengthening integrity and the ability to live independently, or can become an excuse to reject society and assume
an adversarial stance. There can be a narrow line between a
constructive approach, and a destructive one—and distinguishing between these is a challenge for all with Uranus-influenced
values. The "prophet's task" is never easy, and is so liable to
self-delusion; but adhering to the inevitability of change and
recognizing society's need to accept this is correct, and one
lesson that repeatedly needs learning and rediscovery.

The Aquarius influence has numerous similarities to
Uranus, emphasizing individuality and attraction toward
non-conformity and social reform. Aquarius favors a scientific, detached intellectualism that enjoys involvement in
progressive thinking, and these shape conditioning values.
Humanitarian idealism can be displayed through commitment
to social causes or pressure groups, and Aquarius has a powerful belief in the concept of world fellowship to connect
together the planetary array of different races as contributing to the rainbow culture; a theme of unity within diversity
is an Aquarian vision that informs values. This sense of social
participation tends to be activated, and despite unpredictability,
private values are identified with progressive social aims, supporting constructive reforms and the extension of human
rights and freedoms. A taste for the unknown and unusual
may increase an experimental impulse, and a preference for
variety can stimulate a periodically changing lifestyle and direction. Interest in releasing potential and taking opportunities
can ensure that resources are applied, although shifting directions and commitments may diminish their effectiveness
whenever focus is lacking.

NEPTUNE (PISCES)

Values are affected by sensitivity, compassion, and idealism,
and can be a little fragile when exposed to the world. Your

impracticality and lack of realism are often vulnerable to disillusionment, especially as values are inspired by a need to live in a perfect world that may only exist in your dreams. Neptune values are refined and have a subtle uplifting effect, raising your sights to imagine a social vision of the world which may be possible for humanity to create, or equally possible, may lie forever beyond the human capability to attain; this vision could be the coming shadow of a feasible future or the shadow of a fantasy.

You may hope to apply these values to open a way beyond materialism and the confines of physical existence, believing that your sensitivity reveals something else beyond. Often these become embedded in artistic, cultural inspirations or aesthetic appreciations of creativity and imagination, and your aspirations may be reflected by Neptunian values. Connections and channels between levels are established through which inspiration flows.

The dividing line between reality and illusion may be narrow, and an otherworldliness may dominate your personality. Defining your values, attitudes, purpose, and direction may seem too difficult, as these shift with inner tides. Mysticism, day-dreaming, and imagination can be confusedly interwoven, and unconscious motives slip through to influence choices without recognition. Values may appear diffuse, adaptable, or flexible to others, as if no firm center actually exists. Escapism and evasion of responsibility interact with genuine compassion and the impulse to serve others.

Identity boundaries are indistinct and an urge for union prompts a mystical search for oneness with something greater, either by social-cultural involvement or religious quest. The attraction of social participation can be offset by your need for seclusion, and conflicts between these may be experienced.

One effect of Neptune values is to dissolve materialism and the past, while introducing a seed of a possible utopia which may be awaiting birth on a higher level. Clarity is an ongoing requirement when Neptune's values are active; the imagined joy of satisfying future dreams is opposed by current reality, and yet in this interplay something new is born. Without visionary dreamers, progress would be slowed and limited. The real challenge of these values is to ensure that you achieve some tangible result, that imagination does not absorb all the energy; otherwise plans dematerialize into empty space, and your resources and potential fail to manifest.

The retrograde Neptune deepens inward turning toward creative and imaginative channels, and highlights the gap between actual reality and the idealized, perfect dream-world that you would prefer to experience. Disillusionment and worldly disappointment may intensify your need to escape from mundane demands, although evasiveness can result in fears of involvement and commitment, losing opportunities for partnerships and social interaction. Attention is necessary to avoid the excessive participation in imaginative fantasies and self-deceptions, or these may diminish your identity. The urge to serve others will be present, but may remain an intention instead of an action. Actually doing things may be a problem, as thinking about things is more satisfying; you may dissipate inspiration through inactivity and failure to anchor ideas.

Your personality and values tend to be unstructured, and if you lack order and discipline, clarity and self-definition become irregular, causing confusion and loss of meaning and purpose. This can result in being impressionable and dependent on others for direction, which can leave you vulnerable to others' needs and being taken advantage of as a victim or martyr. Certainty is hard for you to find, and a feeling of being "blown by the wind" may diminish potential. As time passes, you can dream your life away and options slip unconsciously from your grasp. A reversal of attention may be required to utilize your talents and sensitivity in ways which assist personal integration and social contribution; discovering this direction will bring a liberating cohesion into your life.

The Pisces overlay on personal values has a passive and adaptable effect; it lacks easy definition. Often the nebulous values inhibit decisions, as at each crossroads a reassessment of intention, aim or need has to be taken. Values have a strong compassionate quality that may either inspire genuine efforts to assist others, or cause a reaction against the empathic suffering that proximity evokes, requiring Pisces to retreat from worldly pain. Values possess an unworldliness and intangibility that elude clarity, often formed by psychic and intuitional impressions at points when decisions are required; consistency is lacking and fluidity rules. Others may make accusations of indecision and loss of principle, integrity, and values; Pisces transcends structures and barriers, making understanding difficult and self-insight hard to attain.

Demonstrating sensitivity is a primary path to using natural talents and resources, and an impulse to introduce more harmony and aesthetic pleasure to life can become an ambition and a way to transform idealistic dreams into an actual experience. Neptunian values attempt to awaken people to a higher appreciation of life's beauty, stirring sensitivity in all spheres of life and pointing to the universal wonder and mystery that those bound to mundane concerns often forget. Through partnerships, Neptune perceives the mystery of the other, and bows down in genuflection, placing the partner on a pedestal until disillusionment offers the opportunity to see the rest of existence with a truer reflection.

PLUTO (SCORPIO)

When placed in its natural house Pluto and Scorpio indicate a deep influence in forming active values, with an opportunity available to make a positive social contribution. However, to fully achieve this, a radical transformation as a preparatory step is required.

Consensus values may have been adopted by your early social conditioning. Pluto initiates a reevaluation process, where absorbed values may fit uneasily with emerging adult characteristics, and an inner abrasion results, casting doubt as to the validity of existing values. You question their current personal relevance. An impulse to create a unique life path may confront existing values and attitudes, launching an inquiry to determine values that are personally meaningful. Life can feel unfulfilling, and you may search for a new way forward. This is the cyclic nature of Pluto and Scorpio energies, where the end-phase is encountered and the prospect of rebirth becomes possible.

To attain renewal, Pluto demands a purgation and elimination of any psychological values, beliefs, attitudes, or tendencies that have reached the end of their constructive contribution, and that are now restrictive. This situation may be met in several contexts—the recognition that your life has fallen flat and feels meaningless, lacking direction; the collapse of intimate relationships; employment problems or a lack of career progress; the disillusionment of political or religious ideology. All of these can trigger a reassessment of life priorities, which will re-form your creative values.

Within the psyche, a movement commences to "push out" agitating feelings, thoughts, or repressed and disowned fragments into your conscious mind, so that a redemptive healing can occur. This experience can be painful, as "darkness" pervades the conscious mind like an invasive inner shadow, tainting everything. Pluto's subverting activity can cause "life-subsidence," where personality structures can either suddenly or slowly collapse as deep roots are severed.

Possible separatist values and attitudes are exposed in a stark light, revealing their inadequacies; self-images may be irrevocably shattered and a new worldview becomes essential. A new relationship between self and other is crucial, and this often introduces greater awareness of possible social interaction and contribution, as if an awakening has occurred. The old personality and value system can be shed like a snake's skin, and a reinvigorated self may emerge onto life's stage if the process has been successfully undergone.

Two choices are possible: you may resist the process of renewal, in which case future suffering will be self-generated,

and life still remains unsatisfying; or you accept the need for
the old to die, transforming any unintegrated psychic debris
or releasing this prior to a new rebirth phase. The first choice
produces disempowerment, and the second allows a reempowerment to occur.

Any tendency toward psychological isolation can be
changed by realizing that by cooperative togetherness, new
socially constructive values can be applied that inspire radical and beneficial transformations for all. Awareness of how
individual choice and actions can make a vital difference is
empowering, both in assuming greater self-responsibility
and engaging in more effective social participation. Resources
are assessed in terms of new values; selfishness is diminished
by a service orientation, which enhances your meaning and
purpose. The challenge of Pluto influenced values involves
the transition from adopted values to uniquely individual ones;
this can be traumatic and difficult, with reactionary patterns
and psychological resistances opposing the embryonic new
direction struggling to be born.

The retrograde Pluto turns this process into a distinct inner
event, where few signs of subjective conflict may be observed
by others. A sense of self and worldly discontent may be pervasive, requiring some type of search to pacify, even though
you may not consciously register this. Psychological pressures
are internalized, and desires and impulses tend to be controlled
by repression. Questions proliferate as to self-knowledge,
values, meaning, and life-direction; your inner state can be
confusing, complex, and lacking harmony. Social interaction
is difficult; perhaps you are alienated by antisocial attitudes,
feeling isolated and not really accepted; this may be just your
personal feeling rather than a fact, but a loss of relatedness
is likely.

From this detached position, an objective view of society may be formed, allowing intensive questioning so you can
challenge conventional values and attitudes. The opportunity
is to develop values that assist self-integration and that suit

your personality, utilizing the outsider vision as a means for self-regeneration and rebirth. If this is evaded, the probable result will be increased alienation from social participation, possibly breeding additional resentment and anger without providing you with renewing options.

Scorpio inspired values can be those of the scorpion or eagle, either selfish or inclined to contribute to social progress. Priority is given to whatever increases intensity, and values are driven by passion and emotion more than rational thought. The need to feel at-one with personal values and attitudes is most important for integration, and a cold analytical perception can be focused on all major life issues to determine the most apt path; once options have been carefully defined, intuition decides the eventual choice, that gut-feeling which Scorpio relies on so heavily.

While Scorpio often displays an authoritarian and dominating nature, resistance is made to others attempting "power-over" tactics; passive acceptance of consensus values is rejected, and questioning these can lead to the renewing process, where you can create a meaningful value system. Scorpio values reflect needs to explore, probe, and penetrate deeply into life, as if in quest of reconnection, and this instinct provides the foundation for ongoing inquiry. Values are informed by desire to discover the truth, and nothing less really satisfies. Principle and authenticity are admired in others and prove a guide to personal behavior. Once selfishness is transformed an altruistic spirit is released, and your endeavors will then reflect the value of service; a self-image as a warrior for the disadvantaged may then motivate your new values.

4 Power, Manipulation, Compulsion, Obsession

WE TEND TO HAVE CULTURALLY confused, ambivalent reactions to the issue of power, especially as we recognize that the ego is inclined to manipulate others for self-aggrandizement and to satisfy desires. Self-assertion often becomes a display of attempted "power-over" others, and because of general misuse an ambiguous set of associations have accumulated around the term power.

We have all experienced the manipulative use of power throughout our lives, from childhood's submission to parents, teachers, and social conditioning, to adult situations with demanding and insensitive employers, lovers, and friends, and various encounters with the power vested in government, religion, bureaucracy, or even majority social attitudes. A common reaction to these clashes of will is that power is a dirty word, and that power corrupts, and absolute power corrupts absolutely, with a suspicious gaze fixed firmly on those who strive for positions of power in politics, business, management, often disparaged as power-mad.

We know the temptations that can occur in these influential spheres; those inflated egos that lose sight of humanity; the greed for money that proves irresistible to many with weakened integrity; the lust to be number one poised unsteadily on the edge of obsession; the seduction of power. How do we know this? Simple, these latent tendencies exist within everyone. All are vulnerable to the fatal attraction of manipulative power exploiting others to fulfill our desires. Even saints are not immune to egoistically dominating others, and religious power can be one of the worst abusers of "power-over" tactics existing in the world, infiltrating minds and hearts with repressive dogma and condemnatory images of being human sinners from our first breath.

Our social structures allow "power-over" hierarchies to develop in most contemporary organizations—government, military, church, corporations—and reflect egoic needs to be superior to others. Positions in hierarchies are considered to define individual status, the level of importance and personality quality, and are grasped to create an identity. These positions also create existential fears if external threats are made to erode personal power. More managerial energy and intelligence is expended on maintaining or expanding departmental empires than is applied to work efficiency.

Those intent on assuming positions of socially coercive power reinforce and favor the hierarchical model, and certainly our patriarchal culture has seen the supremacy of attitudes, values, and beliefs that support male preeminence, openly denigrating and devaluing women's qualities and roles, diminishing their power by a conditioning process that reduces female confidence and self-esteem. One of the main strategies for this was the religious dominance of a Father-God, whose projected masculine attributes were obviously the most important in society and which have created our current Western civilization. Fortunately social changes are now correcting this imbalance as women have become more assertive again, and slowly and almost grudgingly, women's rights are now on the social agenda for improvement.

Power becomes a central issue in potential individual and social transformation, and is an underlying theme of 8th house concerns, especially directed to relationships and use of shared resources, but the implications of this stretch far wider than just intimate and domestic power struggles. The 8th house ruled by Pluto, and Pluto's natal position, are spheres where we experience power and domination, both against and by ourselves, and also where opportunities exist to reclaim self-empowerment. How we use personal power sets our life boundaries, influences all relationships, and determines the extent of self-expression and the liberation of our innate potential. Personal power is rooted in our being, and if we are disconnected through losing wholeness then our ability to be powerful is also forfeited.

Power is neither good nor evil, it is neutral and an instrument of whoever wields it. Misused power can destroy the world by wars, nuclear and bio-chemical weapons, and cause great suffering by certain political decisions such as prolonging Third World starvation and poverty by refusing a radical redistribution of world wealth. Or creative power can initiate constructive radical changes, improving the quality of life for masses of people.

Choice determines probable consequences. Power is simply the capacity to act, the power to change attitudes through social influence, an ability to cause or prevent change. How we respond to power, and how we use it will determine our lives and our world; this is the critical question for humanity to resolve during this next century, induced by the decisive turning-point of creating weapons for possible world destruction. The atomic bomb symbolizes the power for self-annihilation, and parallel to this is the next step that demands a collective world responsibility to avoid eventual genocide. A balance of destructive and constructive power is required, a transformational symbol that synthesizes our choice, and one counteracting image opposing the nuclear mushroom cloud is Earth viewed from the Moon as one world, our fragile planetary home in the midst of space.

There have been two basic reactions to power issues— one is asserting power-over others, and the second is powerlessness, losing power to others. The source of either tendency is often located in childhood, when infantile desires are met by the frustrating opposition of parents and teachers, resulting in anger when needs are ignored or denied, and a recognition that others limit the child's wishes. Children's willful yet doubtful assertiveness is regularly defeated, forcing retreat deeper into themselves to hide and comfort their wounds. The need to socialize children and their lack of awareness is met by the imposition of parental power, which often inadvertently fractures the psyche into acceptable and unacceptable types of behavior, forming the dark side and repressive nature (as examined in chapter 6). As a consequence of this, we develop ambitions to reassert personal power by gaining positions of authority, or we tend to submissively relinquish power to others.

Power over others is a directive force aiming to influence people to act in specific ways; we all try to manipulate to some degree, whether it is with children, lovers, partners, employers, through ideas, beliefs, attitudes, or political actions. At one extreme, this is imbalanced, excessive self-assertion attempting to pressurize others into conformity or to fulfill personal desires irrespective of any cost to others.

When there are hidden feelings of inadequacy, insignificance, and fears of losing ego-controls, then compensatory "power-over" attitudes and actions may emerge, often to feed a deluded belief of superiority and to convince the ego of its importance. In attempting to dominate our outer world, we hope to minimize our fears of being overwhelmed by inner pressures and needs. When we lack genuine self-possession, we substitute actions to possess others or external objects, enforcing controls on the outer reality as a surrogate demonstration of egoic power. With the "power-over" tendency, we attempt to dominate whatever we fear, unconsciously becoming dependent on others or objects remaining responsive to our will, as our ego-securities rest on this, and the examples of losing authority and power (politicians, managers, businessmen) often parallel an inner psychological crisis and failure of meaning and direction.

"Power-over" strategies utilize personality strengths and qualities to manipulate people, and will be displayed by either those who are genuinely confident and believe in their right to lead others, or by those who exert manipulative power over others to counteract insecurities and a weakened, fragmented psyche. A recent example of this was the media psychoanalysis of Saddam Hussein, connecting his brutalized childhood with his adult ruthless quest for ultimate power, and his intolerant, malicious maltreatment of those who disagreed or obstructed his will.

With "power-over," we can ask: what do we gain from dominating others? Does this buttress insecurities? What needs does it satisfy? Do we misuse manipulative power? How? Do we use our power to assist others? How could we use our power for mutual benefit? Do we see ourselves as superior to others, and so justify domination? Would we be willing to be dominated by others in the same way we dominate them? Review attitudes to power, and see if new expressions can be created which are not exploitative but support all concerned.

Powerlessness develops by repeated experiences of being overwhelmed by external power, first met in childhood and then continued into adulthood, but is never transformed by personality resistance to oppression, as capitulation occurs to lessen painful conflict. Outer influences impose attitudes, beliefs, and values that may ignore our individuality, confining freedom and options within a conformist social framework. Feelings of powerlessness and helplessness are derived from a sense of inadequacy, inferiority, low esteem, and a wounded psyche, and such individuals become submissive victims to those intent on domination. When lacking power, others become the channels for our fate; we are dictated to by government, teachers, parents, doctors, employers, priests, experts, lovers, often pushed around by the decisions of others unconcerned with our needs and desires. We are victims of our abdication of power, perhaps failing or even refusing to claim it originally, fearful that with power also comes responsibility and the challenge of making decisions, a situation which we feel unable to cope with as self-confidence has been lost.

With powerlessness, we are not self-possessed but possessed by others, allowing this to continue despite storing painful feelings of anger and resentment. We are oppressed by others controlling and dominating us, possessing what we want or preventing our needs being satisfied. We feel beset by immovable obstacles perpetually frustrating us, and even when others are not directly hindering, then our inhibiting secret fears, resistances, and unconscious motives block our path forward. We feel trapped by ourselves and others; we disown self-responsibility for our lives, and instead create deceptive images of ourselves as martyr and victim, thinking, "It's not my fault, it's not my responsibility...it's them," projecting and misplacing power into the external world. Energies are dispersed by self-pity, and dependencies increased, fearful of losing the surrogate centers that crucial people provide in our lives, afraid that everything would collapse if they were not present to shape our lives. Powerlessness may attempt manipulating others by weaknesses: illness, hypochondria, and other dependencies may be used to persuade others to do their bidding, but then this swings into a "power-over" context and most helpless, disempowered people become the passive victims of others' asserted desires and decisions, losing autonomy.

With powerlessness, we can ask in which areas of our lives have we lost power and autonomy? How and where do we give our power to others? What do we gain by being a victim, martyr, or dominated by others? In which situations do inhibiting inner fears insure we are powerless? Which fears and life obstacles prevent self-assertion? Why do we allow this to continue? Identify those inner voices that repeat defeatist messages, those conditioning patterns that keep us powerless and helpless to change our unsatisfying lives. Define our needs and desires and what we do want in life, and take steps to achieve and satisfy these.

Most people display a mixture of "power-over" and "powerlessness" in their lives, although with our current political systems we all contribute to surrendering considerable responsibility for our country to the ideals of democracy and our elected representatives, a situation that may have inherent dangers if the state assumes greater powers and exerts increasing authoritarianism, like the warped governmental "power-over" regime portrayed by George Orwell in his *1984*, and symbolized by his image of "Big Brother is watching you." The power role of government is interesting, in that it relieves individuals of responsibility and also performs unsavory actions as our intermediary or agent, albeit nominally in our name, and our sense of detachment from national power enables us to evade guilt or plead ignorance and no responsibility for any state decisions with which we may disapprove, even though we have colluded with transferring power into that hierarchic political system.

As 8th house issues engage greater social and cultural attention, this question of power-response is one which will increasingly occupy individual consideration, and an emerging alternative way to deal with power-issues is empowerment, where power is individually and collectively reclaimed and shared responsibility determines decision-making. This is also a major theme addressed by the human potential movement, and most self-development work is concerned with the aim to extend autonomy, freedom, potential, and self-responsibility. Through empowerment we can reown personal power, learn to trust and respond to its needs of expression, and discover how to apply this in right relationships, which in Gandhi's *satyagraha* philosophy of non-violent revolution is summarized as, "I do not intend to coerce you; but neither will I allow you to coerce me," a declaration of both compassionate self-rule and awareness of right relationship. With self-empowerment, we assume responsibility for our lives and decisions, we accept our power to take risks to reshape our lives for greater enjoyment, taking control and ensuring that we satisfy our inner needs and physical needs without abusing and exploiting others, or perpetuating the old "I win—you lose" syndrome associated with "power-over" tactics.

We are still a long way from making real progress in this direction, as a historical tradition of social behavior needs to change, not just individually but also collectively on a planetary scale. In this context, we sense the birth of a new power paradigm, a shift to a different social system produced by transformed values and in transition to a less or non-hierarchical cultural structure. Through self-empowerment, our destiny is to become socially influential and contribute to social development, by wielding a cooperative, creative power that flows from an integrated state of being. Then our vision is of collective benefit, where the ideal is for all to win and enjoy an improved quality of life. When self-empowered, we can encourage and assist others, promoting their growth, too, as a natural radiance of our power, reframing lives to discover self-esteem, integrity and purposeful meaning. Jerry Rubin, one of the leading radicals of the 60s counterculture, later admitted that, "It's the spiritual movement that's truly revolutionary. Without self-awareness, political activism only perpetuates cycles of anger…I couldn't change anybody until I changed myself."[1]

The transfer initiated by self-empowerment involves a radical shift from divisive, self-assertive power to *integrative* power, where self-centered independence is transformed by realized interdependence, and the part recognizes its true role within the whole. Both self-assertive and integrative power are socially necessary, and need binding together in a planetary perspective and systemic context. We detect the connections between integrated inner power and external power, and see that both must remain balanced or they become unhealthy and corrupted.

A sense of universal connection promotes social concern and care, and generates trusting attitudes that do not polarize the world into "us and them" distinctions; the need for enemies disappears and is replaced by a willingness to cre-

---

[1] Jerry Rubin, cited in Marilyn Ferguson, *The Aquarian Conspiracy* (Los Angeles: J.P. Tarcher, 1981; London: Paladin, 1982), p. 225.

ate mutual cooperation and compromise. The feeling of union with life has to extend its transformative influence to include social action; William James said, "I will act as if what I do makes a difference,"[2] and this belief can inspire our social contribution, not as a dream to personally change the world, but by translating intentions into action, manifesting social idealist visions into actuality, and combines re-creating our individual lives with supporting social re-creation. What better task can engage our talents for a lifetime?

The emerging hope for this collective venture into redefining power and its social and cultural reflection has been termed the *Third Way*. The strength of this direction comes from the conscious fusion with something greater than the limited personality—call this soul, spirit, planetary vision or divine plan—and because of this sense of union and merging has 8th house connections related to the mystery of the other. This Third Way provides a new vision of human potential, and is based on reempowerment concepts and government by the higher Self.

During the last century, Thoreau had a vision of a new stage of government beyond democracy, where individual conscience is recognized by the state as "a higher and different power, a context for all authority,"[3] referring to the prospective self-empowered individual. Now we observe a variety of modern examples of a new political framework coming from self-empowered individuals. *Pneumatocracy* envisages the coming rule of the spirit, where people are empowered through enlightened inspiration to self-rule, extending the idea of democracy, and declaring that pneumatocracy is neither left nor right, but uplifted forward beyond the limiting, dualistic mind, and seeking to clarify a new direction for humanity to evolve toward harmony and integration. There are a

---

[2] William James, *The Varieties of Religious Experience* (New York: Longmans, 1935).
[3] Henry David Thoreau, cited in Marilyn Ferguson, *The Aquarian Conspiracy* (Los Angeles: J. P. Tarcher, 1981; London: Paladin, 1982), p. 216.

proliferation of terms for this new cultural direction that is being anchored, all of which include the fundamental recognition that use of power requires awareness and responsibility to each other, and that power plus love is a vitally needed humanizing force that can transform planetary relationships. Other terms for this new power dynamic include cooperative capitalism, enlightened global humanism, participatory divinity and synergic politics.

From the first seed of personal empowerment comes the expansiveness of synergetic power, where by working together with creative vision to think globally, act locally we can simultaneously benefit ourselves and others, increase mutual group satisfaction, energy, creativity, respect, concern and shared responsibility. By dealing with the 8th house issue of personal values and shared planetary resources, we then meet decisive interlinked questions of how we utilize power in all our social relationships.

OBSESSION AND COMPULSION

Due to the close connections with unconscious needs, potent desires and hidden motivations indicated by our 8th house, we may be liable to psychological possession by compulsive and obsessive demands, especially when we deny recognizing and accepting these. The degree of compulsive and obsessive behavior is determined by how adept we are at channeling our desire-energies into satisfying our needs, or whether we choose to ignore and repress them as unacceptable. Socially conditioned attitudes may inculcate a self-rejecting temperament, and often compulsion and obsession are linked to inner conflicts when distorted instructions of how we should behave clash with how we want or need to behave. Each individual psyche has tendencies to create repetitive life-structuring routines of thoughts, feelings, and actions, and this looping pattern can become possessed by obsessive or compulsive needs.

In the 8th house, probable obsessive issues can include sexuality, death, power, money, resources, desires, and the need to surrender and merge. Obsession occurs when part of the psyche is dissociated, projected, and attached usually to something external to ourselves—a person, an object, an aim, an idea or belief—and this desire or need is internally exaggerated, devouring energy and attention, and proceeding to dominate other voices of the psyche, dismissing and excluding their needs as insignificant, and possessing the individual consciousness by usurping personality power. Psychic balance is disturbed, and the only voice heard of importance is the ceaseless obsessive demand for satisfaction. The obsession becomes a message that "I must have...," or "I cannot live without...," "Having this will give meaning to my life...," and essentially we fall victim to the mercy of this projected attachment. In some cases, the obsession can operate as a surrogate anchor and purpose to a life, which may otherwise be slowly disintegrating, due to personality stress and fragmentation. The focus of attention becomes narrowed as the obsession obliterates any broader view. Individual freedom is replaced by subserviency to obsessive power, and the dream or intention of appeasing this insistent, urgent demand preoccupies consciousness.

The power of obsession is associated with a misidentification of psychological survival with our projected attachment to a person, idea, aim, or object; remaining in touch with this projected part of self through possessing the outer "screen" is crucial to avoid further disintegration. Mild degrees of obsessive and compulsive behavior are common in our lives, especially when provoked by powerful emotions which we often deal with by projecting their energy due to fears of being overwhelmed and doubts that we can extend ourselves to contain heightened feelings. Love and sexuality are two primary stimulants for obsession, and falling in love exhibits several traits of projection, possession, and loss of control. The 8th house obsessions evoke ambivalent feelings o

revitalized life—an agony and ecstasy—and the need to surrender to something other or greater than ourselves under-
pins the fundamental thrust of this sphere of life; we can be
both excited and repelled by obsessive projections, and these
can also serve to transform our lives even if without our
volition.

Obsessions assume a power which exceeds due psychological proportion, often superseding rational controls
and leaving us vulnerable and exposed to the focus of our displaced power. A collector's obsession has displaced part of
his or her identity into possessions; a lover's obsession is with
the beloved; an idealist's obsession is with the ideology or faith,
and all are dependent in some way. The expansive nature of
obsession magnetically attracts mental activity and emotional energies into its interior orbit, using them as fuel to extend
and insinuate its control even further over the psyche.
Repetitive anxieties, fears, compulsive actions, paranoia,
thoughts, desires, emotions can all emanate from this contaminating source, gradually increasing pressures to risk all
or nothing in pursuit of the obsessive desire, causing irresistible
urges which may be contrary to the individual's better judgment. Obsessive compulsions have been the downfall of
many, creating intense anguish as the compelling urge to act
in a certain manner battles other convictions of right behavior. "I couldn't help myself, I just had to do it…," is a classic
excuse for compulsive actions.

While the term *obsessive personality* is often meant with
disapproval, implying a neurotic and unhealthy personality,
there can be positive effects from compulsive behavior and
this is often demonstrated by successful individuals in all spheres
of life. To become successful, the individual usually needs talent and determination, concentrated on achieving objectives.
This often requires the deliberate channeling of obsessive
needs and interests toward fulfilling ambitions; the busi-
nessman attentive to business expansion; the artist, possessed by imagery, symbols and visions which he or she
seeks to portray; the musician, haunted by inner melodies;

the writer, experiencing the birth of fictional characters out of the substance of the psyche; the priest or mystic, yearning for the elevating touch of the beloved God; the altruist, dedicated to serving and healing others.

In these, and in many more possible examples, obsessive and compulsive tendencies may serve as the foundation for a career or vocation, determining direction and lifestyle and becoming the specific channel of personal expression. Few creative individuals are immune from some degree of mild obsession by their artistic muse, even if only temporary, as for example when writing a book and the themes preoccupy conscious attention for the duration of the literary process. Even astrologers do not escape from an obsessive preoccupation with their vocation, as knowledge of planetary influences can be distorted into a fear of decisive action unless the planetary positions are perfect. If this occurs, then the consequence of their studies has not been liberating, and has instead awakened parts of the personality that are unintegrated and imbalanced.

In the following section, 8th house planets have been considered in the context of how their obsessive, compulsive, manipulative and power-over traits may manifest, especially when these have negative repercussions and the state of inner possession is harmful to both personality and relationships. Obviously the degree to which these may manifest will vary, from negligible to considerable, and the whole chart configuration may need assessing to modify evaluations. Yet being aware of the possibility of such compulsive characteristics may help encourage us to look again at our behavior and inner life to see if these are activated, and if so bring awareness to adjust them and minimize any mischief and damage they are causing.

SUN (LEO)

You may have a compulsive need to be someone special, asserting your solar potency and individuality to impress others and to gain respect and admiration. Your ambition is to become influential, holding positions of authority, responsibility, and power, as achieving these will confirm your self-image as a leader. There is a definite link between your self-esteem and self-worth and the degree of power you possess, irrespective of where this is demonstrated in your life. This urge to distinguish yourself from others has an egocentric foundation, biased toward acting in ways that impose dominance and control on others, and which usually emphasizes your needs and aims as the highest priority to satisfy. This tendency for "power-over" others is often displayed in a working environment, intently pursuing the grail of career achievement and aiming to reach superior positions. Willpower is one of your favored qualities, and combined with a manipulative and devious mind may enable you to successfully play the career game.

Underlying this compulsion are needs for security, status, affluence, expansion, and self-improvement, but care and awareness is necessary to adjust how you chase after these goals. While you present a proud, confident, and almost overbearing personality to the world, you recognize that you actually feel less certain about your identity and skills, and any manipulative attempts to become the center of attention is to convince yourself of your importance. This insecurity generates a stressful need to continually assert yourself, imposing compulsive pressures to succeed and develop your skills and talents; you may rarely feel satisfied, or at least, not for long, and you create grandiose dreams to force you ever-onward.

These ambitions include searching for greater power and influence, and may assume an obsessive quality that ignores realism, practicality, and your actual abilities; failure to achieve these may be especially bitter and disillusioning, although the seed for this lies in your own excessive fantasies. This compulsive expansion may need modifying, or becoming a victim to this may prove your own undoing, stretching too far and failing. Moderation may be a valuable quality to introduce into your life; believing in the efficacy of willpower may not always be sufficient for success. After all, your willful intentions are not yet as powerful as the scale of the Universal Will, even if you desire to emulate that!

Relationships are often the focus for your assertiveness, at work and at home. This is where you intend to demonstrate your power and purpose, and where both compulsive and manipulative behavior is prevalent and most easily observed. You tend to be highly demanding and expect others to submit to your preeminence, often creating a melodramatic, theatrical personality which you believe will impress them—your mask of power. Sometimes this may work, but others may perceive this as an inflated role that you are playing, and question your sincerity, especially when they sense a childish, self-indulgent personality that demands everything their own way or it's tantrum-time. Insecurity leads you to play to the audience, fearing that if attention is withdrawn then the actor fades, diminished into insignificance. But if this is true and all you have to offer is a facade, then spending time on developing your real inner qualities and strengths would be a much wiser investment of effort—then you can impress by what you are, rather than what you pretend to be.

Issues of "power-over" others and self-empowerment are important to explore, as these hold a key to genuine prospects for self-improvement and better relationships. Striving to dominate others while intent on resisting any domination by others will always create imbalance and possible antagonism. Mind that you do not take undue advantage of a partner's intimate feelings by becoming dictatorial in relationship, over-sexually demanding, possessive, and using intimacy to release compulsive pressures, or assuming a right to do whatever you please. A possible Casanova Complex may develop, fuelled by career status and power, which attracts you toward hedonism and infidelity as an assertion of the benefits of power and self-importance; your gullibility to flattery may undermine your position, and others may equally manipulate your desires and complexes.

Obsessions can develop around health, especially as you grow older, and the aging effects on appearance may disturb you more than you admit. Work can easily become obsessive—a preoccupation that you cannot resist—and compulsively grasp your time and energy.

A compulsive search for understanding may develop, perhaps stimulated by attaining ambitions and then wondering, what next? Or, by the shock of failure or relationship collapse. This may lead you to explore life's mysteries, occultism, death, or various taboos as you consciously reconnect to unconscious forces that have been driving your choices and actions, and gain insight into their nature. To discover your inner truth and to face your real nature, stripped of masks and needs to be special, you have to drop egoic claims and pretenses. This may not be easy, but this painful encounter can be very liberating and productive, creating a life-renewal and increasing fulfillment prospects by reducing compulsive urges. Another sphere that may require attention is the compulsion to seek wealth and ostentatiously display your worldly success by conspicuous extravagant spending, surrounding yourself by material possessions while still feeling unsatisfied and empty within.

MOON (CANCER)

Your expression of power and manipulation often occurs in intimate and domestic relationships, and is connected to compulsive needs for security and stability incorporated into the fixed routines and structures that shape your lifestyle and partnerships. You assert these needs by emotional manipulation, either passively, by acting helpless or as a self-effacing martyr, or by emotional demands, smothering and possessing a partner or family by the sheer weight of love that you are pouring out in a dependent manner.

Your compelling impulse is to fuse emotions with others, either needing them to receive your overflowing love, or being needed by others, reliant on your support for security and protection. Dependency is the key issue which needs resolving, and you may become possessed by unconscious emotional complexes, secretly directing your manipulative relationship actions. Often the roots of these complexes lie in unresolved previous experiences, even dating back to early childhood and emotional exchanges with parents. The influence of your mother may have been significant, and women remain important in your life. Childlike feeling-patterns are still active in your adult responses, perhaps symptomatic of emotional deprivation, unrealistic emotional demands, and repressed emotional needs. These patterns interfere with and mold adult relationships, despite the need to integrate and heal your wounded inner child.

You may be bound to cultural traditions of relationship conditioning which dictates how you form intimate partnerships, assume roles that may be unsuitable, and which diverts attention into simply satisfying security needs, especially emotional and financial ones. Home is your sanctuary from the world, your anchor and defensive walls, and often you project emotional attachments on your possessions, investing them with great personal significance and obsessively linking them to your sense of well-being; the more possessions and money you can accumulate, the more you hope to feel secure.

Your emotional state dominates awareness and partnerships, and moods and feeling responses color your worldview. Obviously emotions fluctuate and pass through lunar-like phases, and you can swing from optimism to pessimism quite rapidly and confusingly. Manipulative power over others comes from your emotional controls, especially if a partner relies on you for mothering, nurturing, nourishing, and protection; then you may be tempted to pull their strings, empowered by their dependency. Equally, however, this may happen to you if your dependency needs are paramount, and this leaves you vulnerable to a partner's actions. Neither position allows individual growth, and can prove mutually inhibitive and destructive.

Emotional stress and tension is likely through overcharged, capricious and protean feelings, which pose difficulties understanding, integrating and containing. Through your emotions come complexes, compulsive and obsessive behavior, repetitive desires and needs that demand satisfaction, yet are rarely sufficiently satiated for inner peace. Emotions drive you and dictate compulsive relationship needs. Often you use your receptive, psychic, empathic and intuitive sensitivity to manipulate others to meet your desires, even though you may not always recognize how you do this. Unconscious pressures leak into the domestic atmosphere, and either overt or covert emotional manipulation encourages others to bend to your demands, in the name of love. Or you may observe your receptivity to others' feelings and thoughts—even if not spoken or openly communicated—and you become manipulated by your impressionability and dependency, reliant on their good opinion of you.

Either you impose your emotional needs on others, or their needs are imposed on you; this appears the only options available to your perspective. However, this symbiotic dependency is not inevitable and can be changed into a more healthy relationship. Over-assertiveness or passivity are not the only answers, nor is withdrawing into a reclusive shell, brooding with self-pity, nor a tenacious possessiveness, clinging on to a partner as if your life depends on it, which emotionally, you believe it does.

These compulsive actions can be renewed by exploring their unconscious connections; understanding can diminish dependency, and show you how to become more self-contained, discovering an emotional well-being that does not rely on the presence of a partner as a vital support. Otherwise, you are disempowered by your need, and likely to become an emotional victim at some stage. Obsessively organizing your physical lifestyle for protection and security by ritualizing daily routines and insuring its smooth running does not negate the emotional chaos that can erupt through lack of insight. Neither does a shrewd, thrifty approach to finances shield against losing a partner. Your externally directed caution and possessiveness may be misplaced; you cannot control others and the outer world forever, and attention should be rediverted to replace any resistant infantile emotional patterns that have outlived their effectiveness.

MERCURY (GEMINI, VIRGO)

This implies possible compulsive patterns related to communication, information acquisition, intellectual logic, rationality and perfectionism. Your mind is prone to nervous restlessness, sometimes overloaded by absorbing information that simply accumulates without being synthesized into meaningful order. Knowledge is equated to mental security, and you believe that the world can be understood by compulsively collecting fragments that you hope one day to piece together to comprise a revealing picture. However, this hunger is never abated, and your obsessively logical outlook is tainted by an analytical and critical attitude which continues to sever and divide reality, focused on obsessively examining the details of pieces rather than looking beyond to see their context. There is always more to scrutinize and categorize, and you place all into order and eventually find that scattered interests disperse energies and make activity less productive.

Power over others and manipulation may come through intellectual display, as you can be very mentally stimulating and knowledgeable, even though this may not make any genuine difference to your well-being. You may enjoy manipulating others' minds, perhaps through teaching articulate and literary skills, or juggling information to justify and prove your arguments and beliefs. Almost compulsively you apply a dissecting intellect to other points of view, often dismissing their logic while rarely applying this scalpel to your own beliefs, arguments, and attitudes, as if considering these as beyond questioning. This penetrative talent may be effectively destructive, yet substituting an alternative may prove beyond your ability. Being critical is easy, establishing perfectionist standards and then comparing these to judge others can be done, yet this narrow discrimination may only create dissatisfaction.

Your mental state is often characterized by compulsive inner agitation. You may be liable to self-condemning inner messages, born from self-criticism and perfectionism rejecting and repressing parts of your personality into the unconscious. Your quality of thought can be more inconsistent, changeable, and less reliable than you believe, although quickness of thought may disguise this, and may become fixated on interests that assume an obsessive quality. With such a mental emphasis, you can devalue your physical instincts, emotions, and intuitive nature, as these fail to fit your intellectual, rational assessment of life, and, indeed, cause you some discomfort and discomposure.

Relationships may form primarily as mental exchanges of ideas, information and verbal communication, and you find it difficult to express feelings and non-verbal contacts. A sense of detached lack of feeling may interfere with intimacy and socializing, despite your superficial diversity of many acquaintances and friends attesting to popularity. You may compulsively analyze relationships, obsessively going over situations or reliving conversations in an anxious quest to extract meaning and understanding. Memory-loops may develop, especially if there is a pattern of partnership failures, haunting you by the unresolved past. Intimacy may be characterized by ritualized behavior, perhaps even obsessive attractions to fetishist practices. Sometimes you feel almost disconnected in relationships, a symptom of non-involvement and lack of total commitment. Sometimes your memories remind you of successful strategies used to cunningly manipulate others into supporting your schemes, amorally using them to further your aims.

Mental health concerns may worry you, and an undercurrent of anxiety is often present, perhaps emerging as psychosomatic and hypochondriac illness which stirs obsessive traits. A fear of life and personality disorder is present, and mental controls are established to prevent chaos. Work may channel several compulsive patterns, such as self-demands for fastidious industry, conscientious efficiency, and organization, possibly allowing a latent workaholic complex into manifestation. If you find an intellectually stimulating career, then this will assume great priority and consume most of your attention and energy.

Your inquisitive questioning may unite instead of divide once you redirect your sights from detail to context, and from the part to the whole. This perceptive, observational ability may allow you to discern connections that are less apparent to a superficial glance; if you search for meaning rather than to possess information, a radical shift of mind may become possible, one which allows you to discover universal interrelationship rather than becoming lost in the fascination of fragments. Your role as a distributive channel of knowledge can be transformed to one of disseminating wholeness, embracing yourself and others rather than locking yourself away in a limiting corner of your own making through continual analysis.

The retrograde Mercury deepens contemplative and introspective tendencies, where concerns are inwardly directed to study mental interactions, intellectual pursuits, conceptual and abstract thoughts. Mind is highly active and may pose problems of relaxation, continually sifting impressions, thoughts, ideas, and self-images, evaluating and revising them to conform to a perfectionist standard, imposed by critical analysis. This inner turning may make you receptive to intuitive insight and imagination, and you are more aware of a hidden meaning to existence, which you strive to locate in all experiences and create a cohesive intellectual structure to reflect its presence. Sometimes lost in mental preoccupation, your interest and communication with others is variable, sometimes eager to share your insights, sometimes taciturn and reserved. Communicating your complex thoughts often proves difficult, and you are uncertain as to whether the effort is worthwhile. Power over others and manipulation becomes irrelevant, as your intent is self-discovery, although this can assume compulsive elements, and mental narcissism may be evident.

VENUS (TAURUS, LIBRA)

Love, pleasures and relationships become the focus for manipulative power needs, compulsions and obsessions, centered on a search for balance, harmony, and union and the gratification of personal desires. Others may be manipulated by exploiting their desires and your own physical attractiveness, seducing them by the allure of sexuality, sensuality, and love. Venus in the 8th house is especially enchanting, promising exquisite experiences capable of enslaving anyone's desires.

Who becomes enslaved varies—it may be you, afraid of being alone and desperate for someone to love you, or perhaps falling victim to your own projected anima-animus image of the ideal lover obsessively possessing you, or vulnerable to a diminished self-esteem, ready to offer yourself to anyone who shows interest. Alternatively, you may assert seductive power over others, manipulating their feelings and expecting them to give love and financial and material security in exchange for your company. Sexuality and money may walk hand-in-hand here, although not always in harmonized step.

Compulsive issues related to love are at the heart of this, and much depends on if you love yourself as a state of self-acceptance; if so, and you avoid exploitative "power over" manipulation, then balanced relationships are more possible, but if you have suffered a loss of self-esteem, then distorted compulsive behavior is more likely. Self-rejection can lead to compulsive pleasure-seeking as a compensatory action, indulging in sensuality and materiality to appease insistent needs. You need to be loved, and this can be indiscriminate, perhaps experiencing multiple partners while failing to realize why you feel so unsatisfied. Obsessions with sexuality can develop, and fascinations with libidinous and libertine behavior provoke compulsive desires and choices. Your impulse to merge becomes either possessing another or being possessed, seeing no other way between these imbalanced extremes. If you create high expectations of the perfect partner and a permanently harmonious relationship, then you are liable to be disappointed and disillusioned, and if you attempt to force a partner to change to match this ideal as a sign of their love for you, then this creates a recipe for tension and conflict. Romanticism is fine in its place, but is an inadequate substitute for real life and accepting human frailties.

Your need for harmony may be replaced by a compulsive avoidance of relationship conflict, where you change or ignore your needs and desires in favor of your partner, molding yourself into the partner's image and minimizing disagreements, compromising, becoming compliant, malleable, and adopting a mask of pretense. You are disempowered by this action, vulnerable to your partner's domination if he or she chooses to assert this over you. Relationship balance requires mutual sharing, cooperation, and interdependence, and this is the aim to be worked toward.

You may feel envious of others' material success, and can be possessed by compulsive hunger for prosperity and possessions, enticed by a materialistic attitude which equates security with money. Greed is likely to drive your actions and decisions, especially concerned with physical and emotional satisfaction, and whose pursuit can lessen awareness of others, dismissing their feelings as inconsequential. Compulsive motivations may increase extremist actions, although analyzing these may reveal their contradictory nature and that they are suddenly expressed after a period of previous indecision and confusion, as if pressures are released through a surprise eruption.

Beauty, style, fashion, and environment may become obsessive preoccupations, where the harmony of appearance supersedes the virtue of reality. The recognition of inner beauty may become secondary to superficiality, distorting perceptions and evaluations of people. A creative and artistic spirit may emerge from this, and beauty could become an obsessive theme in your artistic endeavors.

Retrograde Venus redirects attention from outer partners and the world, and looks inside for union. Relationships are less attractive, and a preference for a solitary, more ascetic self-exploration may assume greater importance. A complex self-image and sense of self-esteem is active, bridging indulgent narcissism, feelings of being unlovable, a reserved and over-sensitive temperament, and a reflective need to establish inner beauty by harmonizing the multifaceted psyche and forming an alternative value system. Individuality is more unconventional, and less common sexual appetites and interests may lure unresolved, obsessive energies. Reactions to love are ambivalent, often complicated by dissatisfactory experiences and confusion in giving and receiving love, and may require clarity and insight to bring these back into right balance.

MARS (ARIES)

You have a compulsive need to master your world, proving your power and satisfying innumerable desires. You adopt the attitude of "I am the master of my fate, I am the captain of my soul," partly attempting to affirm your potent identity by combatively challenging any obstacles in your way. Your expression of power often has an abrasive, aggressive quality, and you are competitive and manipulative when possessed by an insistent desire. Relationships prove a contentious arena, whether social, work, or intimate, and this is mainly due to your inclination to dominate others as the means to self-fulfillment. Preoccupied with compulsive needs, one casualty is your awareness and sensitivity to others, often disregarding their needs and feelings. As your manipulative skills lack subtle strategy and your aims may become obvious, interpersonal conflict is likely, and you are quickly angered when desires are blocked. Unconscious pressures spill out into argumentative fights, and your own unresolved stress can work against others cooperating with you. You hate feeling frustrated, and may begin acting recklessly as restraining controls are cast away. To discharge this energy build-up, your bellicosity may turn into cruel, violent and coercive behavior as your awareness is diminished by the exaggerated obsessional desire filling your mind.

Satisfying every desire is seen as marking the limits of your power, and you are often prone to take risks for progress, acting impulsively, impatient to succeed, yet lacking discipline and organization, and failing to prepare your battle plan. You love action and prefer a busy lifestyle, often compulsively filling the hours with frenetic obligations, keeping the energy-level high; yet this minimizes time for quieter reflection, and while you are self-motivated, you often become your own worst enemy inhibiting progress. Instead of directing power over others, declaring a me first attitude, hustling to the front of the line, you really need to regain power over yourself, because the likelihood is that you are dominated by desires and unreceptive to much else in life.

Sexuality can be an arena for abusing power, manipulating partners, and compulsive action, and you may devote time and energy to the excitement of the "sexual chase" and orgasmic release. You may make considerable physical demands, and sexuality conjures needs to control and dominate, as if a contest for supremacy and one which you intend to win.

Unease with feelings and compelling physical instincts may also awaken darker unconscious emotions, and lust, jealousy, possessiveness, anger, resentments, and hostility can interfere. These are unresolved desires previously frustrated and stored in the unconscious, which often serve as the roots for obsessive and compulsive behavior, and can damage your relationships and cause depression unless properly discharged. With excessive energy you are faced by choices of right expression; this can easily be mishandled and become aggressive and destructive, or assertively directed for positive results. There is a narrow line between them with your temperament, but right choice will determine if you succeed in your declaration that "I want the world and I want it now."

You find it difficult to live in a moderate manner, but you could live with greater awareness, focusing your ambitious desires more effectively. Your compulsive outward directed energy can be rechanneled into pioneering enterprises, which could create the opportunity to receive most of your desires. Your self-reliant, individualist nature could become a strength, as your momentum to initiate things could be purposefully used. Asserting independence could be a route to achieve the money, power, and success that you intensely crave, as your tactless and egocentric style may not always meet approval when working for others, and the external world will often refuse to bow to your demands. Business and financial deals may especially appeal, and while money may be a root of any obsessive conduct, this energy may be turned to your advantage.

You can be direct, optimistic and idealistic in your attitudes—even though this does not always improve your relationship awareness—and with a modified compulsive nature may be attracted toward applying your combative energetic temperament to support a social cause, becoming a dedicated crusader for your beliefs. This however requires a shift from self-centeredness and compulsive fixations, but could provide a genuine alternative path to positively utilize and transform your desire-energies.

Retrograde Mars amplifies these traits of high energy, intense desires, crises of action, and sexual compulsions, yet makes these more difficult to satisfy as the way to externally assert them appears to be blocked, and volatile energies turn inward with pent-up angry frustration. Self-confidence is lessened, denuding your power of much forcefulness and diminishing its effect over others; you are more resistant to asserting your desires, confused over how to discharge this restless energy and yet pressured by compulsive desires. Contradictions may accumulate, especially related to issues of power and sexuality where erratic behavior is likely. You may act passively and then suddenly and surprisingly explode when blocked desires overload your defenses after a period of heavy brooding and struggling to keep the volcano cap in place. Compulsive drives force you to act, even though you fail to understand these subconscious motivations. Sexuality may either be obsessive, repressed, or viewed with disinterest, and again may erupt compulsively and erratically as an imbalanced part of your nature. Possible frigidity or impotence may result from this inner tension. There may be attractions toward self-destructive and self-abusing behavior, a twisting of your natural energy flow inward to agitate unconscious compulsions. Alternatively, you may redirect these powerful energies into penetrating inner reflections to explore your psyche, discovering the root of both desires and compulsive traits, possibly rebalancing and integrating them for greater harmony.

JUPITER (SAGITTARIUS)

This implies a compulsive search for "more," although this probably involves a crisis of direction connected to your beliefs, moral principles, and over-optimistic dreams for the future. You believe that answers do exist to universal questions, and may compulsively investigate various religions, philosophies, esoteric teachings for their solutions, obsessively committed as a student. You may voraciously absorb spiritual studies, probing universal mysteries, accumulating multiple answers yet have difficulty in assimilation and application. After all, which one is right? Are any right? Or are they all attempts to rationalize the ineffable?

This impulse to grow and expand by knowledge can inspire your approach to "power-over" others. Being a student is not sufficient, your pride and over-confident self-image shrugs off this role as soon as possible; you may have a compulsive need to become a teacher, self-proclaimed, self-righteous and possibly self-deluding if this latent complex assumes control. A tendency for exaggeration may transform your acquired information into truth and gospel or revealed holy inspiration, and many want that hotline to God. Some fall victim to inflated egos, opinionated, intolerant, and eventually hypocritical, overextending a belief in personal power to dominate others. Your values and beliefs form a center to your identity foundations, and you like to impose these on others, manipulating minds and worldviews to conform with your own—acquiring followers is an appealing development.

An alternative direction for this compulsive search for understanding is where a genuine inner contact is made, one not dependent on serving simply as a channel for unconscious self-interested motivation. Through this obsessive ambition to know, an inner guide conveys wise inspiration, collaborating together for growth and manifesting your purpose and destiny. From this source may come genuine prophetic insight—clarifying insight—defining your ethical stance and affirming idealistic intentions, awakening you to universal abundance. The problem is distinguishing between the productions of a self-seeking ego and an inner wisdom that you can contact and perhaps disseminate to others.

You have to deal with possible compulsive immoderation, indulgence, and excess that attracts, those extravagant tastes for quantity and quality that may increase an obsession with mammon, money and acquisitions. If this takes possession, then your quest is diverted into worldly success and power, and the numinous quest replaced by a lust for materialism. You often manipulate others by using their resources for your gain, perhaps through shared partnership finances, business, or investment. Yet you may be a compulsive giver, generous and altruistic, gaining a sense of importance from your power to indulge others or share your abundance. If the world dominates your focus, the quest for meaning may be declared a taboo zone, pushed away from attention and religion and occultism deliberately repressed.

Mundane, routine life makes you discontent, and you strain against restrictions, always expecting more from life and others. You anticipate and demand satisfaction, perceiving yourself as a favored one, and can carry this attitude into intimate relationships where heightened sexual appetites can assume compulsive overtones of manipulative power. This also can generate fears of being possessed—complicating, distorting and confusing sexuality.

Retrograde Jupiter poses questions of right direction, and you may struggle with the conditioned impulse to search in the world while the Jupiter impulse magnetizes an inward turning. Your inner life assumes compulsive attention, with self-contemplation, and exploration becoming a priority. Asserting your unique individuality and worldview is predominant, although this does not require others to be oppressed by being pressured to agree with your views; you are relatively indifferent to their opinions, provided you can remain true to your values and principles. You trust in an inner abundance and spiritual riches rather than material gain, and your compelling need is to discover these for growth. You still make high demands and expectations, but these are of yourself instead of from others. Being reliant on inner direction, you trust these intuitive feelings and messages, and prefer an adventure of the psyche to a worldly excursion. The power you seek is over your own drives and compulsions, and this you hope to attain by self-understanding.

SATURN (CAPRICORN)

Your own compulsive self-restrictions can simultaneously be a way to exert "power-over" others and manipulate their attitudes and actions. Saturn in the 8th house agitates unconscious pressures which often assume a self-negating function, based on disowning self-images and your inclination to be overly cautious, defensive, or repressive. You may have an obsessive need to control and organize yourself or others, derived from inadequate self-esteem and fears of losing control and allowing chaos to enter. You erect boundaries against emotions, anxiety, pessimism, guilt, shame, insecurity, passion, despair and paranoia; yet these still encroach into consciousness. No inner barrier is impermeable, and even though you believe in the shielding power of conformity and conservatism to order and regulate your life, you often only succeed in increasing inner stresses by self-repudiating actions.

The impression of social and parental conditioning has marked you, leaving behind unresolved psychological patterns of an incomplete self-image, fragmenting your wholeness and divorcing parts of yourself by a perfectionist ideal of how you should be in distinction to how you are. You are more compulsively self-rejecting than self-accepting, and as a consequence of repetitive reprimands and recriminations by introjected condemnatory voices replaying previously absorbed admonitory commands, you have lost touch with yourself. Instead you have substituted a set of rigid controls to structure yourself and life for security and stability, failing to recognize that this obsessive defense is actually imprisoning you and virtually guaranteeing dissatisfaction. In the name of self-preservation, these limiting behavior patterns restrict options and opportunities.

Complexes and fixations shape your lifestyle and expression with others, who may perceive you as remote, indifferent, or hard to know, closed to deeper relationship. To compensate for private inadequacy, you may be driven to assert authoritarian power over others by exploitative and domineering behavior, probably connected to your singleminded ambitions—which may become obsessive—and allowing few distractions that enable any worldly progress to be possible. Your reliable, responsible temperament can be well disciplined, focusing attention on your tasks, and being able to impose control, order, and organization is an obsessive skill you can utilize for career benefit. In addition, your compulsive submission to right behavior is reflected by qualities of scrupulous honesty, and so others can trust you to discharge your duties efficiently. However, there is an inflexible dimension to your self-control, and you can become obsessed with fulfilling rules and regulations, serving the letter of the law rather than the spirit, which is not always apt or sensible; any touch of instability and deviation unsettles your need for predictability.

Your harsh and inhibiting attitudes often manipulate others' choices, especially those dependent on you, and instill a restrictive voice in them, similar to the prohibitive messages that you receive from your conscience, which is more a creation of conditioning than inner wisdom. Your fears and controls proscribe others' freedoms, even psychologically depressing any who are especially receptive and empathic. Your perfectionist evaluations and judgments of others reflects your own inner critic and this can negatively impinge on others' self-image, when the real root of disapproval is your own repression. Even if you do not overtly seek to control others, this subtle influence is still "power-over" people, and perhaps should be transformed by refining your attitudes. A distrustful, fatalistic, narrow attitude is one that attracts oppressive dark clouds, leading to despair, depression, and reduced life-enjoyment. Do you really want others to act similarly, magnifying your own limiting worldview and diminishing optimism and joy even more?

The 8th house issues of intimacy, sexuality, death, values, and resources are likely sources for compulsive and obsessive traits to gather around. You may have resistances to intimacy and sexuality, and your control need is a protection against change and death. You fear involvement with primal experiences of life, as you recognize that these are more powerful than your defenses, and your barriers will not hold forever. Letting go and merging with something greater may fill you with panic, and you hate imagining emotions running free, especially those blocked for so long—the anger, rage, envy, jealousy, passions, and lust for power that you strive to ignore. You may try to minimize the importance of 8th house issues in your life, while unconsciously experiencing and displaying their effects through compulsive behavior. Money may become an obsession, where thrift and miserly attitudes conceive security as material prosperity. Health fixations may develop from excess anxiety and fears of illness, aging, or death; emotions may become blocked, causing psychosomatic symptoms as a consequence of repression, and, if continued, perhaps resulting in an inability to exchange intimate feelings.

Retrograde Saturn intensifies personal demands, doubts, criticisms, and a sense of inferiority and inadequacy. Self-condemnation is deeper, and the repressive conscience conveys its message with a stronger voice. Rejecting trust in the world (and others) instills a defensive posture, often by retreating from involvement and building rigid controls that increase a solitary temperament—one uncomfortable with either superficial social contact or intimate relationships. Negative fears, caution, morbidity, and melancholy combine with a guilt-ridden and self-denying personality that anticipates frustration and failure, almost passively conceding to this as a form of masochistic penance for imagined sin. Fatalistic and pessimistic stoicism often attracts negative experiences to confirm this worldview, and as you tend to resist change you may ensure that discontent continues.

URANUS (AQUARIUS)

You may have a compulsive need to be different, asserting your identity in an unconventional, non-conformist manner, rejecting social expectations to be predictable, responsible, and controlled by the conditioning process. You may perceive stability and security as a trap, almost akin to death, and instead demand your right to follow your own impulses and oppose any restrictive laws and rules. Your self-image may be based on rebellion, justifying your disruptive behavior as promoting change, awakening others to the excitement of chaos that liberates all prisoners, believing that deviation generates innovation and progress. Yet in your search to transcend limitations, your affirmation of independence and individualism may infringe on others' freedoms and rights; inadvertently or uncaringly your manipulative "power-over" others can contravene their choice of behavior.

Society cannot continue to exist if everyone is intent on rejecting community commitments and acting in knee-jerk contrary and extremist ways; freedom expressed in such an immature, juvenile manner is simply destructive and non-productive, destabilizing for little positive effect, although a social balance is necessary between conditioned responses and free responses, so that neither unconscious stagnation nor license becomes preeminent. These compulsions to break free of obligations and mundane routines by making sudden disruptive changes may have mixed consequences, often sweeping away what is still good along with the stagnant, repressive patterns. Your ideal is a state of absolute freedom, which is a dream and fantasy rather than a likely reality in your life. Yet this drives you onward, looking for change and new experience to experimentally stretch further into less-charted realms. You look for the beyond, attracted to taboos, sexuality, death, and mysteries to probe more deeply than the majority immersed in the consensus mass-mind. You look toward the future and beneath the surface, edging closer to an isolated unique position.

There's a pioneering spirit that is driven by curiosity, and this turns your idealistic nature into one that is prophetic, awakening intellect and intuition to grasp new visions and seed-ideas for social reform that are overshadowing humanity to create the future. You may become obsessed with a role as an original, innovative thinker, offering a blueprint for human progress and a utopian state of freedom that together can be created. Radical ideas may flow from you, and you feel compelled to communicate these to others, receiving variable reactions; some see them as impractical, others as possible. If this path is taken, then you actively seek to manipulate others to contact your vision, and care is needed as to how you respond to their critique, or any imbalance could expose you to being labeled a fanatic rather than recognizing what you hope to contribute to society. Try to ensure a detached, impersonal and logical evaluation of any such schemes, and this can counteract any excessive and obsessive distortions.

Crossing taboo lines excites your attention, and sexuality is one sphere where experimentation is likely; you may, however, be less involved emotionally—mentally curiosity rules—and a detached witness may observe and assess your sexual experiences. Underlying this is a compulsion to be free of all instinctual and emotional needs, as interfering with a mental exploration of life, and you need to avoid disintegrating your nature by this tendency.

Retrograde Uranus extends this rebellious compulsion for absolute autonomy and freedom, and the search to shatter restrictions may produce eccentric and unstable behavior, especially when external pressures are acutely felt. The inner battlefield may seem a constant state of existence, both at war with yourself and with society, alienated and fragmented, yet driven to discover psychological freedom from conflict and stress. This can empower inner inquiry, and most energy is diverted into self-transformation rather than outer revolutionary activity; in particular, psychology and metaphysics appeals, both as the root of personal problems and as the root of collective socialization. You may intuit that understanding yourself will give crucial insights into how society is created and operates. You are compelled to redefine your individuality. Instead of feeling detached and separate you can introduce greater wholeness and participation into your life. If this can be achieved, then new insight and ideas may be grasped. Being simply a rebel without cause, and acting contrary just to reinforce a false individuality is futile and unproductive, and the retrograde's inner turning is an opportunity to induce greater awareness of your compulsions.

NEPTUNE (PISCES)

A compulsive need to lose yourself and merge with something greater is a key impulse in your personality and life-experiences, driven by an unconscious pattern prone to sacrificing something for the sake of reconnection, regeneration, and purification. Your malleable, flexible and impressionable personality may allow you to adapt and flow with life, yet often moves you perilously close to becoming lost and confused. Drifting through inconsistency of purpose and clarity, you may feel paralyzed when faced by decisions, often looking for something or someone to act as your savior.

Compulsively you weave imaginative, escapist fantasies, dreaming of your ideal, perfect life, secure, stable and emotionally peaceful, you can indulge in your own interests without the world interfering. Yet you often prefer to maintain these dreams, illusions, and unrealistic expectations without testing them in the crucible of life; you can concoct magnificent visions, but have difficulty translating them into tangible form.

The need to merge may awaken a mystical search, inspiring escape into an otherworldly paradise, where blissful love, light, and wisdom can enable you to transcend mundane reality, and where your heightened emotions and psychic sensitivity can flow at peace with spiritual life. The fascination of spirit, esoteric teachings, and the promise of joining the company of high beings will inspire your efforts, and you can easily become obsessed by such endeavors, especially if you devote yourself to a charismatic guru or teacher to whom you can surrender and act submissively and selflessly. The quest may obsess your life, and all is consumed within that fire. The mystical path may also motivate you toward compassionate service to humanity, alleviating suffering and encouraging evolutionary growth as a compulsive "server." Discrimination is vital when aiming at mystical heights, as your imagination and uncritical impressionability may be deceptive, and you can equally find yourself lost in the byroads of glamour and illusion as walking the narrow straight path.

Another sphere where this compulsive need to merge may lead is involvement with idealistic political doctrines, intent on social redemption. Uniting with a group for political action may seem apt to actualize your vision of a perfect world, and you can see yourself as a martyr for the cause, yet be undone by your addictive nature which is essentially dependent and has to follow someone or something such as gurus or political visions. Your submissiveness can be exploited, and you may prefer to see only whatever supports your illusions.

Personal artistic creativity may also attract compulsive and obsessive tendencies, where expressing your imagination becomes dominant and preoccupying. The "I am an artist" self-image may be both an anchor and yet also cast you further adrift, as mediating the artistic impulse can dislodge many personality foundations when perceptions of the world take on different hues.

As your temperament is more sacrificial and submissive, there is less of an overt display of "power-over" others, yet you still manipulate others by your spiritual, political, artistic, and intimate expressions. Relationships often assume a symbiotic dimension, and you compulsively project a perfect lover image, superimposed on your partner as part of an obsession for an ideal union, in which you can melt away in the arms of your lover, abandoned to love. Yet while you are eager to lose your identity boundaries, the likely consequence is complications, confusions and heartache when your lover is revealed to be only human after all. Romantic disillusionment is probable, and when obsessions are projected, they may be difficult to bear. You manipulate lovers by empathy, or by acting as a martyr or victim to their lack of consideration, and are often parasitically dependent on them for stability and security. Intimacy may be rife with sexual fantasies, and you may be liable to compulsive promiscuity, searching for sexual escape and forgetfulness, or see sex as a means to serve others. You may be obsessively concerned with defining a fairly fluid and changeable sexual nature, uncertain as to your real needs and tastes.

The impulse of transcendence which is so powerful may form obsessions attached to self-destructive fantasies, often diverted into addictive behavior connected to alcohol, drugs, and sex. Wanting to break free of boundaries may activate psychosomatic illnesses and death urges.

Retrograde Neptune reinforces this need to redefine and transcend a limited self, and stimulates imagination, sensitivity, and otherworldly traits even more. The inner vision dominates attention and is affected by unconscious complexes and compulsions shaping its form. Self-delusion is probable, and escapist impulses hard to resist as the obligations of mundane reality find little interest. Fantasies may absorb obsessive energies, and these can find fertile ground within creativity, spirituality, politics, and sexuality, and you can easily be manipulated by your impressionability. Acting decisively and achieving tangible results may be difficult, and disciplined organization is not usually one of your talents. Addictive behavior is likely at some stage, and unless you understand your compulsive motivations, and adjust and purify them, you may experience dissatisfaction and disillusionment when dreams dematerialize into evanescent fictions.

PLUTO (SCORPIO)

Compulsive needs to dominate others and assert personal power are likely, exploiting and manipulating people to satisfy your needs and desires, forcing them into subserviency. You may look for opportunities to display "power-over" others, and can use your penetrating psychological insight to cunningly manipulate others' actions and choices in your favor, often by subversion and undermining their positions.

As Pluto is connected to the repressed unconscious, latent compulsive and obsessive tendencies are more prevalent, often stirred into activity by attitudes and encounters with primal forces and the problem of integrating the personality dark side. Pluto can function as a conduit for repressed energies and disowned aspects of self, which are either kept firmly out of sight by controls and self-denial, or which periodically erupt by compulsive behavior, discharging energies with little concern for their impact on others or their destructiveness. These repressions include several causes for compulsion and obsession, such as needs for revenge, violence, lust, passion, envy, jealousy, greed, power, sex, money, possessiveness. All of these can promote extremist attitudes and behavior, possibly negative and damaging to all concerned, unless corrupt and contaminated energies are healed and transformed into positive channels of expression. Many Pluto-driven personalities feel dominated by inner compulsions, and lack the knowledge or ability to harness these powerful energies and instead fall victim to obsessive possession, where the repressed self can emerge with a demonic nature.

Inner battles may proliferate, tensions increase as you seek to impose a determined will on the world, attempting to change anything that resists your intentions. Often this "power-over" others is compensation for a recognized loss of inner power, where despite efforts, compulsive desires still preoccupy your mind. While utilizing compulsive power to achieve ambitions may generate an effective momentum, you fail to shake off these psychologically consuming patterns until your ambitions have been taken over by them. The need to satisfy desires may erode ethical principles, and can also subvert your own integrity.

Intimacy and sexuality can attract these compulsive energies, and often serves to release aggressive feelings by physical assertion. Emotions are highly charged by sexual activity, and there may be inclinations toward "power-over," sexual obsession, and sadism, when volatile repressions extrude. The question of directing libidinal energy may be important to resolve, met often either by mastering its influence in the psyche or repressing to some degree. Men especially have connections between dark-side-sexuality-aggression and tendencies to engage in power struggles and breaking taboos. The destroyer image lurks close to consciousness, and this is related to both a deathwish and rebirth impulse inherent in Pluto's influence.

The deathwish may be compulsively displayed by a preoccupation with death, after-lives, reincarnation, out-of-body experiences, and a need for freedom from insistent inner drives. This includes a contradictory attraction toward control and chaos, an apparently mutually exclusive polarity yet connected through renewal and rebirth processes of destroying the old to make space for the new. These are the experiences of transformation, the breaking apart, and the later reassembly and revitalization inherent in regenerative change. Often compulsive patterns strive to initiate this crisis in the psyche as a means for an integrative, healing self-restitution. If enslaved by inner demons, two options are available—either submit to their domination, or become master in your own house again by self-understanding that eliminates the power of these intrusive, disowned fragments of self who have usurped power by your self-ignorance and lack of attention. Much of Pluto's fascination with occult and magical powers is a need to reassert control over an unruly unconscious mind, and to renew self-discipline, psychic balance and create a context in which to explore and unify the repressive dark side.

Retrograde Pluto may find these compulsive tendencies even more oppressive and demanding, and the dark side may feel almost overpowering and resistant to controls. A sense of alienation increases tension, while emotional stress and psychological pressures may generate phobias, complexes, fixations, and distorted, imbalanced behavior whenever repressions accumulate by self-denial, expelled in periodic outbursts of uncontrolled self-destructive emotions, eliminated like a psychic purgative. Difficulty may occur in expressing personal power, emotions, and sexuality, and an extremist, confrontational nature may provoke regular relationship crises, and with hostility to others may form adversarial attitudes. Yet this interior battlefield can be transformed, and the healing power of Pluto released through an inner revolution, when a compulsive search to understand the mysteries of the psyche and life can unlock the gates to rebirth, reshaping the personality, and reowning those neglected, festering partial selves locked away in the underworld's dungeons and in pain ever since. This may involve cleansing past conditioning—often based on control and repression—which may have been unsuitable for your temperament. Peace can come when an overloaded desire nature is emptied, cutting the roots of obsession and compulsion and substituting self-mastery through genuine insight as the dark side is raised into the light for regeneration.

5 Sexual and Emotional Union— Crisis and Catharsis

THE 8TH HOUSE IS THE ARENA OF intense, catalytic intimate relationships, when Eros incites the individual to seek identification with "something greater than the limited, separate self." This is an instinct that motivates us toward sexual and emotional contact and also awakens mystical aspiration. These involve sexual and emotional union by experiencing the intimate interaction of self with others, and the mystic dissolution of subjective barriers between self and reality to realize oneness and nonduality. Through both approaches we can experience a profound self-encounter—either self-reflection by a partner, or by comprehending our holistic self.

Sexuality is more complex than just physical coupling may suggest, or as openly discussed socially for we tend to emphasize body-sexuality rather than discuss the subtle emotional, mental, and spiritual interactions that also occur. Despite the modern social advances of sexual liberation an immaturity still remains, preoccupied and focused on physical attributes alone. Unease persists within collective attitudes, as is evident when greater public controversy and opposition is aroused by television and film occasionally transmitting mild sexual acts and stirring media censorship into urgent action, when nightly news-scenes of mass starvation, war, poverty, and deprivation are considered less obscene. In such a juxtaposition, the imbalance of collective moral attitudes is starkly and vividly displayed.

It is intriguing and perhaps surprising that society remains uncomfortable with sexuality, an activity from which all life springs and which most adults engage in regularly. We fail to recognize the crucial role that sexuality has played and still plays in social formation. Society is a gathering together of individuals for communal support and mutual benefit, derived originally from small family groups of nomadic hunter-gatherers for security and protection, and eventually forming permanent settlements which later became villages, towns, and cities. A cohesive force for this was the need for sexual bonding—the primal, natural instinct for mating and procreation. In this context, sex is a source for human development and a builder of civilization, as evidenced by the tradition of marriage and the social foundation of the nuclear family system.

Scorpio is naturally channeled through the 8th house, and a powerful sexual force is a major characteristic of this zodiacal energy. Scorpio represents the driving force of the sexual impulse; this is the urge to merge and become whole by the dynamic regeneration of union, where the self is either expanded or joins with others to constitute a greater organic whole. Similar to the dilemma of the unconscious mind—wanting to become conscious and yet remain unconscious—Scorpio symbolizes the dilemma of duality, as one powerful part of the psyche seeks to transcend its limiting separative existence, while another fears the breakdown of individuality and apparent loss of self.

BRIDGING ISOLATION

From subjective isolation comes the need to bridge the separation felt between ourselves, others and the world. For many, the only available course to move beyond egoic confines is by sexual activity, which offers a temporary respite from an insular experience and at least satisfies insistent physical instincts.

Feeling separate is ultimately unsatisfying, and it is a recognition of our incomplete aloneness. Sexuality becomes not merely the discharge of physical needs and tensions but also a search to discover emotional security; we hope to merge with another through love, become a couple, a married partnership and family unit. Achieving this simple aim is, however, fraught with difficulties, and intimacy often deteriorates into a notable source for personal suffering when relationships are disharmonious or collapse in acrimony. In striving to break separative barriers we can meet emotional battlefields in which many are damaged and broken.

Our existence is conditioned by the ceaseless interplay of dualistic opposites, and our life experience is founded on the "meeting-place of self and others." In the 8th house this becomes the crisis of union and the problem of successfully uniting men and women with different emphases, needs, thoughts, and sexuality. Through intimate relationships, we encounter "fate" in the disguise of lovers and long-term partners. These relationships invariably prove catalytic in our lives, producing both positive and negative consequences; intimacy engages us in our most profound and traumatic experiences, perhaps offering bliss and pain in equal measure and posing critical emotional choices and decisions.

Eros is a great teacher for humanity, although his messages and our ignorance of the power of intimacy may result in his lessons being received through emotional tears and pain. The strains of intimate failure can provoke a personality purgative, discharging twisted emotions as the antidote to containing them. As a process, this is difficult to endure, and cathartic release is often felt as a disintegration and loss of control, yet the restorative quality of this emotional restitution is important for psychological health and balance. If we deny cathartic responses, we may succeed only in intensifying inner stress and increasing emotional and mental "pollution." Modern psychotherapy recognizes the therapeutic virtue of catharsis as a self-healing process, and often encourages emancipation from carrying unnecessary bondage to the past, where emotionally charged memories still remain unintegrated and previous wounded feelings are still raw.

In love deep exchanges occur, and these encounters can stimulate considerable emotional turbulence which may both enliven and frighten people. To many, the power of sexual and emotional feelings, desires, and needs is disturbing, almost a shock to the self-image because of its compulsive quality and physical sensuality.

Within relationship there is a close relationship between sexuality and death. Intimacy demands temporary relinquishment of closed personality boundaries, we relax egoic defenses when opening to a lover. The separate self extends a welcoming hand for contact, and in the merged space created by passion and emotion, both partners can be interpenetrated by anothers' "being" during union.

When genuine emotional resonance exists, intimacy can be extremely revealing for both partners, as identity controls are suspended and the hidden self can be exposed by a lover's gaze; more than clothes are stripped away in intimacy, personality masks are also dropped when vulnerable feelings are shared. Unless the experience is mutually limited to just physical union, noone emerges from intimacy the same as when they entered; something has been transmitted in a psychic exchange that is capable of reshaping reality. By the opening of the "I" to welcome the other, a sense of "we" or "something greater" is touched, shifting awareness by insight into relationship. When physical virginity is lost, this is the start of maturity, as symbolically this change represents the movement beyond self into greater awareness of others, and initiates the adult quest for a partner and completeness.

THE IMPRESSION OF SOCIAL ATTITUDES

Contemporary sexual attitudes are still contradictory. Despite an apparent preoccupation with overt sexual displays, we retain taboo associations surrounding sexuality, and demonstrate fascination, antipathy, and ambivalence to the range of human sexuality. Fear of a liberated human sexuality often comes from reluctance to deal with life's primal energies, which are recurring themes of an 8th house exploration. We fear rousing the primitive savage concealed beneath our civilized facade; we fear disrupting the carefully constructed social cohesion that controlled sexuality has helped develop; we fear liberating the orgasmic potential of people, in case their awakening to an ecstatic reality is the spark to ignite demands to change society, as demonstrated by government oppression of Wilhelm Reich's controversial orgone energy experiments and studies of human sexuality.

Repetitive media attention influences us to believe apparent demands and expectations of sexual performance. We wonder if our bodies are the right fashionable shape? Do we "do it" right? Are we technically adept? Do we have sufficient orgasms? Or do we condemn ourselves for unattractiveness, lack of interest, relationship caution, minority sexual preferences, and fears of intimacy? With such profuse sexual information and comment we may compare and measure ourselves against the media rule, feeling inadequate if our experience fails to equal the golden sexual peaks. It is understandable that few remain unscathed by social sexual pressures; with such ambiguous and restrictive attitudes met on our passage to adulthood, secret fears and disquiet regarding certain areas of our sexuality are to be expected. Our sexual defensiveness may deny that we have any hang-ups; but in all honesty, few approach intimate exposure without some anxiety, and perhaps those that do have simply erected impassable walls around their mind and emotions, leaving only the experience open of physical contact.

Our society appears primarily biased toward sexuality as a physical release and turns away from its potential for ecstatic sensuality and a mystical path. Modern sexuality has a devalued quality devoid of reverence, and tends to be misused as an adjunct of exploitative personal power. We have lost the understanding of sexuality as a path to rebirth, failing to comprehend the sacred contact that can be made through sexual union.

Many only experience a soon fading, partial, and temporary sexual satisfaction, not realizing that their deeper search is to transcend isolation by intimacy and to reconnect their fragmented wholeness. Neither social, moral, cultural, nor religious teaching encourages us to discover the higher dimension of sexuality, usually preferring to enforce prohibitive instructions to control our sexual self or to perceive our body instincts as inferior, lower, or animalistic; in these twisted and distorted impressions lie the roots of shame, fear, and a disgust for sex that ruins intimacy for many.

The author Henry Miller once commented, "For some, sex leads to sainthood; for others, it is the road to hell…all depends on one's point of view."[1] This point of view is often dictated by the type of sexual conditioning received. For many, the road to hell is busier than the road to sainthood. Media glee at the discovery of sexual scandals remains a bane of those in the public eye, fuelled by an overly-righteous and hypocritical media intent on manipulating public attitudes and ambivalent reactions of sexual fascination and condemnation.

If personal sexuality is not honored as a bridge between body and soul, and a meeting of heart and mind, then the energy flow is incomplete, promising much and delivering less satisfaction than expected. When an individual has been molded by negative sexual conditioning, doubt, fear, and self-censure interrupts spontaneous natural expression, crippling the prospects for a healthy and liberated sexual union.

Sexual and emotional communion may be inhibited by suspicion and apprehension, obstructing shared communication and intimate relaxation. Guilt and shame may accompany sexual and emotional needs. Inherited taboos and attitudes can imprison, choking spontaneity and diverting energies into repetitive self-disparaging messages which reinforce low esteem, fears, vulnerability and opposition to intimate exposure. We may be so tightly controlled that bar-

---

[1] Henry Miller, *The World of Sex* cited in Margo Anand, *The Art of Sexual Ecstacy* (London: Aquarian Press, 1990), p. 83.

riers remain even when making love. We may refuse to open to our partner. We may maintain a certain separation, perhaps through exploitation, manipulation, and the need for conquest to affirm personal power. Our dark side may be agitated by sexual and emotional intensity, or old resentments, rejections, humiliations, possessiveness, rage, passions, and jealousy may be discovered and rise into awareness. Intellectual self-images and resistances may interfere with natural sexuality and emotional interaction, blocking a relaxed response to physical pleasure and the ecstasy of the moment.

INTIMACY AND SURRENDER

Questions of trust and surrender become important in intimacy. Unless we let down our defenses to a partner, the deeper levels of personal communion remain closed and the relationship is reduced to a relatively superficial experience. Many feel afraid when intimacy touches vulnerable feelings. Many dislike personality exposure, often evading and withdrawing from contact. Yet through a lover's acceptance, we are given an opportunity to uncover fears (and even those demons and monsters) of our repressed self; in genuine love, intimacy can serve as a liberating path to heal wounds of self-rejection. Partnerships rely on trust, as both have handed their hearts to the other for safe-keeping; if this trust is abused, relationships lose cohesion as this fragile, bonding connection has been severed. Individual tendencies to trust or distrust intimacy can reflect underlying attitudes to the universe, and these may change over time as experiences accumulate and as these attitudes shape personal lives.

Intimacy requires some degree of surrender, and there can be a misunderstanding of what is involved. Many interpret this as losing free will and personal power, which is actually submission to another, and in our patriarchal culture this often implies the supportive role of women to men. Partnership submission is a warped intimate interaction, and one that is always imbalanced and liable to manipulation. Surrender is a different process, and one which can create an holistic partnership of equality and mutual benefit. The word surrender comes from *render* meaning to melt, and *sur* meaning to the highest, thus a "melting to the highest." A genuine partnership experience is when both are renewed through union, accessing the highest potential of their relationship.

CHOICE AND REGENERATION

The regenerative impulse can enter our lives through the channel of sexuality. Adults look for a compatible partner, and hidden affinities and resonances attract people into relationships which can become transformative and mold their future. Intimacy is a conduit for fate; as the two become "one" something less tangible slips through in the passion of love. This may be a constructive or destructive force, depending on the aptness of our choices and our ability to integrate the stimulating energies unleashed by sexual activity.

Through relationship, we open doors that can determine our future; we may have created the basis for a happy, enduring, loving partnership or to an eventual slide into recrimination, antagonism, and rejection as separation and divorce provides the only option when love wanes or personality friction is too damaging and dissatisfying. We may inadvertently choose a partner who brings demanding burdens and obligations in his or her wake, perhaps through illness, psychological problems, addictions, dependency; or whose talents, inheritances and financial acumen bring us greater material liberation, wealth, and abundance, enabling our lives to be more fulfilling and pleasurable. We may choose a partner to match dominance-submission needs, and intimacy revolves around power struggles, which may ignite passionate feelings or destroy them.

Careful choice is needed to intuit what a partner may introduce into our lives, otherwise through ignorance we can face problems of adaptation, cooperation, and compromise that neither can successfully bridge. Each relationship will bear fruit; it is a mutual creation whether this is a bitter or sweet fruit and whatever consequences result from our merging. Relationship crisis can lead to either psychological breakdown or breakthrough.

THE GATE OF SEX

All esoteric and occult teachings study energies within the body which are capable of raising the individual to a transcendent state of consciousness. Awakening these regenerative forces is the intention of yoga, magic, and mysticism, and much attention is placed on animating chakras and the kundalini fire by various meditations, breathing techniques and ritualized practices. Within most spiritual paths are veiled mystery teachings which involve working with sexual energies, and these are often disguised by symbolic imagery to protect understanding by those unready for such knowledge. The sex force revealed by Scorpio and the 8th house is a path to attain liberation from the confining, separate self, and this is through the ecstatic experience of oneness, a taste of which we savor in the intimacy of love.

Beyond personal cathartic relationship lies the potential mystical sexuality of maturity, where intimate needs can expand to embrace the whole universe instead of merely a single partner. The impulse for union with a lover extends into a quest for the Beloved and Divine Lover as sought by Bhakti Yoga and Sufi paths. The nonprocreative use of sexual energy enables the experience of a higher, unified level of existence. Elisabeth Haich states in *Sexual Energy and Yoga* that, "The secret of sexual energy…is to lead his consciousness step by step…to God…. Just as sexual energy has helped man out of his spiritual state into the body, so it can help him to return to full awareness to his divine primal state of wholeness."[2] It is this

---

[2] Elisabeth Haich, *Sexual Energy and Yoga* (Santa Fe, NM: Aurora Press, 1982), pp. 154, 24.

state that we have lost, and our race memory dimly recalls a paradisaical golden age of conscious unity and our fall from grace, enshrined in ancient legends and biblically linked with sexual consciousness and shame. The spiritual path is a return to this state of communion, a reaffirmation of liberated ecstasy.

Social conditioning does not make this return easy to achieve. A rebirth of a cultural ecstatic spirit is often oppressed by fears of unleashing little understood primal forces which we refuse to concede are part of our nature. We prefer to close down our sensitivity to life instead of opening our perceptions wide, and this is the situation that imprisons us and ensures we remain fragmented. A new understanding and integration of the Dionysian ecstatic joy of life awaits our rediscovery, and this can only become possible when we reperceive ourselves through holistic awareness.

SPIRITUALITY AND SEXUALITY

One prevalent Western attitude to spirituality and sexuality is that of division—the two do not meet. This continues gnostic beliefs in the profanity of material forms, physical bodies, and the natural world, all "ruled by the powers of evil and darkness," and repeats dualistic, ascetic-inspired Manichean doctrines that initially appealed only to repressive personalities.

Celibacy became commonly associated with the spiritual life, the priest's way of renouncing human frailty and temptation as a presumed mimicking of Christ's life without a partner. This is now contentiously questioned as to the validity of Western biblical interpretations and actual Judaic customs two thousand years ago. Alternative traditions have built on suppositions of a married Jesus and the lineage that followed, especially connected with the Merovingian dynasty in Europe. Roman Catholicism refutes these heretical suggestions, and reaffirms their priesthood's apostolic succession from St. Peter as a nonprocreative lineage, denying that Christ and sexuality were ever introduced.

Celibacy becomes not simply a free personal choice, but is implicitly identified to follow as a way to the spirit. One consequence has been the cultural loss of an exalted human sexuality and reverence to the sacredness of primal energies; we deny the deepest roots of our lives, and disconnect our psyches from an ecstatic potential by regarding sexuality as almost an impure, secret, and shameful act. Our attraction and need rubs painfully with fearful insecurities and an admonishing vision of God casting us out from the edenic garden because our sexual innocence has been lost. Our attitudes become confused and contradictory, yet socially we "worship" sexuality while maintaining taboo restrictions, persecuting homosexuality and having an unhealthy fascination that emphasizes the value of the body but dismisses the spiritual potential of sex.

This 8th house issue indicates that personal integration may involve a regenerated sexuality, requiring the acceptance and understanding of the sexual impulse expressed on physical, emotional, and mental levels, and alludes to the opportunity for further exploration of the mystery of duality.

One philosophy that is unequivocal about this higher direction is Tantra, a Hindu approach often misinterpreted, distorted, and condemned by social repression, yet whose message is one that a Western culture suffering from an attitudinal division—which perpetually separates the opposites of spirit and matter, of secular and transcendent, of male and female, and of body and soul—could learn from. The Tantric holistic perception enables divisions to be healed, by reuniting fragmented opposites within a vision and experience of unity. The Tantric path is one of reconciliation, where opposites no longer divide but reveal their complementary nature. It is this schism between opposites and self-other that the 8th house mystery explores, and which is a root-cause for both cultural and relationship crises.

Tantra vehemently disagrees with social and religious traditions of dividing flesh from spirit, seeing this as a primary reason for suffering. The aim of Tantra embraces the whole being, body-mind-spirit, rather than repressing or disowning vital aspects of human nature as unsuitable for spiritual congress. Sexuality becomes crucially important in Tantra for personal understanding and social integration. Tantra views sex as a gate to ecstatic enlightenment and intimacy as a path to self-realization. Tantric meditation practices seek to discover the divine self in a lover, and through intimate contact and fusion, gain a reflection of wholeness and experience oneness. When self and other are united, a regenerative insight is attained as fragments reemerge in communion.

The sage of the Tao Te Ching observed that when opposites no longer damage each other, both are benefited through the attainment of the Tao. Therefore the wise identifies opposites as one, and sets an example for the world. This is the essence of nonconformist Tantric and Taoist paths which, enflamed by the spirit of universal acceptance, are deemed subversive, dangerous, and taboo by dualistic societies; yet these traditions hold insights that could help heal both individuals and society.

Tantra uses the image of Shiva-Shakti, male-female, the polarity of opposites as a teaching tool and cosmological symbol. Shiva is the ecstasy of consciousness and his consort, Shakti, the ecstasy of energy. Their spiritual and sexual union generated the universe as an erotic act of love, a joyful dance reenacted in all living beings. Tantra invites us to participate in this by dissolving our divisions of spirit-sexuality-matter and those contradictory illusions defining what is either sacred or profane. The Tantric attitude weaves fragments together again, all those disparate and disunited conflicting aspects of self that can turn life into hell, and continues this process of renewal until an inner harmony is restored.

Applied to both self and intimacy, Tantra accepts everything in life. Concepts of taboo and forbidden acts, thoughts, and emotions are dissolved; divisive judgments are rejected; labels of good and bad are cast away, taking each experience as an opportunity for self-discovery; opposites are seen as complementary not antagonistic, and boundaries between the acceptable and unacceptable are replaced by an holistic vision. However, Tantra can be misunderstood and misapplied as an excuse for license and irresponsible permissive action; the true Tantric expression is displayed when the holistic self is awakened and demonstrates responsible right relationships.

Sexuality can indicate life-affirmation; a healthy sexual attitude free from repressions is liberating for both individual and society. As the Reichian Bioenergetic therapists believe, regular orgasm is regenerative, releasing blockages that can accumulate on physical, emotional, and mental levels of the human organism. To Tantra, sexuality is self-energizing and affirmative, a natural way to worship the mystery of life and connect to the sacredness of matter and the divine essence of the human being and is certainly never an excuse for denial and repression.

Tantra encourages exploring sexuality for self-understanding, which provides a remedy for feelings of unease, hostility, and fascinated enslavement which can characterize socially conditioned attitudes. Tantra opposes asceticism, morality, and social controls, rebelling against "power-over" people and all cultural taboos and prohibitive beliefs born from separatist perceptions. Instead, Tantra asserts sexuality as a spiritual path; a way of acceptance that dissolves futile and fallacious ideas of opposites, pointing toward the prospect of feeling oneness with the world, by fusing the within and without and merging as the wave and ocean. Certain elements of Tantra are included in the Dionysian cult, where non-conformism challenges cultural convention, and a mystical, joyous, and glorifying attitude provides a rebirth when dualism fades.

If the 8th house emotional and sexual issues remain troubling to anyone, the Tantric doctrine counsels an exit from a dualistic impasse. For personal concerns, a variety of self-help and therapeutic techniques exist which enable greater integrative insight into these sometimes difficult and alienating intimate experiences. One repercussion of intimacy can be to increase awareness of isolation and separateness, particularly poignant when apart or when relationships cease. While heartache continues to shake emotional turbulence, the sudden awareness of aloneness is even more disturbing as an unchangeable fact of life.

SADO-MASOCHISM

The controversial practices of sado-masochism have several connections to major 8th house themes active in individuals and society. These include responses to power, control, domination; heightened emotional, sexual and spiritual experiences; cathartic release of personality pressures; transcending the separate ego to unite with something greater; issues of self-image and self-esteem; compulsive, manipulative and obsessive behavior; and the close interplay of intimate pleasure and pain.

Sado-masochism is a minority practice and an individual preference that provokes social taboos. It is considered by mainstream attitudes as sexually deviant and perverse. When scrutinized more reflectively, automatic collective antagonism against sado-masochism can be observed embedded in unconscious and evasive reactions. It appears that the prime sin of overt sado-masochism is the conscious display and elevation of certain tendencies intrinsic to most intimate relationships and endemic throughout most societies.

The often conditioned recoil from public discussion of sado-masochism reflects an avoidance of how relationships operate, both those of intimate partnerships and between individual and society. In particular, the hierarchical, elitist cultural structure relies on a minority retaining and assuming social power. Whether this is based on aristocratic lineage, political influence, business skills or wealth, social relationships often function in terms of "master-slave" as a parallel to sado-masochistic partnerships. The strange thing is that in our free and democratic society this situation is allowed to continue. Power is freely given away by individuals as if imitating a masochistic role; our conditioning directs us to do this in favor of authority, and we unconsciously acquiesce to this loss of autonomy. Sado-masochism is a variation of the social "leaders-followers" tendency, and can reenact this drama in a more intimately conscious and deliberate manner.

Recent decades have seen male cultural power being adjusted by assertive female demands to acknowledge their rights and equal status. As many women recognize—and more than most men—social power vested in men has often abused women, taking advantage of their subservient position. For centuries, many households have been male-dominated and the woman has been a servant or slave to her master, an attitude reinforced by conventional religious teachings. The man naturally assumes power and control as the master of the house, and the woman effectively assumes a self-denying, masochistic servile posture. This role-play remains socially prevalent, despite modern ideals of sexual equality; such engrained cultural attitudes cannot be dispelled quickly.

Sado-masochism, on the other hand, ritualizes the social relationship instinct of dominance-submission. This collective behavior pattern can be heavily distorted when abused by "power-over" others—as in crime, violence and rape—but in sado-masochistic practice it is an agreed relationship between consenting adults, based on mutual needs and desires parallel to other types of intimacy. Negative socio-cultural reactions against sado-masochism is often a collective rejection of recognizing and accepting the truth of sado-masochism's psychological insight into the nature of existing social structures. The fear is that wider public awareness of how they are manipulated by unconscious ignorance of domination-submission traits may awaken them to reassert mass-power, and that, of course, is dangerous to powerful elites and cannot be allowed.

Sadism is the preference for control, power, and domination expressed by exploiting and enjoying power over others, demanding or forcing submission to exalt egoic supremacy. This often involves a diminution of relationship awareness, because one cannot be a "master" unless "slaves" and followers exist. Sadism is associated with cruelty, torture and inflicting pain on people, and is often displayed by worldwide state oppression as exposed by Amnesty International reports. The attitudes of those in governmental power often become harsh and impersonal, as their connection with the people becomes atrophied and distorted, resulting in a loss of humanity and disregard for human rights. Many states currently utilize sadism to frighten and threaten their citizens into silence and conformity to their dictates; Saddam Hussein's Iraq is an example, Stalin's Soviet communism, Hitler's Nazi Germany, Pol Pot's Cambodia-Kampuchea, and Idi Amin's Uganda are other notorious regimes linked with oppressive state violence.

The sado-masochism axis within intimacy is displayed in most relationships, where personalities polarize power roles. One naturally assumes command and the other follows, and although this may not include openly imposing pain and cruelty, the "power-over" tendency is actively manifested. Power struggles occur at some point in most relationships, and occasional re-definitions of this balance may also occur. Some relationships are founded on unrecognized and unconscious sado-masochistic tendencies present in their participants. Many men exploit their wives in ways that edge extremely close to sadism, by vindictive or stress-derived physical violence and emotional or mental abuse. The covert intention of this disregard for equality, individual integrity, and freedom is to reassert power and domination.

The sadist focuses on control techniques suited to different levels—from physical bondage, pain and slavery, to emotional humiliation and mental torture—probing intently at exposed personality weak spots. In sadomasochistic partnerships, this type of relationship is based on agreed consent and trust, and includes a mutually intense sexual arousal and a desire to satisfy subjective needs, preferably through the ritually dramatized production of an exciting, heightened sense of reality.

The purpose of the sadistic role is to experience "uplifting power," a feeling of primal potency and universal will, similar to imagining yourself as the God of a personal universe. This elevation of egoic supremacy is balanced by the alternative need for egoic destruction, mirrored by the polarized sado-masochistic roles. Sexual intensity and release is part of a process aiming to experience an ecstatic egoic transcendence, a higher unity and universal oneness that equates to the objectives of Tantric, holistic, and spiritual paths, although approaching the mountain top from another route. Obviously, there can be varying sado-masochistic levels and individual ambitions may differ as to their preferred level of intensity, but what characterizes these practices is that they are deliberately pursued, so that these intimate subtleties are also recognized and enjoyed.

The sado-masochistic partnership can unite personal needs for power and control matched with another's need for punishment and submission. The masochistic role is often assumed by someone with low self-esteem, repressed feelings, misplaced devotion, dependency needs, and guilt. The sadist may be living out compensatory fantasies, becoming a master or mistress in domestic privacy to rectify external frustrations and failures or to extend worldly power and authority in more intimately intense areas.

The peculiar sense of masochistic pleasure is vividly portrayed in many examples of Christian saints or yogic fakirs and ascetics. These adopt a self-denial technique, often rejecting their bodies and physical reality, and instead welcome the painful prospect of martyrdom and paths of pain, deprivation, and death for their beliefs and to experience the transcendent ecstasy they hope this can provoke. The practice of flagellation for "sin" is a masochistic pursuit which for certain temperaments introduces a sense of strangely satisfying shame, a validation of their unworthiness; the practice of confession to the authority of the priest can be seen as a religious variant of ritualized self-humiliation.

The masochist's need is for the sadist to diminish their ego because of their innate abjectness; the sadist's need is to diminish the masochist's ego, and thereby assert their own egoic power. Both needs are mutually complementary and supportive. The sadist may dominate the submissive personality by physical restraints and turning them into slaves whose only purpose is to serve the master or mistress in whatever ways are desired or agreed. The masochist wants to feel destroyed and diminished; the sadist to be able to destroy and be exalted. Part of this fuses sexuality and death as ways to transcendence and these repeat the cultural and psychological connections of Eros and Thanatos, although this can easily be degeneratively expressed as sexual humiliation is endemic to many forms of malevolent oppression and persecution.

Once the masochistic ego fades out of existence and the sadistic ego rises to exaggerated heights, the point of orgasmic sexual climax has been reached. Such practices span a broader range of emotional experiences between pain and ecstatic peaks, and these complementary psychological natures provide an opportunity for greater closeness. At orgasm, both hope to feel their connectedness and dissolution with the universe, an intensity that they believe cannot be found by other intimate practices.

The masochist "melts" by surrender and submission, and the sadist enters a heightened self-referential state; both techniques can use sexuality and ego-destruction for a temporary transcendent "death" to a limited personality, allowing both to contact a new personal perspective. The sadist takes pleasure from a vicarious participation with the masochist; both need each other to rise toward a higher state, and the sadist is transformed by empathy with the masochistic experience. Sado-masochism can be a shared two-way exchange, as the sadist contains the masochist and vice versa, and mutually explore a dual role-play together, enjoying both opposites and discovering the point where neither is preeminent.

This intensity is partly generated by elaborate dramatized ritual, which increases foreplay arousal by including elaborate costumes, fantasies, fetishism and body piercing. These inflate expectations and excitement by a symbolic drama which adds an evocative atmosphere to intimacy. The use of masks is another sado-masochistic practice that many observers find disturbing (often appropriated by numerous horror movies) or by the preference for leather and rubber-wear and specific clothes and accessories. These controversial indulgences are viewed with negativity and suspicion, even though they may parallel conventionally accepted styles of fashion, where provocative body-display receives public approval even when more sexually explicit. Compulsive and obsessive tendencies can find certain needs met by fetishist practices.

Obviously, there is an element of unorthodoxy about these sexual preferences when considered from a consensus viewpoint, but the sado-masochistic parallel to 8th house sexual-emotional catharsis potentially catalyzing insight is intriguing. The resemblance between sado-masochistic practices and acceptable social relationships is noticeable, and cultural censure of these intrinsic human traits condemns this issue to the fringes of allowable inquiry. As humans, we only replicate the dominant-submissive group and sexual patterns of the animal kingdom, although in our "sophistication" we pretend otherwise and collectively create another source for repression.

In essence, sado-masochism reflects a primary theme in social interaction, one which permeates cultural conditioning. Our avoidance of socially acknowledging this determines rejecting or recognizing similar traits in our own behavior. The truth is that as children of our culture all of us are biased toward either assuming a controlling, active, and dominant role or a submissive, reactive, and passive role. We may vary between these in different circumstances but our prevailing characteristic remains constant. In a culture not founded on a master-slave hierarchy, sado-masochism would have different cultural emphases and reactions.

Astrology can provide insight into how these tendencies may operate within the individual, and how the axis of dominance-submission may be sublimated by their social attitudes and behavior. In most personalities latent masochism and sadism exist, because these are two fundamental reactions to life; either a compliant, resigned fatalism, surrendered to a socially determined future, or an intention to take command and impose a personal will on the universal fabric, shaping it to match desires.

The outer planets' influence can suggest certain of these unconscious tendencies, even though it must be stated that this does not imply a definite practice or predilection toward sado-masochism. Jupiter, Saturn, Uranus, Neptune, and Pluto can attract individuals toward a heightened reality. Saturn is especially liable to control preferences; Jupiter and Uranus need new horizons, experimentation, and innovation, and are willing to traverse taboo demarcations; Neptune enjoys imaginative fantasies and subtle perversity which can manifest through sacrifice, martyrdom and surrender; and Pluto seeks transformation and power. Hard planetary aspects between these (or to the personal planets) can hint at unconscious tendencies that require awareness. Mars is also significant whenever desires and assertion are important. The outer or transpersonal planets resonate deep within the unconscious, linking the individual and collective, so how individuals deal with these psychic channels is collectively mirrored by society and culture, and as previously noted, the threads between sado-masochism and society are quite entangled.

Signs with affinity to masochistic inclinations can include Cancer and Pisces, two water and feminine signs; Scorpio has great capacity for emotional pain although it prefers the control and domination role, along with Aries, Taurus, Leo, and Capricorn. Libra and Virgo can sometimes vary between the two roles, and Virgo can have an interest in S/M fetishist ritual. Gemini and Aquarius can be mentally curious and intrigued by this complex intimacy; Sagittarius is concerned mainly with freedom, and can take minimal interest to involvement in such a partnership. A powerful Neptune may be attracted to the costumes, theater, and imaginative fantasies of sadomasochistic ritual; Pluto can see an ideal role as master-mistress; Uranus can love the non-conformist experimentation.

Houses that may activate sexually cathartic issues can include: the 1st house, a need for clarity and redefinition of identity; 2nd house, an exaggerated need for possession; 3rd house, a need for intimate, inner communication and sharing; 8th house, a natural residence for these issues, where individual-society taboos may be faced and a gate to the unconscious is opened; 10th house, where needs for social power may overlap into intimate relationships and impose "power-over"; and the 12th house, where another door to the unconscious is discovered. The 12th house is a natural repository for repressed energies; this influence may not be so obvious, as a planet there is often unexpressed or disowned—yet hidden effects may emerge elsewhere in the chart. The tendency for sacrifice in this 12th house has connections to the masochistic impulse, and the need for atonement and transcendence parallel possible aims of the S/M partnership.

Investigating 8th house issues may lead into difficult and controversial areas, and poses questions of how these may be handled with clients, especially as an astrologer may gain insight into their sexual nature, inhibitions, and repressions by 8th house reference, noting how they merge with others and on which primary levels—suggested by planets, sign, and element.

SUN

This implies that you look for intense intimate relationships which make you feel alive and invigorated, and where you feel free to assert your individuality through partnership. Yet your perception of relationship may remain self-centered, focused on personal needs and pleasures and can lack sensitivity to partners. The element of your Sun-sign is significant, indicating the probable level at which you evaluate your relationships to determine how suitable and fulfilling they are. An earth element may look for physical satisfaction and creating a comfortable material life; water looks for emotional accord and genuine feelings, a loving and trusting partnership offering mutual respect and relaxed enjoyment; air looks for intellectual stimulation, a mental exchange of shared or compatible interests and affinity of worldviews; fire may search for a partner who is enthusiastic and spontaneous, an imaginative, creative personality who sees life as an adventure and chooses to live intensely.

You may actively pursue intimate encounters (unless challenging aspects disperse your confidence) and expect highly physical sex and powerful emotional release, especially enjoying a sense of sexual control and dominance. You prefer experiences with depth, enabling contact with an innermost being which awakens an enlivening, integrative principle to reshape your personality. Through transformative intimacy, you can discover a less self-centered perspective, one which extends your worldview and which opens to higher insight, encouraging greater awareness of partners and social relationships. Your identity can be expanded, dissolving a limiting self-preoccupation and bringing renewal through intimacy. This sphere of life may provide important teachings, and perhaps through emotional and sexual cathartic relationships a new liberated identity is forged, even if via paths of disillusionment, disappointment, and pain.

An integrated Sun will increase personality confidence and a relaxed acceptance of your sexual nature, allowing your inner magnetism, power, and possible psychic sensitivity to flow within social contacts. Awareness of sexual affinities will be strong and rarely far from consciousness, and this could become distracting unless integrated as a natural level of existence and not exploited or abused. Your immediate response to people is often based on intuitive feelings or a sensitive physical response, which determines your reactions even when rational logic may suggest other forms of response. Superficiality is exposed by this deeper perception, although you may tend to take social advantage of this and can become involved in control and power trips, especially if concerned only with personal pleasure and when those domination traits take precedence. While perhaps not consciously recognized, intimacy can become a path of change and development for you, a way to discover an inner force that guides you toward your solar destiny. Sex and emotional intensity are the magnetic attractions drawing you onward.

Your sexual and emotional integration can be suggested by planetary aspects to the Sun, as can compulsive pressures indicated by the planets concerned. When positive aspects are made (trines, sextiles, and certain conjunctions) you feel more free to express individuality and personal needs—a relaxed personality secure in intimate relationships and willing to open to a loving deep interaction. If aspects are more challenging (squares, oppositions) then you can be less comfortable, perhaps overly assertive, aggressive, too self-centered, or conversely, inhibited, and lacking confidence. Intimacy can frequently collapse into tension and conflict, as personality frictions erode feelings and compatibility, or unwise choices sow seeds of dissention from the start of affairs. You may find it hard to build a good relationship, or make excessive demands of a partner without acknowledging that you, too, have to compromise and change to harmonize with others. Your desire nature becomes too expectant, and you can attempt to force partners into submission by dictatorial attitudes. Or, if dissatisfaction increases, you turn to compensatory escapist actions, rather than attempting to resolve partnership crises.

Intimacy can become a battleground for realization, where awareness of relationship issues is slowly born from the anguish of failure and confronting your separatist attitudes.

The 8th house solar path traverses the heights and depths of sexual union, taking the personality on a journey into the depths of its nature, offering a cathartic renewal through ecstasy and pain; the relative balance of these experiences depends on how you express individuality—either with awareness of others or by narcissistic egotism.

MOON

This implies a response to emotional and sexual encounters that is reactive, receptive and feeling-derived, and the primary levels that require stimulation and satisfaction are physical and emotional gratification. Security and stability are essential for your deeper, intimate relaxation, and relationship structures and behavioral parameters are often established on rhythmic repetition and predictable expectations, enabling an almost automatic, reflexive, or mechanical level of partnership exchange to develop. This may generate feelings of safety while eventually limiting and restricting emotional flow and changes, and areas of intimacy can slip into routine, losing spontaneity and diminishing deeper satisfaction and excitement.

The Moon rules instincts, emotions, and feelings, and your basic level of life response is by "gut-reactions," a psychic or intuitive sense that assesses the environment, outer stimulus, and other people. This evaluation determines any sexual responses, and depending on the degree of lunar integration, you will look either to nurture and care for a partner, or desire care from a partner. Dependency issues are likely, focused around needs to love or be loved. Releasing emotional and physical pressures is necessary, and instincts seeking intimacy and relatedness will dominate choices. Sexual and emotional insecurity and inhibitions may be likely, often as a consequence of childhood experiences and formative parental relationships, and several subconscious needs for safety and protection may be traced back to those conditioning years.

Your emphasis on feelings may produce either demands for self-satisfaction or an impulse to serve and satisfy others, dictating the nature of your intimate experiences; finding a balance between "giving or taking" may prove difficult, yet worth the effort.

The lunar self's changeable nature may pose relationship challenges, as emotions display tidal ebbs and flows, and moods swing between high and low, confusing both yourself and partner. Inconsistency may distort habitual relationship patterns, and you may feel uneasy when unconsciously assuming a passive role that is often adopted. Sometimes your needs for satisfaction rise and demand acknowledging, and these should not be avoided or repressed, or else future problems are created and self-denial will inhibit vital energies from being released.

While security is an instinctive need, and one expected in long-lasting relationships, there can be an attraction toward a deeper intimacy, where you experience mysterious levels of heightened sexual emotion, which evoke powerful physical sensations, shaking you by turbulent emotions, uncontrolled feelings, and passionate excitement. Such rare experiences can prove important in liberating emotional tensions, and although the loss of inner control can feel disturbing, you may submit to a need for surrender and transformation. When you re-emerge from such sexual and emotional encounters, you may be renewed and more integrated as a result of personality disassembly and reassembly.

The 8th house Moon may either attract an important relationship crisis which becomes pivotal in your life, or set in motion a series of powerful intimate encounters that continue until needed changes have been undergone and key lessons understood. Pain and pleasure can be intermingled, and emotional insight and awareness of habitual personality patterns is required, or else you may fall victim to unconscious instinctual needs directing your life without your volition. Any dependency traits require rebalancing and understanding, or else your individuality remains compromised and reliant on a partner. You cannot afford to remain unconscious of your instinctual and emotional needs, as these make you increasingly vulnerable to the choices and actions of partners, who may control and manipulate your weaknesses. Possessiveness and emotional smothering may occur, and others may find your demands excessive and uncomfortable, especially those who need independence and freedom and dislike routines.

Emotional release through intimacy is crucial for a sense of well-being, and if this is blocked by fears, self-denial, or inhibitions, then feelings and sexuality can be distorted, perhaps becoming overly passive and allowing others to dominate, emotionally closed through defensive postures and reluctant to experience intimacy, or alternatively, emotionally and sexually demanding, frightening away possible partners through excessive needs. Maintaining a balance is important, and identifying the complexity of your emotional nature through verbalizing feelings or defining them by analysis may be valuable in discharging repressed energies and gaining an objective insight into how they shape your life-responses. Unconscious automatic behavior needs renewal by awareness, and this is the Moon's main message, or you may discover that fulfillment evades your grasping hands as the cost of self-ignorance.

MERCURY

There can be mixed reactions to sexuality and emotions, an ambiguous response to experiencing intimate intensity, and confusion added by awareness of duality and the contrast between reality and imagination. Mercury reflects the principle of the separate individual mind, and your primary attraction to a relationship is to discover opportunities for a deeper mental communication with a partner, where your thoughts, ideas, and personality can be shared and expressed with someone who ideally has a similar or complementary

worldview. Common attitudes, beliefs, and values are important for harmony, and areas of disagreement serve only to divide
rather than enrich your relationships.

You prefer an intimate mental union, where compatibility
also exists on intellectual levels for real satisfaction. Sexual
tendencies may emerge from the type of mental fantasies
that you imaginatively create, and you may observe that
internalized "mind sex" can excite you more than actual
physical sexuality. This depends on whether you enact your
fantasies and desires in real life or fail to find a suitable partner. Indulging in erotic imagination can offer more variation
than bodies can comfortably perform, and multiple partners
can be visualized in the midst of a monogamous relationship.
Sexual curiosity is strong and can be at the forefront of your
consciousness, active even within the most mundane of situations, often providing a temporary inner escape from boredom. If any sexual obsessions or desires for idealized partners
exist, then these will form the centerpiece of regular fantasies, even when unable or unwilling to pursue these into
reality, and can sublimate energies and needs through private
compensatory mind-plays.

An interest in understanding human sexuality, physical
sexual techniques, and minority sexual practices and "devi-
ations" is likely, used both to enrich knowledge and insight
into personal tendencies and to stimulate erotic fantasies.
Discussing sexuality can appeal, prompting imaginative sce-
narios and sparking off sensual attraction between potential
or actual partners. While your fantasy level is highly activated,
you can experience disappointment with real sex, which is
often felt as too physically focused, misconnecting with the
mentally satisfying inner films. Technique may dominate
feelings, and while a proficient lover, genuine emotion may
be lacking or withheld. Emotional anxiety and undefined
fears of union and intimacy may be present, mainly resulting from mental suspicions and panic at losing control. You
may find that relaxing into physical pleasure and emotional

release difficult to achieve, and this inhibits a full experience; for some, sex becomes totally redirected into mental imagination, voyeurism, and fantasies, and is detached from
physical action due to such fears.

Love can be resisted, and wariness about the potential
transformation and depth of self-encounter can result, perhaps trying to stop this from occurring by insisting on a
rational, analytical dissection of emotions and sexuality. This
apparent quest for understanding can distance you from
experiencing powerful emotions, and serves primarily to
restrict possession by heightened feelings. An unease with
physicality may be observed, with a need to dismiss lower
expressions, particularly if following certain development
paths or influenced by spiritual abstinence and self-denial.
Yet, as you still need a meaningful loving relationship, you
would benefit from rebalancing inner priorities and coming
to terms with your less developed feeling nature, learning to
accept them as equally important as your mind.

This can become a route to greater integration and insight,
even though confronting possible fears may be painful.
Relationships may be encountered which provoke radical
changes, and sexuality and emotional passions may stimulate the birth of a renewed self-image. Whenever love strikes
you, the arrow penetrates deeply, breaking down the posture
of a detached, objective intellectual stance and demanding that
you face your real nature. The consequence can shift inner perspectives and allow an understanding of the duality-union
interplay within yourself, society, and the universe. Part of
this experience comes often from a one-sided love affair, where
you may fall for someone who, like yourself previously,
resists depth and commitment. You are left struggling to
deal with newly awakened and agitated emotions which
have broken down internal controls and are running riot
through your personality, unlocking doors to a variety of
feelings, needs, and compulsions that have not been acknowledged before.

Fantasies and sexual interests are strongly influenced by
the specific planets that aspect Mercury, as Mercury leans toward

an asexuality; a Uranus aspect implies needs for experimentation, freedom, and inventiveness, while Neptune emphasizes imaginative, idealistic, and romantic fantasies—an unreal partnership that often generates confusing dissatisfaction instead of fulfillment. A Jupiter aspect implies expansion through understanding the sexual-emotional-mental interaction, while Saturn suggests a limiting self-discipline, order, and control, perhaps mentally repressive traits denying emotional and physical needs. Challenging aspects may point to a splitting of imaginative fantasies from reality, with possible attractions to unconventional sexual and emotional interests or repeated frustration within relationship. Excess idealism or criticism may interfere in developing partnerships, as few match high expectations. The major lesson to be discovered is that real sexual intimacy can engage all levels of yourself, and any tendency to divert this energy into any one restrictive level only results in the diminution of the transformative and fulfilling potential of the experience; opening yourself to this can be your key to understanding the 8th house mysteries.

The retrograde Mercury may be liable to obsessive thoughts causing disruptive sexual fixations and inner preoccupations, but much of this is symptomatic of an unintegrated sexuality, where mental activity is emphasized to the detriment of emotions and physical contacts. There can be a reticence toward intimacy, and you may be uncertain as to the necessity of such relationships in your life. You enjoy your own company and maintain a solitary, reserved attitude, protecting your privacy and often evading opportunities for deeper contact. Your prefer an observational stance, intrigued by sexuality but not convinced of your need and responses. There is a seriousness to your temperament and you may believe that others misunderstand you. Insecurity is present, and this increases hidden fears and reluctance to become involved.

VENUS

In distinction to Mercury's mind focus, Venus is the sensual and emotional outreach for union through loving and sharing. A powerful appetite for this exchange is active, and emotional and physical desires determine your choices and decisions. If they fail to be satisfied, then relationships collapse. Your sexuality is quite physically and sensually demanding, and intimate emotional intensity is expected; affinity and compatibility on these levels is given greater priority than intellectual accord. The search for love and relatedness can monopolize your attention, as this is equated to life-fulfillment, purpose and the culmination of desires. Love is believed to conquer all, and when gripped by its passions, logic and rationality is defeated, as you welcome the transformation of self that heightened emotions and sexual ecstasy can create, even if this has less positive effects on the rest of your life. A willingness to surrender is evident, yet this can also leave you vulnerable to less scrupulous partners able to manipulate your feelings.

Venus intensifies your capacity to receive and give love, the range of emotions that you can experience, and defines what attracts your interest. If a partner appears mysterious, inscrutable, or enigmatic, then your curiosity is immediately provoked. You often believe in a "fatedness" of intimacy, where "union was meant to be," perhaps by reference to renewing "karmic relationships." If a prospective partner offers a challenge to your attractiveness, then you find it hard to resist the temptation, drawing on your seductive powers to gain their attention. Sometimes you attract unsuitable partners, and your ability to choose may require additional refinement and discrimination; perhaps less so in physical attraction than in inner compatibility which becomes more important as the relationship continues.

Planetary aspects can shape specific interests: Uranus can encourage less conformist sexual and emotional needs to develop, where freedom is emphasized and individuality clashes with desires for close union; Neptune provides an inner picture of an idealized partner, perhaps unlikely to be met in real life, yet is used as a standard of assessment and comparison, much to others' detriment; Pluto may introduce themes of control and domination into intimacy, either submitting to another's power or imposing your skill at manipulating emotions and sexual desires; Mars may increase an emphasis on physicality to the exclusion of subtlety, or disregard emotional resonance in favor of sexual passion. Any planets which aspect Venus in this 8th house can indicate the presence of compulsive tendencies which interfere with relationships and determine specific desires which require satisfaction. When Venus is in an earth or water sign, you may act with passive receptivity, expecting partners to take care of your needs and fulfill desires; in fire and air signs, you are more extroverted and outwardly directed, searching for and clearly demanding your requirements in a partner.

Through opening to intense sexual and emotional experiences, you may discover that your need for love becomes a path of expansion, taking you beyond seeking self-gratification into a sensual exploration of existence, transcending separative barriers by allowing the triple unions of partner, self, and universe to reveal the mysteries of life.

The retrograde Venus suggests discomfort with love, sexuality, and intimacy, as emotions and affections are hindered by inner defenses. Reclusive tendencies and emotional self-containment combine to decrease dependency needs, and a vacillating sexual nature which intermittently blows hot and cold is hard to sustain in an ongoing relationship. When desires are awakened, you need immediate fulfillment and expect others to provide satisfaction; yet when you are disinterested, you dismissively resist others' needs, asserting your freedom of choice and action. Your self-image has an independent streak and the nature of partnership still remains a mystery. The pursuit of an ideal lover may spawn unrealistic hopes and expectations, yet you rarely modify these to conform to reality, and often decide to wait rather than enter any "imperfect commitments." Secretly you dream of total involvement with a lover, where mutual possession and union is experienced and the power of love sweeps away all emotional wounds, anger, and resentments that have accumulated in previous encounters, as you may repress vulnerable feelings and find them difficult to discharge in daily life. Conventional personalities fail to excite you, and your preference is for less orthodox partners. Love and pain may appear entangled, and this can provide cathartic experiences when you allow intimacy. Feeling out of your depth and confused by complex, contradictory emotions and desires, relationships can become a transformative channel for renewal, even when experiences are painful if someone unlocks your emotional floodgates.

MARS

One insistent need that you probably register is for physical action and satisfaction in relationships, as sex invigorates you by a regular release of physical and emotional energies. If intimacy is unavailable, then inner pressures accumulate which you find uncomfortable and disturbing, unless able to constructively redirect these energies—perhaps sublimated through creativity or purposeful work. Your sexual expression may contain impulsive, aggressive tendencies, and is a major channel for self-assertive behavior. This powerful sex drive can pose difficulties through its urgency, and finding responsive partners can be problematic, especially if you insist on the priority of your pleasures rather than mutual enjoyment. Partnership fails to attract your interest, and deep emotional and mental intimacy is less to your taste, impinging on preferences for independence and self-sufficiency. You enjoy competition and the challenge of the hunt when looking for a partner, and once desires are stimulated, your pursuit can be persistent and not easily rejected. You can choose to be perceptive to a partner's needs, yet often disregard them by selfishness; learning partnership sensitivity is necessary to experience more profound levels of sexual interaction, and realizing that physical coupling alone is just a superficial temporary union and ultimately unfulfilling.

There can be an adversarial and confrontational quality to your personality, one which you exploit as self-assertion, striving to dominate and control others to submit to your desires. You enjoy an aura of power and mystery surrounding you, as this creates an attractive, intriguing image heightened by manipulative secrecy regarding your motivations and intentions, while carefully observing and interpreting others' responses before choosing your time to act. A sense of seductive timing is often present and applied.

Yet relationships can become contentious, partly because you may resist real intimacy, short-circuiting the exchange of personalities and energies by protective barriers and survival instincts which deny genuine emotional union. The truth may be that you fear losing control of powerful, complex emotions that remain unintegrated and unconsciously active; you feel the existence of these pressures, and resist releasing them. Repression can breed potentially destructive and violent passions, and you are uncertain whether your volatile nature is strong enough to maintain adequate defenses. One lesson is to investigate these and understand your psychic dynamics as a preliminary step to reorientate energies into more positive, constructive channels of expression; yet, you may find reluctance to self-inquiry as this is an opposite direction to your normal external focus, and you may deny that self-knowledge has real value or purpose. However, perpetual control can become psychologically dangerous, a liability to explode as a release of uncontrollable pressures, damaging yourself and others; understanding can defuse stress and heal personality fragmentation and ignorance.

Restless desires to impose your mark on the world and explore new territories can make you unreliable in relationships. You may lack patience, and others can find living with you too demanding for the returns, and relationships can easily degenerate into mutually unsatisfying experiences. Blocked emotions require liberating—even if through a cathartic turmoil—until you reconnect to greater wholeness and consistently recognize the existence and values of others. Intimate communication can be improved, and compromise would bring additional benefits to be enjoyed.

Certain planetary aspects to Mars may inhibit or distort your expression. Uranus can make an intermittent contact, almost like a "stop-go" signal, turning desires on and off, and interfering with consistency and personal clarity. Pluto may amplify passions and aggression, especially when emotions are disowned and repressed, creating a dominating personality exploiting "power-over" others by forceful manipulative controls regarding sexuality and finances. Neptune dissolves purposeful aims, making them difficult to focus and define, and diverting attention into unrealistic aims and attempts at perfection. Jupiter can encourage excess ambition, extravagance and indulgence, a ceaseless demand for more that is hard to assuage; while Saturn can impede action by fear and caution, even to the extent of causing sexual and emotional frigidity and impotence, or a low level of intimate desires as inner blockages accumulate.

The main recognition of the 8th house Mars is for deeper relationship, where self-centeredness is exposed by enhanced awareness, recognition, and respect for others, so that your assertive power can be redirected for the good of all rather than just chasing personal desires. The value of emotional and mental affinity is also discovered to be equally important in intimacy when you awaken your holistic being, and is not simply disregarded as irrelevent or unnecessary.

Retrograde Mars implies sexual inhibitions and a reluctance to take relationship initiative, mainly due to worries about rejection, inadequacy, or emotional desertion. Confidence is lacking and doubts multiply, making intimate relaxation difficult while desires are frustrated. You dislike being emotionally dependent and are afraid to open your heart to another's safekeeping. These restraints may enforce a solitary lifestyle, where repressed feelings and needs are signs of an alienating self-denial. Compulsive tensions may increase from unconscious pressures and may be experienced as a variety of inner battles, where passivity and aggression are locked in uneasy balance. Desires require a healthy discharge or rechanneling, and you should ensure that this retrograde influence is consciously modified and integrated, or an unconscious self-imprisonment may result.

JUPITER

This implies potential expansion through encountering "the other" within sexual and emotional intimacy, and these experiences can provide you with greater self-understanding and awareness of others' needs. You may approach prospective relationships with an optimistic and trusting attitude, perhaps almost an innocent and naive one, although more painful contacts can quickly shatter illusions. Your deeper sexual and emotional nature remains an unexplored territory, requiring intimacy to evoke added awareness as others provoke previously unrecognized emotions, needs, and desires when activated by the influence of love and sexual activity. Self-development can come through the light of consciousness peering deeply into your dark inner depths, illuminating corners of your psyche and revealing areas that have been ignored. One way for personal growth is through this inner door to sexuality and emotions, which will demand learning the lesson of intimate relationships, breaking down self-centered barriers and preoccupations and acknowledging the reality of others.

Received social and religious morality may interfere with your instinctive sexual and emotional nature, as prohibitions and "standards of right and wrong behavior" may reverberate in conditioned attitudes. You may need to confront these to realize their influence on your choices, or to become free from their restricting hold. When such conditioning exists, you may observe inhibitions to sexual activity and emotional involvement, rather than feelings of confidence, ease, and relaxation; or note beliefs that certain types of sexual behavior are wrong, sinful, and socially condemned. Passively accepting these psychological social introjects may erect obstacles which prevent future growth, and considering your dominant sexual and emotional attitudes might be worth discovering to see if these really fit and liberate instead of imprison you.

The issue of partnership expectations and judgments is important when making choices for intimate contact, and you may make over-expectant and unrealistic assessments which interfere with your decisions and appreciation of partners. An image of a "perfect lover" may stand between you and intimate satisfaction. You may continually compare others to this sought for ideal, failing to register the merits of your actual partner. Restless dissatisfaction often spoils enjoyment. The type of suitable partner may be indicated by the sign(s) of this 8th house. You tend to make either wise or foolish choices of intimate partner, dependent on your degree of self-knowledge and capability to recognize a complementary partner for a harmonious relationship, with whom compromise and cooperation can be easily and consistently achieved. In particular, you are attracted to those who have a mysterious aura of depth, perhaps with a promise of adventure and a touch of the "unknown" surrounding them; those who could inspire you, or project a sense of intrigue and danger may also prove appealing.

Your taste can vary between emphasizing "quality" or "quantity" of partners, and Jupiter's influence can unbalance sexual and emotional priorities if not properly integrated into the personality. Tendencies toward extremism and excess may be present, or an alternative fearful reaction of retaining control and preventing these powerful, primal energies to dominate. While casual, temporary intimate encounters may excite and revitalize jaded familiarity, you prefer the benefits of a more committed, long-term relationship as offering greater satisfaction and the strengths of partnership. When a degree of trust, openness, and commitment has been established with a right partner, you can be very giving, proving a reliable source of strength and understanding, and you can grow into an insightful and caring lover.

When Jupiter's planetary aspects are harmonious, there are less inhibitive barriers preventing or distorting sexual and emotional fulfillment. You can become a creative and liberating individual, and are perceived as a loving, guiding personality at ease with your own nature. Aspects to Mercury, Venus, and Neptune especially exaggerate sexual and sensual imaginative fantasies, often shaping the type of intimacy that you prefer giving and receiving; with Pluto, the emphasis is desires and deeper needs that require expression, often with an even deeper level of emotion and sexuality to be contacted and explored. With challenging aspects, Jupiterian thoughtlessness may contrive interpersonal problems which result from self-centeredness, or when excessive optimism and lack of realism cause poor judgments. An attraction to risk-taking, illicit affairs and immoderate, less controlled sexual-emotional activity may overshadow other areas of your life and personality, indicating a need for understanding and rebalancing compulsive psychological patterns.

The retrograde Jupiter tends to value quantity of sexual partners more highly than quality of intimacy, and displays a restless sexual attitude, rarely content and satiated. There is a distinct physical curiosity about others, a sense of personal power from body-knowledge, and this overrides any emotional or mental compatibility and interest, which immaturely remains secondary in importance. A taste for unconventional relationships and behavior may be also apparent.

SATURN

Parental, cultural and religious conditioning may have influenced your emotional and sexual attitudes, and conformity to social standards perhaps has created an inner rigidity that you find hard to relax. Unease may be felt with this aspect of yourself, requiring growth into your sexual and loving self as essential for integration. Saturn functions as a teacher, pointing out that an encounter with Eros' transformative power of love is a means to understanding self and life; you may shrink away from this, fearing the threat of emotional pain and recognize the presence of repressions, inhibitions, self-imposed limitations, and cautious disciplines that obstruct deeper sexual and emotional involvement.

Moral codes may agitate guilt if transgressed and you favor social conformist behavior. You may feel uncomfortable in situations of possible intimacy. These feelings can be acutely felt, especially during earlier life and young adulthood, yet this pain also may indicate an area of possible growth in later years when you confront it and the transforming lesson is learned. These issues will demand considerable time and effort to resolve, and dismantling restrictive inner patterns can touch on all aspects of your being, posing questions of any conformist and conservative tendencies, and exposing your inclination to submit to the opinions of others and to assume majority attitudes.

Your intimate relationships become a major concern, and where emotional and sexual interaction occurs, there is also potential for decisive turning points where either mutual commitment is reached or the partnership collapses. These issues may confront you with phoenix-like transformations, reflecting death and rebirth as a consequence of emotionally cathartic suffering whenever love fades or is rejected. Recognize that your feeling nature demands greater examination and a healing cleansing, as emotions may remain an ongoing source of conflict and difficulty. On this 8th house battlefield, Saturn encourages self-understanding and emotional mastery through intimate crises and traumatic experiences that you may find unavoidable at times. Observing why and how this pattern operates in your life, and the reasons for it, may help you move through dispiriting and painful periods with awareness, reaping valuable insight through converting "negative into the positive" and "the painful into the beneficial" for future growth and integration.

Central to partnership intimacy is sexual union, the intensity of emotional and physical oneness with another. There may be a needless fear of sexuality, as if it is an "unclean" sphere of life. Underlying this you'll find a peculiar fascination with sex, a preoccupation and source of concern. Love is a potent mystery and you feel insecure in its company, yet simultaneously recognize its irresistible attraction. You may observe fears of vulnerability to emotional intensity, perhaps trying to resist or protect this by defenses. You may feel inadequate or fearful of physical sex, which can create personal anguish and repudiating intimacy. This is not usually a problem of physical functioning but reflects emotional withdrawal and dread of submission, emotional rejection, a partner's domination, or losing self-control.

Certain types of behavior can result from such fears. One is being friendly and loving, with a surprising tendency to become inhibited or freeze in the bedroom; another is to be an efficient, if mechanical, lover, blocking the flow of emotional openness between partners to inadvertently create a disturbed and unsatisfying intimacy. Over-compensatory tendencies may emerge, even physically promiscuous behavior, as if demonstrating that no problem exists while avoiding genuine emotional exchange. Or doubts and fears are masked by religious or moral conditioning which provides an excuse to minimize adult sexuality, adopting a celibacy based on fear and evasion. A distorted sexuality can be born, founded on twisted emotions and impersonal sexual attitudes, where bodies are distanced and detached from being real personalities. The taboo areas of sexuality may exert compulsive fascination, and the darker recesses of love, sex and emotions may attract exploration. None of these expressions are healthy or respect personal wholeness.

Challenging planetary aspects to Saturn suggest a lack of confidence, or a negative self-image that diminishes self-esteem regarding emotional and sexual desirability, and this prohibits relaxing into an enjoyable and fulfilling sexual relationship. Insecurities can be disguised by the appearance of a hard, cold persona, where emotional repressions distort sexual activity and may spill over into other social relationships, especially in the form of authoritarian traits. Feeling inwardly uncertain, sexuality can become a channel for domination and control needs, where one extreme can create the often formalized, ritualized order of sado-masochistic practice.

It is possible that until any repressed emotions and needs are met, healed and stabilized through understanding, you may experience only emotional disillusionment and pain in relationships. Part of this may stem from early childhood, where physical contacts and emotional needs were not properly acknowledged, and this may have formed a pattern of self-isolation and emotional defensiveness that still operates, making it difficult to open to others. Yet, your deeper needs still exist and make demands; only by searching for "union" to transform these can you die to the old and be reborn into the new. Your partnership choices become more crucial, as you may unconsciously fall victim to insensitive, demanding partners who harm your emotions even more by disregarding your hidden vulnerable sensitivity.

If you can allow this emotional catharsis to happen when relating to a suitable partner, and permit a temporary loss of control by trusting and being swept away by love, then you could receive a new perspective and become free of emotional conflicts. This may not be easy, but attempts to cleanse and heal emotions will prove extremely beneficial; the support and understanding of a loving partner may also prove instrumental in helping you make this change. Admitting the existence of inhibiting patterns is a first step toward inner resolution. Saturn exists in this house to cast a light into a dark area of your psyche; even though the light may expose facets you wish to retreat from and ignore, this is the only way to embrace wholeness.

Saturn retrograde increases the possibility of important karmic relationships, rendering you highly impressionable to their effects. Part of this may be because your solitary character restricts intimate encounters due to limiting fears and doubts. Sexuality and intimacy evoke your insecurities, and you feel unable to relax inner control. Early experiences, religious and moral injunctions and parental admonishment may have connected sexuality with a self-rejecting image and sense of shame. Traditional sexual attitudes and a critical conscience may encourage greater caution than is necessary, and apprehension can produce a psychological or physical frigidity coupled with a self-flagellating attitude toward relationship failures. Breaking free from this self-limiting cycle can be difficult, and you may require the support of others to encourage a genuine affirmation of your needs and desires.

URANUS

A confrontation with boundaries and restrictions related to sexuality, emotions, and relationships is inevitable, as the Uranus influence strives for individual freedom from unconscious conformism and passive conventionality. The principle of discovery is actively creating a need for experimentation and liberation from mass moral standards, refusing to be limited by unnecessary restrictive social sanctions in order to find what is true and right for yourself. This assertion of individuality may lead to non-conformist behavior and unorthodox relationships, which may disturb others still bound by social conventions. You can discover a path to growth through rejecting social pressures and instead following your inner messages wherever they lead. Feelings of greater excitement, vitality, and enjoyment of life are experienced when you pursue your own truth and search for freedom. You may recognize this impulse perpetually looking for novelty, variety, change, and growth, or else when this is denied, a devitalizing and dispiriting feeling casts a dark shadow over life as boredom encroaches.

In relationships, this often results in a desire for new experiences and different partners, even prior to the constraints of possessiveness making unreasonable demands for commitment and repetition breeding predictability and diminishing excitement. Your reliability as a partner may be questionable, both in fidelity and responding to the inevitable demands of a committed partnership. You dislike any restraints on your freedom, and as your desires and interests often fluctuate on and off, these changeable attitudes can be confusing, sometimes appearing as a disinterested lack of genuine concern. Emotionally you may be indifferent, cold and self-contained, and could be accused of an impersonal detachment even in the midst of emotional situations. While sexual passions can be awakened, your emotions are more resistant to becoming engaged.

Casual social relationships may suddenly and urgently become physical affairs, even with relative strangers, and you may feel the thrill of being swept along by forceful desires, when any opportunity to appease curiosity and explore another is presented. The need for multiple relationships may also be indulged; some of these intimate contacts may have a fated inevitability, which seems unavoidable in hindsight. These may have the power to change your life, often in a traumatic, revelatory manner, providing life lessons and teachings that can inspire profound self-insight, enlightening the issues, motivations, and prospects contained in your partnership patterns, and awakening you to unrecognized needs and desires.

Uranus will work changes through your sexuality, and such activity can become extremely important, possibly determining important choices by its demanding voice. One pattern could be the periodic upheaval and changing of relationships when points of commitment and decision are close; or partners could suddenly and shockingly leave you. Your sexual range could be quite varied and unconventional, especially if aspects are made to Moon, Venus, Mars, Neptune, and Pluto. How you express sexuality can affect the formation and dissolution of relationships, and you may need increased intimate emotional content or else imbalance can occur. Perhaps discovering the intensity of emotional union could stimulate a rebirth of your instinctive patterns, a realization that a deeper long-term relationship could bring a level of satisfaction previously unknown.

With harmonious Uranus planetary aspects, sexuality is considered as a relaxing, liberating and fun activity, with relatively minimal inhibitions to distort interpersonal sharing. There can be a preference for minority sexual tastes and practices, and sexual exploration will be given a higher priority.

With challenging aspects, this liberated response is obstructed by fears of social attitudes and reactions against less acceptable preferences; this can create unnecessary guilt and shame, causing personality fragmentation and disowning of self-rejected facets. Pressures can accumulate, with needs for freedom resulting in compulsive demands for independence which can destroy potentially viable partnerships. Such stresses and tensions can destroy relationships unless constructively and positively rechanneled. This Uranus influence will also heighten attraction toward unusual, individualistic and unconventional partners, where both personality and sexuality refuse submission to predictable conformism.

Retrograde Uranus tends to exacerbate the direct Uranus characteristics, where needs for change, variety, experimentation, unconventionality are more internalized and perhaps less easy to discharge through relationship and outer interaction. Unusual sexual and emotional experiences may provide unorthodox encounters which increase prospects for personal awakening, and can be an important factor on your path.

NEPTUNE

The impulse motivating Neptune's influence is to transcend boundaries of self and body, present in both the paths of sexuality and mysticism, and which often causes confusion within sexual identity and activity. As Neptune inspires imaginative fantasies related to sexuality, death, occult mysteries, and mystical visions, a deep undercurrent is added to sexual encounters where things may not always be as they seem. You may search for heightened sensual, emotional, and sexual experiences—which, if not found, can lead to discontent, stirred by a belief that such experiences do exist if only the right partner could be located. Part of this is a projected psychological reflection of "the divine partner" via lovers, and is inherent in the play of anima-animus archetypes, which can overshadow real people with glamor and unreal illusions, placing them on an idealized pedestal that they are certain to eventually fall off. These visions of an overly-expectant idealized partner capable of providing transcendent, blissful sex and emotional uplift may often turn into confining illusions rather than actually met in real life.

Your emotional and sexual nature is complex, where tendencies for sacrifice and selfless love can dominate. This can create sexual promiscuity, through the impulse to be sexually sacrificial and giving in an indiscriminate, unrestrained manner, which can also include a need for ecstatic loss of self, forgetting mundane obligations for a brief escapist respite. Dependencies may become common, based on partner-reliance and desires to be possessed and absorbed as a form of self-abandonment and abnegation, becoming lost in the "beloved" as a distorted travesty of the mystical quest for oneness. Alternatively, a desire to possess and control a partner may dominate, using subtle manipulation and weaving a glamorous spell.

For some, sex may become a way toward union, touching that greater overshadowing force that is dimly intuited, and which is the attraction of Tantric, Grail, and Arthurian Mysteries, hoping to utilize sexuality as a path to ride the waves of orgasmic release (inwardly or outwardly directed) to attain higher consciousness. Another approach could be a deliberate renunciation of sexual activity by resorting to celibacy or offering sexuality as a sacrifice to a consuming and obsessive ideal, given for the reward of a purifying, transforming, redemption.

With challenging Neptune aspects, fears of losing control through intimacy may be barriers inhibiting passion, and love. This can create relationship disappointments, perhaps caused by personal resistances, unrealistic expectations, sexual illusions, or failure to accept sexual preference, and an inability to integrate sexuality.

Part of your sexual nature may be disowned through lack of confidence and sexual and emotional anxiety; it is only allowed expression within restricted, defined parameters and becomes partially dissociated and detached. It can be difficult to define Neptune-influenced sexuality, feelings and attractions, as they can be too fluid and changeable, overly impressionable to different partners. Part of your self-inquiry requires understanding what you actually want and need from sexual intimacy.

You may be attracted to partners who offer "an escape from reality," or to engage in"lost and found" relationships that incorporate dependency and rescue issues. With a compassionate heart and a preference for giving, you may be vulnerable to many a hard luck story, and can easily be manipulated by others, making you a victim of self-deception and romantic disillusionment. Your readiness to surrender and to serve the needs of others can leave you open to abuse, even if you try to justify this by invoking spiritual service. Your intimate relationships will benefit from a new perspective, as glamor and illusion often distorts reality, clouding objective clarity.

Yet it is by entering the mysteries of love, and searching for union between the emotional and sexual dualism of self-other, that insight and intensity is released, revealing new areas to understand. Through intimacy—even tumultuous and painful intimacy—you can awaken intuition and find creative or spiritual outlets. In the end, the sacrifice that is required is not to the other, but of the lesser self to the Self, and by that action will you find the renewal that attracts your aspirations.

Retrograde Neptune intensifies these inner tendencies, where fantasies may revolve around unconscious needs for martyrdom, self-sacrifice, atonement and becoming a victim of love. When these patterns are operative, relationship choices are affected by unconscious manipulation, and as you are liable to build a romanticized lover's image, you may fall into a self-deceptive trap. Partners can be unconsciously chosen for their ability to emotionally punish you, to demand your sacrifice and martyrdom and turn you into a victim. The only remedy for this is self-understanding, so that these impulses can be observed and taken into account when making intimate choices.

PLUTO

In Pluto's rulership of its own house, the emphasis is firmly placed on a complex reorientation and restructuring of your physical, sexual and emotional levels, intent on regeneration and rebirth. An impulse for transformation will exist, sometimes offering a potentially deeper and more involving relationship than is usual, or by attracting partners who will evoke an almost consuming and obsessive love that has profound effects on your self-understanding and future life direction.

Pluto demands redirecting attention from yourself into an awareness of others to improve the quality of relationship. Intimacy becomes a source of development, and with hindsight, you may notice turning points in your life that are marked by the starting and ending of key relationships. Your intimate experiences often involve powerful undercurrents that may not be apparent to observers, and complex interactions lie beneath the surface, often not fully recognized or understood.

Emotional and sexual needs can be powerful, insistent, and obsessive, and even when ambivalence may exist toward intimacy you are continually drawn toward relationships and prospective sexual encounters. You need life-intensity and heightened feelings, so passions need to blaze. There are tendencies toward psychologically absorbing partners, or entering into consuming types of relationship, partly reflecting the presence of Thanatos, whose death urge conditions the psyche's need for transformation and release from physical imprisonment. This can emerge distorted and misapplied— perhaps through destructive expression, an attraction to risk-taking to satisfy compulsive desires, or the tendency to destroy partnerships or lifestyle stability whenever pressures accumulate, rather than finding constructive channels for a creative redirection. Personal volatility is likely, and although this can be masked by an impassive appearance of self-control, a moodiness and liability to provoke periodic emotional crises can reveal a smouldering inner volcano prior to eruption. When some partners register this darker presence within your personality, they may feel disturbed, or react by withdrawing more from intimate depths.

Your relationships are often characterized by issues of power, domination, and manipulation, all closely connected to satisfying your strong desires. You prefer "power-over" partners, often insisting that others support your needs or change in ways approved by you, molded as adjuncts to your purpose and personality. Your powerful will remains disengaged unless desires are active, yet when applied your will becomes fixated and obsessive until aims are achieved.

Your confidence is founded on feelings of control, and even if emotionally dependent on a partner, you still need to feel that you dominate the relationship in order to remain empowered. As you are so self-controlled, these needs enter your relationships, resulting in psychological manipulation and sexual control, and you need insight into how these tendencies are operating. If self-centered exploitation of others is unchecked and excessive, this compulsive element in your nature can damage relationships unless inner change and reorientation is achieved.

Sexual needs could become exaggerated, and emotional demands proliferate when primal issues of life, death, security, or emotional and physical desires are over-emphasized.

While driven toward intimate intensity, there can be a simultaneous repulsion which confuses and is a consequence of fearing ego loss. This may result in relationship evasion by an irrational, projected distrust of psychological "invasion" by "the other." Such complex, often contradictory patterns may be noted, and these can help you recognize that a psychological reconciliation between contrasting impulses is necessary. Desires need raising to the light for understanding and these 8th house issues demand real awareness and insight, prior to renewal; otherwise, you may be driven into situations by obsessions that keep you bound to unconsciously encounter your "negative fate."

Any Pluto planetary aspects increase undercurrents, making available insight through experience of the aspected planet's principle characteristics and corresponding psychological impulses. Compulsive traits often flow between Pluto and aspected planets, so consider carefully the nature of these relationships; harmonious aspects indicate paths of creative potential, and challenging aspects suggest needs for inner rebirth and transforming corresponding issues. For instance, a Pluto-Mars aspect indicates a preference for a physical level of control or manipulation of others, where willful action can dominate or leadership positions are exploited for power. Pluto-Mercury implies a need for mental control and influencing the thoughts and attitudes of others; Pluto-Moon favors emotional controls, taking advantage of feelings and security needs. All of these are derived from fears of losing identity and power if unable to control and dominate, and this requires dealing with if this compulsion is to be healthily redirected. Once properly integrated and understood, the need to assert personal power can be channeled into helping others to reclaim their own power and affirm their uniqueness to the world.

Retrograde Pluto is very sexually potent, although this may permeate the whole personality rather than be just physically limited. The "urge to penetrate" is a primary psychological force, and you will be attracted to explore beyond superficiality and probe less well-charted areas of intimacy and sexuality. Sexual mysteries can fascinate you, and all shades of sexuality can intrigue study and curiosity. This facet of your personality requires acceptance, or else repression and control may distort this energy into perverse channels. Sexual experience and love is a likely source for inner rebirth, although this will be painfully achieved by cathartic experience, and can cast you into black depths of rejection and frustrated emotions. The power of your emotions will "burn you, " either as genuine love or as complexes, fixations, or obsessive desires. Pluto energies are always abrasive to the personality, and you have no exit to escape them. The sooner they are faced, the sooner integration and understanding dawns, and the better your intimate relationships will become. Evasion only prolongs an uncomfortable attrition.

8TH HOUSE SIGNS

The sign on the 8th house cusp can suggest how each individual deals with the experience of his or her sexual and emotional nature. Each sign indicates a personal bias toward one of the twelve types of expression, and our demonstration of sexuality and emotions is likely to reflect the cuspal sign characteristics. As previously mentioned, if a secondary sign additionally overshadows the majority of this house, then these tendencies can also be considered, as some people may resonate more strongly to the secondary sign rather than the cuspal sign.

The nature of each 8th house sign is like a "backdrop" to any planetary activity, and the sign-planet affinity or disaffinity can either strengthen or weaken a particular planet's power, so interpretations should consider how each planet-sign combination may actually interact. Some may be complementary, such as an 8th house Jupiter in Aries, or Uranus in Sagittarius, where shared tendencies may be invigorated and emphasized; or some may be less suited and require adjustment for effective interaction, such as Saturn in Pisces, or Neptune in Aries. Astrological relationships can provide insight into psychological dynamics, highlighting motivations, desires, and drives that may not be openly apparent, yet which affect sexual and emotional expression, and determines the tone and likely outcome of intimate relationships.

ARIES

Physical and sexual assertion may be noted as priority is placed on personal satisfaction and emotional expectations. Emotional needs and sexual desires may feel insistent and urgent, and a direct bluntness may characterize your search for intimate union. Preoccupation with personal pleasure may interfere with relationship awareness, and the subtleties of intimacy and a gradual building of erotic tension may be disregarded by haste. Patience can be quickly lost with any relationship that is slow to develop or when a partner attempts to restrain new stages of development until he or she is ready.

Impulsive and spontaneous intimacy is often preferred— the sheer energy rush of excitement proving attractive. You need to feel in control and dominate the relationship by asserting your personality and assuming initiative and direction. You enjoy reaching for new intimate horizons and pioneering new experiences. While you can relax into this relationship rush, others may find it too disturbing and try to withdraw. You can find your emotions suddenly engaged with a partner, almost compulsively so during the initial contact, and short, intense affairs may suit your temperament more than committed partnerships.

There can be an immaturity that keeps intimacy at a superficial level, mainly focused on physical pleasure rather than communion on several levels; long-term relationships may not be easy to sustain or be possible until age, experience and gradual maturity makes you able to respond positively and appreciate their benefits. You may need to understand that deeper relationships grow slowly, and that they pass through inevitable changes over time; the temptation to jettison them when difficult phases occur should be wisely resisted, at least until efforts are made to resolve a shifting partnership situation. You may feel uncomfortable in situations of sexual and emotional commitment and responsibility, but running away is rarely a permanent and satisfactory solution.

Planets in Aries are often charged by a forceful, compelling energy, which dispels hesitancy and indecision by an urgency to act. This forcing of planets may make some more effective and demonstrative, possibly clarifying sexual and emotional needs, while others may become overly exaggerated and too self-centered, perhaps even operating destructively in relationships. Uranus in Aries may find a need for variety magnified, so that promiscuity, multiple partners, or short-lived relationships are experienced; the need for experimentation may create difficulties with some partners; the intermittent sexual and emotional desires may confuse others, as needs fluctuate between red hot and ice cold. Neptune in Aries may have an exaggerated imagination, perhaps creating a romantic ideal of intimacy, portrayed as a knight in shining armor, either as the rescuer of a damsel in distress or waiting for the handsome hero to sweep her off her feet, or being liable to self-deception and uncertainty of sexual and emotional needs. Pluto in Aries amplifies domination, control and power traits, which invariably imbalance relationships, or destroy the potential of genuine partnership. Venus in Aries may find greater satisfaction of needs when these are openly disclosed to partners.

TAURUS

Sexual and emotional needs reflect possessive tendencies and desires for stability and security. Often a partner is psychologically considered as a possession. You may expect a monopoly of another's attention and affections, and will rarely forgive any deviation from your retentive embrace. Trust is important and suspicions or reasons for jealousy and threats to your possession will feel extremely disturbing and painful. If you are involved in an intimate relationship, then your partner is genuinely and highly valued; while the psychological possession is active, a form of displaced physical and emotional dependency is also projected onto a partner, which, if the relationship fails, can be a shattering and cathartic event for you.

Intransigence and obstinacy can interfere with intimate harmony, and communication may collapse when contentious situations occur. Emotional and physical satisfaction is your priority in a partnership, and if these levels are fulfilled then mutual support is freely exchanged. When material desires are not met and finances are inadequate your emotional and physical security is disturbed and this can eventually effect sexual relations, too; decreasing libido may create a gap in partnership contact and communication. You can be susceptible to external influences, and emotional stability is sometimes very fragile.

Emotions need to be strong and sexuality a very physical experience; intimacy may cease if these diminish and become lukewarm. Intellectual discussions of sexuality or imaginative fantasies rarely inspire your attention; the preference is for actual, sensual hands-on experience, and sexual games appear as mere irrelevancies and distractions. There's a sexual earthiness to your preferences, and with the right partner, you can be extremely loving, reliable and supportive. Long-term relationships are more suitable than short affairs, and mutual monogamy is generally expected. There can be a predictability about your partnership expression, but the security of this can be highly valued by many, and once your love is given then it rarely fades away. Closeness, warmth and intimacy are enjoyed and your partnerships are always firmly anchored and lifestyles established before you can feel content.

Planets in Taurus have a magnetic and attractive quality, which often operate with seductive allure, a key factor in drawing partners together. Your partner may need your particular qualities in some way, and you tend to exploit this as a possessive tie. Planets which have affinity to the physical level, or to material and emotional desires are more easily activated by Taurus than planets which resonate with intellect and intuition. Uranus in Taurus is a disruptive influence, disturbing security and stability needs and is an uneasy presence, bringing the threat of change to everything that Taurus is devoted to establishing. Venus in Taurus heightens the romantic spirit and your attraction to pleasure, comfort, luxury, and sensuality—making love a priority of life. Saturn in Taurus emphasizes order, control, and defenses against unwanted changes, attempting to impose an inflexible will and stubbornness on reality. Mercury in Taurus may interfere with sexual and emotional expression, diverting attention to mind and intellect and rupturing a natural energy flow. Mars in Taurus may exaggerate physical needs and pleasures, and physical prowess and power may replace a more subtle approach to intimacy.

GEMINI

A Gemini 8th house implies extreme curiosity about sexuality, intimacy, and regenerative union, with an appetite for intellectual knowledge, information, and analysis of experience. Gemini may turn sexuality into a field of study, so that by accumulating physiological, psychological, and objective insights and data, new light may be shed on your own motivation or preference. Your mental preferences may be favored more than emotions. Emotional needs are devalued in intimacy, and you may consider that mental affinity and ease of communication are better substitutes.

You may display the Gemini changeable and restless nature via flirtation and fickleness; a cool emotional response may resist early commitments and responsibility. Your innate inconsistency and need for freedom to change can intervene in developing partnerships, and short-lived relationships may be more common. An attraction to variety may make monogamy less appealing or easy to maintain. You can sometimes be a frustrating and confusing partner, as others experience the duality of your nature and feel uncertain which "twin"is really dominant. Intimacy with you can seem to be with two distinctly different personalities; this may excite and intrigue some, while repelling others who would prefer you to be more predictable.

Curiosity can be your incentive for experimentation, and Gemini-influenced sexuality can be shaped by the preferences of either partner or by whatever aspect of sexuality is currently interesting you. Your sexual desires are quite mutable and rarely fixed and repetitive; choosing a suitable long-term partner may pose difficulties, unless his or her sexual range is potentially broad, too. While physicality is enjoyed, your main priority is mental stimulation and exploration; you may observe your physical and emotional reactions during lovemaking, evaluating these like a detached witness and researcher. Discovering new sexual techniques or studying the intellectual examination of sexuality can inspire you to seek opportunities to actually experience these. Your sexual self-image is quite open to different types of experimentation, and prefers heightened sensuality to just genital sex. Sensitivity to intimate subtlety is present, and will easily be shared with a partner as part of mutual communication. Eroticism and slow arousal may suit you, and you can evolve quite sophisticated tastes.

Intellectual and verbal communication with partners is crucial, for you enjoy this level of intimacy even more than physical intercourse. You may distrust and inhibit passion as this releases emotional power which feels uncomfortable, and is less controllable and containable. You like the intimacy of personal exposure through mutual sharing, discussing inner realities and the stimulation of exchanging information and knowledge. One "turn-on" can be encouraging imaginative sexual fantasies that can be mutually enacted. Thinking about sex, visualizing alternative partners or sexual experiences may be enjoyed, sometimes effectively substituting for sexual familiarity or lack of a partner. The explorative impulse can edge close to crossing sexual taboos and investigating minority interests, although this is not inevitable. In fact, you can often go long periods without a sexual partner, as if an off-switch has been activated.

Planets in Gemini have a need to be understood, and effort will be directed toward gaining insight into their primary desires and motivations through self-inquiry and observation. The complexity and interconnectedness of personality impulses can provide a fertile ground for you to explore and investigate for a long time, and Gemini extends this to probing and examining both partner and relationship, much to the discomposure of certain temperaments who react against ceaseless analysis and evaluation. Neptune in Gemini inflates imaginative fantasies, and confuses perceptions by deceptive illusions. Jupiter extends Gemini impulses for variety, and strives toward further horizons in enthusiastic pursuit of new discoveries. Mars in Gemini may stimulate argument and intellectual friction in relationships. Saturn in Gemini may control inquisitive needs, imposing conformity and conventional order on an agile, restless, adaptable, and unpredictable nature.

CANCER

You may approach sexuality and emotional intimacy with great caution, defenses erected and ready to retreat into your protective shell at the threat of rejection or humiliation. Your emotional sensitivity is considerable, even if this is not openly displayed. Sometimes your periodic superficial extroversion can mislead observers, as essentially you are a reserved, introverted character, who finds difficulty in communicating your needs and desires to others.

In intimate relationships, you often adopt a nurturing attitude, which some may find protective and secure, while others find it smothering and restrictive. Your sentimentality may similarly polarize reaction, and those easily hurt emotions and moody behavior can easily be dismissed or misinterpreted by self-centered partners. You often evaluate partners by a mixture of shrewdness and psychic intuition; indeed, you should never disregard these inner messages or else you may become involved in unsuitable relationships. Emotions dominate and color your perceptions, and if feelings are not in harmony, then relationship contact and communication is damaged. Romance, imagination, and idealism permeate your dreams of intimacy, and experiences of dependency and disillusionment are likely.

You can hide behind partnerships, building strong defenses around your intimate commitments, often resulting in a possessive strategy and a diminution of freedom. Certain partners may find this severely restricting, and individualists like Aquarius and Aries may find your bindings too tight for comfort. You are prone to emotional denial and repression, especially if no suitable partner is found, and these controlled energies may then disturb inner equilibrium until channels for release are discovered. Your problem is often excess emotion and sentimental feelings; emotions seem to be dammed and accumulate, as if being squeezed through a narrow channel, and can overflow, flooding you with hard-to-handle emotions. Men, in particular, can find Cancer's emotional potency almost frightening, as this sensitivity and vulnerability contrasts strongly with their assumed masculine self-images. Women can redirect these through nurturing a family or by being a loving and supportive partner.

You may respond poorly to freedom needs in relationship, as this seems to oppose your requirements for security, stability, and dependency, casting doubt over trust and fidelity, and eroding the quality of intimacy that you demand. If you choose a suitable partner, then your loving devotion can bond the relationship closer; although if your embrace becomes too possessive and dependent, you can inhibit expressing mutual potential through fear of partnership change.

For you, physical intimacy rests on emotional connections; if emotions are disengaged, then cohesion is lost, as sexual pleasure alone is insufficient to sustain the relationship. Sometimes sexual dysfunctions and unease about physical loving may be symptomatic of emotional imbalance, even caused by excessive emotions and fears of their power. You can have worrying images of emotional drowning, and if previously badly hurt by intimacy, you may resist new involvements due to anxious apprehension. A hidden inferiority complex may also afflict you, and any tendencies to store self-pity and disparaging slights can interfere with your confidence when initiating new relationships.

Planets in Cancer may be weakened and internalized, and can represent difficulties in sexual and emotional closeness and communication. Sensitivity may impede ease of contact, and caution predominate over expressing specific planetary qualities. Mercury in Cancer may be experienced as acting irrationally, with opinions, thoughts and attitudes fluctuating by capricious moods. Moon in Cancer highlights domesticity and unstable emotions. Mars in Cancer can introduce emotionally irritable disputes into intimacy, disrupting harmony; while Jupiter may find its charitable nature extended into productive humanitarian action. Saturn in Cancer may become increasingly defensive and suspicious of a partner's feelings and intentions. Effort will be necessary to manifest the positive qualities of planets in Cancer, and this will require consistent attention to their potential, or else they may remain latent and relatively unexpressed.

LEO

You can be very self-assured, and this encourages confidence in attracting sexual partners. You can project a powerful and impressive self-belief through energetic assertiveness, and this can appeal to those who prefer strong partners. In relationships, you prefer a controlling and dominating role, and at least like to believe that you are "supreme ruler and arbiter of choices." Sexuality and emotions are expressed with warmth and generosity, and an element of intimate play may be displayed. Sexual behavior tends to be relatively conventional, and there is less attraction toward unusual and minority tastes, unless the impulse of domination is exaggerated; then imposing your will and preferences will interfere with intimate balance, and could incorporate distinct controls of a partner's sexuality and emotions. A touch of theatrical drama can intrigue attention, and while other extroverted personalities may initially attract, there can be later challenges related to ego and power struggles. If your Leo-influenced character is not overly intent on domination, your better qualities can be evoked by relationship with a partner who tends to be slightly dependent.

Sexuality is usually integrated into your whole life, and compulsive behavior is less common. Control needs are often redirected into other areas of life, especially through "power-over" others; if circumstances limit this assertion, and any authoritarian trait finds no other release, then intimacy can be the only remaining option. Awareness of a partner's needs may then be diminished, replaced by a self-centered concern for pleasure. Often sexuality is diffused into a general life-sensuality, where enjoyment of the senses becomes your major aim.

There can be hidden sensitivity and vulnerability to others' opinions, as your self-assured image is a defense against the pricking of your ego and pride. The admiration and respect of others is important, and if this is not experienced or relationships fade and collapse, then anxiety and loss of confidence may severely affect emotions and sexuality as a psychosomatic symptom.

The fixedness of this sign may indicate a repetitive sexuality, where behavior slips into regular routines and assumes a predictable response. A partner may need to assume responsibility for introducing variety and experimentation, yet achieved without undermining your sense of domination. You are easily persuaded and influenced by a partner's praise and flattery.

Planets in Leo often assume an extroverted tendency, looking for an audience for their specific qualities. Sun in Leo seeks to impress partners by personality power and charisma, expecting regular applause and imagining themselves as a lead actor in the drama of life. Mars in Leo can find enthusiasms and ambitions ignited, which may decrease attention given to relationships, and often displays dominant and arrogant attitudes which cause friction and argument. Saturn in Leo easily assumes authority and responsibility, taking the reins of a relationship and imposing order and stability on a partner; conformism and conventionality may create intimate limitations, and are often indicative of hidden fears of inadequacy and misgivings. Venus in Leo can be effusively warm-hearted and social, acquiring many friends and partners who respond to your open heart and enjoyable company.

VIRGO

This indicates a complex sexuality and emotional response to intimacy, often dependent on inner conditioned attitudes and your relationship to your body. The conflict is between your need for efficiency and purity, and the issue is how you resolve this in terms of sexuality. Tendencies toward repression or determined expression of sexuality are the two likely opposite responses. If conditioning has introduced ideas of body-negation and disapproval of sexual activity, then a psychological resistance is probable which may inhibit physical responsiveness, relaxation, and enjoyment. Whispered inner messages like "Sex is dirty," "This action is not right," "This is perverted and it's not normal to enjoy this" can be dissuasive influences and obstruct natural relationship development. Mental standards of purity can distort your instinctive feelings and needs, and coupled with uncertainty and unease of emotional involvement can lead you to reject intimacy.

However, if healthier sexual attitudes exist, you can become an efficient and inventive lover. The Virgoan impulse to serve is then expressed as a desire to sexually please your partner, and in accomplishing that, you also derive considerable satisfaction. While conventionality may often rule you, there can be an attraction to sexual techniques that provide alternative practices and that exploit more subtle, individual tastes, and edge closer toward contrived fantasies and "so-called perversions." Attention and energy can be directed into your sexual expression in a particularly effective way, and Virgo-influenced sexuality can act as hot as it can be cold. Sometimes a need to periodically break free from your normal state of control and order can burst through into liberated sexuality.

In this 8th house, compulsive elements may form around sexuality (fetishist tastes are not uncommon) or where fantasies assume greater psychological impact due to connecting with the unconscious mind. Imagination may be limited, but mental study and analytic skills accumulate information about human sexuality, and a thorough discriminative evaluation of this often provides the evocative source for later fantasies.

Emotions can remain unintegrated, and intimacy may partly be experienced as a detached observer, sifting sensations and feelings in an attempt at personal comprehension. Your relationship can also be subjected to this ongoing critical analysis, and matched against high ideals and standards may often fail to attain expectations. A preference for purity and perfection can be destructive to intimacy, and if these tendencies are prevalent, then interference is inevitable. If emotions are regularly repressed, then intimate bonds may atrophy from lack of support causing a gradual separation to occur. Criticism is abrasive to feelings and emotions, and wounding divisions are exposed when awareness is lacking to a partner's sensitivity.

Planets in Virgo can adopt this tendency of high expectations and idealistic standards, and strive to either express these or look for them in partners. The principles of any natal planet will become important in relationships, and will prove either unifying or divisive, depending on how they are handled. Each planet acts as a filter through which intimacy is perceived, and again, this can either clarify or distort. There can be a therapeutic value in integrating a planet in Virgo, and the experience of working closely with this planet can be a source of self-healing by contacting unconscious depths that need understanding and purification.

Venus in Virgo may adopt a perfectionist attitude to intimacy; few may match these standards, and relationship disillusionment is likely until greater realism replaces a hypercritical level of evaluation. Mars in Virgo may find conflicts between instinctive needs and desires and conditioned "inner programs" that hinder satisfaction and frustrate sexual and emotional impulses. Saturn in Virgo may emphasize conformist partnership development and conventional tastes, while Uranus may be inclined to explore broader sexual dimensions. Neptune in Virgo may prefer experimenting through creative fantasies and imagination, and also may create an over-idealized perfect lover who is difficult to find in real life. With Neptune, tendencies of service, sacrifice, and martyrdom may become apparent in relationships, and self-deceptive illusions may prove resistant to discriminative self-inquiry.

LIBRA

Your relationships are characterized by a need for harmony and balance, and your urge for partnership is especially insistent on emotional and sexual levels. You tend to look for qualities in others that are either lacking, or latent in yourself, hoping to achieve compensation by togetherness. Yet a balance is often evasive, and your inclination to continually improve a relationship adds its own unsettling influence. This pressure to change and modify situations in the name of greater stability and harmony can be either constructive or destructive, and your bias toward trying to change partners to fit an ideal role model can be a recipe for futility and argument. One side of Libra's balance seeks emotional stability while the other inclines toward destabilization; the scales are rarely static. You dislike a discordant environment, but inadvertently introducing an imbalanced Libran influence often becomes a source of conflict.

In the 8th house, balance in sexual and emotional union is needed, as there can be excessive movement of the scales, when attitudes and desires fluctuate in irregular rhythms. While partnerships can be mutually attractive and exciting, unresolved differences pose challenges which may not be overcome, and relationships can fail when the balance tips from harmony to conflict. Understanding how this dynamic operates in intimacy may be crucial to increasing your prospects for a permanent, satisfying partnership. Otherwise this restless Libran spirit will confuse others and disrupt communication and lifestyle stability. There can be paradoxical, contradictory, and enigmatic facets to your Libra affected sexual personality, often resulting in a loss of self-knowledge and obscuring of purpose. Sometimes a belief is held that fulfillment waits just out of sight, when things change, despite previous experience and failed expectations. There's an idealistic dreamer struggling with Libra's scales, unsure which side is right and perplexed when balance is actually attained. Life, intimacy, and partnership may remain a step beyond your grasp, always disappointing and disillusioning; the quest to correct this perpetually disturbs the balance.

Emotions tend to be romantic and sentimental, often retaining a slightly disengaged position even during intimacy. Moodiness and discontent go hand-in-hand with your perfectionism, which may diminish the prospects of numerous possible partners. Feelings are changeable and erratic, and combined with your indecision can lead relationships through many ups and downs. Life with you is not tranquil, and searching for harmony brings changes in your wake. You can be manipulated and impressionable, especially by anyone with understanding of your psychological traits, who exploits your need for unity and relatedness. Often your recognition of inner confusion and sense of inadequacy and anxiety can be translated into acting in ways to please and fulfill others' expectations; if this becomes a repetitive pattern, then autonomy is weakened and dependency increased.

The importance of sexuality is as a part of intimate communication, rather than a separate priority. Your Libran-derived ideals include compatibility on every level possible, and adjust each level's importance accordingly. A marriage of minds can be more suitable than simply physical affinity.

Relationships include compromise and cooperation, and mutual equality replaces traditional power struggles between partners, even though you may only develop this after an uncomfortable period of intimate adjustment.

Planets in Libra are often affected by this see-saw-rhythm, where both positive and negative characteristics can be equally displayed. Planetary principles can be highlighted, especially in the context of their ability to unite and relate with other personality facets and natal planets, as the actual quality of such relationships is starkly revealed. Venus in Libra may appear the ideal, loving companion, or display frivolous attitudes, disturbed by discontent and unrealistic expectations. Mars in Libra may be persuasively assertive, ardent in pursuing lovers, or can be argumentative, irritable and disputatious, ruining partnership harmony. Uranus in Libra may be disruptive, unpredictable and a constant channel for change, favoring short-lived, uncommitted affairs and the pleasures of variety. Neptune in Libra adds another dimension to indecisive tendencies, and exaggerates idealistic fantasies and dissatisfaction with the world, or alternatively, inspires artistic and imaginative creativity.

SCORPIO

Sexual and emotional intensity characterize this influence, and in the 8th house, the impulse to probe and penetrate through intimacy is apparent in your need for identification and union. Emotional conviction and steadfastness is usual in your relationships, and once love for someone is acknowledged, monogamy and commitment are naturally displayed. Intimacy is vital to engage your emotional powerhouse, and if relationships are unavailable, then this energy is trapped within your psyche, causing irritation and discomfort. Intimate partnership is seen as regenerative, salvific, and redemptive, and serves to define the fluid water energies by providing a "container" through love for a partner. Strong, passionate sexual and emotional feelings are stirred during intimacy, even though these may not be openly revealed; inner changes can be traumatic and profound despite your self-contained temperament and apparent composure. When a suitable partner or lover is chosen, purposeful perseverance is likely to overcome any obstacles preventing relationship occurring.

You may adopt a mask of impassivity to protect raw emotions and feelings, enabling the preservation of an aura of apartness that can equally attract and repel. Extremism appeals to you and lukewarm sexuality and emotions are of little interest. With such a potent sexual force coiled inside, your range of sexual activity can be considerable, and curiosity in all aspects of sex can extend personal experience. Sexual compulsion and obsession can be near the surface of consciousness, ignited by inner pressures that require regular release, or else they may explode or implode in a damaging way. When energy retention occurs, tensions may be released by violence and provocative behavior, and there can be an uncaring, destructive, and almost "berserker spirit" unleashed at such times of crisis.

Relationships may be liable to jealousy, destructiveness, vindictive behavior, cruelty, domination, and resentments if this energy is handled unwisely. Alternatively, consistent, genuine love may be shared, with trust and faithfulness as sources for mutual development and growth. Either a deep, transformative level of union will be discovered with Scorpio in the 8th, or intimacy will be the scene for repeated trauma and crisis, a realm where complex entanglements with others is inevitable. Lives can be ruined or regenerated through this type of intense experience. Some may find such intimacy difficult to live with; Scorpio's scrutiny and honesty can expose many areas of vulnerability, and under this direct gaze few illusions and self-deceptions can exist for long as faults and virtues are both revealed to investigation. Your trait of enjoying control and periodic needs for an adversary to release pressures may confuse others about your real feelings, and if a partner does not possess insight then neither will they be informed. Even in committed partnership, aloneness is still retained.

Any planet in Scorpio will be significant in sexual and emotional expression, and their principle will reflect an important need that requires satisfying. There can be a degree of repression of these needs, as they are reminders of vulnerability, dependency on others, and an inner weakness that cannot easily be forgotten. With Mercury, this is the need for communication through intimacy and partnership; with the Moon, a need to establish lifestyle rhythms, to harmonize and deal with the presence of deep, emotionally-charged personality patterns. With Venus, the need is to experience intimate emotional unity; and with Pluto the need for transformation and regeneration through love and emotional intensity. With Jupiter, intimacy is a path to expansion, of growth, experience and understanding, a means to discover the abundant life; with Saturn, the need is to impose self-discipline, to contain and direct energies wisely and carefully, ensuring that they are constructive, productive and not irresponsibly dissipated. Intimate security and stability will be prerequisites of this control and self-ordering. With Uranus, the need is to deviate and innovate, to step beyond conformism and assert free independence; the exploration of taboo areas appeals, and a need for periodic change is both liberating and destructive.

SAGITTARIUS

Needs for freedom, independence, and exploration characterize sexual and emotional requirements, and you can resent
feeling restricted in partnerships. This can unsettle intimacy,
especially if a partner is looking for a more permanent relationship, and you can develop a "habit" of apparently losing
interest when issues of mutual commitment need to be discussed. Your urge to explore stimulates curiosity in other
personalities and prospects for sexual liaisons, and you may
be inclined to chase new partners who hint at new exciting
challenges. Your adventurous spirit is ready to welcome new
opportunities; there may be an aversion to the concept of a
monogamous relationship. Even within ongoing intimate
partnerships, you often attempt to shift habitual sexual
expressions into new spheres of activity, although emotional
exchanges may remain fairly static.

Your preference for freedom, spontaneity and excitement may appeal to those who enjoy a lively and changing
relationship, but may disturb others who prefer more stability
and predictability. You are attracted toward risk-taking in relationships, often seeking a partner who matches your high standards. An optimistic belief that this ideal person exists
somewhere may introduce additional discontent into any existing relationships that may be suffering from mundanity or
"imperfection," especially if another's demands weigh heavy.

Sexuality tends to be directly expressed, in a confident,
vigorous, energetic, and assertive style. Once your singleminded intention for a lover is focused, the determination to
succeed and conquer is persistent. Your sexuality may be
physically biased as emotions can sometimes be denied or
repressed for fear of losing personal freedom through
commitment. Companionship and mental affinity is considered of high value, and most Sagittarian-influenced partnerships are founded on a deep level of mutual friendship.

Emotions are unpredictable and passions flow irregularly,
as if a periodic short-circuiting occurs; this transiency of
involvement can suggest why you often resist commitment,

or suddenly redivert amorous attentions to new partners who reawaken your interests. In this 8th house, adventure is often sought by exploring intimate relationships, and there can be a compulsive trait which continually attracts such encounters. Romance, sexual needs, and risk-taking may be interwoven, and intimacy may be used to generate crises that relate to personal growth.

Your outspoken honesty can embarrass partners with perceptive observations, and an emotional realism (or lack of sensitivity) can be too stark for those who prefer a more tactful and diplomatic style of expression. Relationship communication is important, but your directness can often bruise vulnerable feelings, especially when self-centeredness predominates.

If high ideals derived from religion, morals, and ideology, condition your worldview, then these may interfere with your natural sexuality, and cause inner friction and conflict if desires contradict beliefs. Generally, moral conventions are adhered to, although if deviation occurs, guilt is likely to spoil your pleasures and become confusing.

Relationships with dominant partners are unlikely to succeed, and crises can emerge from resisting their demands and expectations. An adaptable partner is more suitable, and one not so willful in temperament, so that independence and relative freedom of thought and action is maintained. Feeling emotionally suffocated by intimacy will either repress your needs or create divisions that will destroy intimacy. A supportive partner is often required, one capable of helping to direct your energies and talents into productive areas, or these can easily be dissipated and wasted. Clarity of purpose and genuine need and desire is necessary, or else your search for an ideal mate can continue without ever knowing exactly what can satisfy this search.

Mercury in Sagittarius indicates a need for mental compatibility, and stimulating intellectual exchange is important in retaining intimate connections. Complementary worldviews and shared interests are foundations for a more per-

manent relationship. Venus in Sagittarius implies a flirta-
tious and changeable attitude to intimacy, probably involving multiple partners, and a self-centered lack of consideration
in relationship. Idealistic partner-images can interfere with
reality, and passions can wax and wane to mutual confusion;
occasional obsessive and compulsive behaviors may intrude
into sexuality and emotional interactions. Saturn in Sagittarius
emphasizes the moral, conventional, and conformist traits, even
though an underlying impulse to break free can unsettle and
cause contradicting messages. Faithfulness and trust will
assume greater priority as security and stability needs pre-
vail. Uranus in Sagittarius extends explorative needs and
preference for variation, and establishing a settled relationship may prove difficult as the impulse of freedom and
change is entrenched in motivating personality patterns.

CAPRICORN

Passion and Capricorn are uncomfortable companions, and
you may feel vulnerable to emotional involvement, as indicated by inner shields against Eros' arrows of love. While there
can be an earthiness and physicality about your sexuality,
engaging feelings can instigate withdrawal and fear, marked
by self-repression, passivity, and restrained caution in affairs
of love. The qualities of this Capricorn influence are more easily displayed in worldly matters—by rationality, discipline,
and organization—and these fail when faced with uncontrollable emotions. If permanent relationships become committed and legalized, then you easily give loyalty and fidelity,
as marriage conforms to acceptable social behavior; the main
difficulty can lie in the approach to deeper levels of intimacy.

Others may perceive you to have a cautious, disciplined,
and serious temperament, finding intimate relaxation and play-
fulness hard to maintain. Affection is difficult to demonstrate, and your emotions may appear cool, unattached, and
disinterested, symptomatic of inner controls and repressions.

Emotional misunderstandings are possible, and substituting a calm rational appraisal of feelings is often insufficient to convince a partner of genuine love. In the 8th house, this Capricorn influence struggles to impose order on sexuality and emotions, energies which can reflect chaotic crisis and trauma, and strive to perpetually break free of all impositions. Your challenge is to understand the various complexities of human nature that do not allow order and control.

Tendencies to redirect sexual and emotional energies into other areas of life may be attempted, such as by preoccupation with your work, career, and social advancement, but this is only achieved by a repressive self-denial, and while possibly successful can create personality imbalance. Distortions of emotions and sexuality may occur, especially if connected to control needs that are projected onto others and the world, as sexuality is redirected for personal power and influence.

Letting go is a Capricorn difficulty, and emotional and sexual intimacy may pose transformative issues for you. Relationships may be fraught with crisis-potential, especially when emotional barriers have been relaxed and feelings engaged; you may be quite emotionally immature, due to these repressive tendencies, and can fall extremely heavily if love penetrates your various shields. Self-control and self-image can all collapse under the madness of love that this combination of inner state and outer experience can provoke; lifestyles can be disrupted and careers destroyed if compulsion subverts rationality. This 8th house position indicates your need for sexual and emotional transformation, and this is unlikely to be achieved easily or painlessly.

Inner attitudes may contribute to relationship difficulty; narrow-mindedness, criticism, severity, pessimism, restrictiveness, conventionality, exacting demands and selfishness can all be displayed by a controlled personality. Others may not acquiesce to these needs for self-importance and defer to your will, and your defensiveness may succeed only in erecting an impassable wall which excludes intimate communication. An impersonality, self-sufficiency and solitariness may restrict opportunities for contact, as does a distaste for frivolity and juvenile fun. Your needs are rarely revealed to others, and even intimate partners have to work hard at discerning your requirements and desires.

Defensive tendencies may be associated with early childhood conditioning, or the impact of restrictive religious teachings, school, and parental education. Transforming these may require exploring these impressionable sources, such as the parent-child relationship. Unlocking these foundational psychological patterns can be traumatic and cathartic, yet provide a radical change in personality dynamics and create an opportunity to achieve greater wholeness.

The Sun in Capricorn fuses self-image with personality controls and discipline, and this identity context can make passionate abandonment to heightened sexuality and emotions sometimes difficult, as any temporary loss of control is equated to loss of psychological control. A degree of detachment is often retained which minimizes intimacy. If obsessive love occurs, the personality shake-up is considerable, and this can result in a cathartic relationship crisis which is either positively or negatively transformative. Mars in Capricorn emphasizes power, assertion, and control, and assumes an authoritarian role in partnership. There can be a tendency for restlessness, when caution and desires clash in stalemate, and frustrations spill over into irritability and contention; harsh words and apparent unfeeling indifference can repel partners. Jupiter in Capricorn may search for expansion through greater partnership understanding and material affluence; morality and conscience may shape relationships, and self-righteousness may distort them. Uranus in Capricorn implies opposing psychological pulls, one for freedom and another for stability and security; dealing with these in the complex arena of human sexuality is probably difficult, and confusion, repression, and change are inevitable.

AQUARIUS

A detached and intellectual approach to sexuality and emotions is likely, and this can diminish passionate involvements, replacing them with relationships that are characterized by mutual friendship and general compatibility of personality and interest. Needs for independence, unconventional behavior, and experience can add an erratic quality to intimacy, and you may be disinclined to accept commitments and responsibility, perhaps appearing evasive to others. Partnerships may need to compete with your enjoyment of a broad and varied social life, and numerous friendships and acquaintances may interrupt relationship progression. Your ideals and humanitarian beliefs are important, and these can make demands which affect partnerships; it is possible that any commitment to progressive causes may create relationship schisms, either by rediverting time and energy or by the clash of contrary attitudes.

While curiosity about emotions and sexuality is strong, this is only part of a wide range of topics that you find intriguing. Sexuality can be approached as a technical and clinical study, and the experimentation associated with Aquarius is derived from ongoing research. New options and sexual horizons appeal, and repetition is seen as only lessening interest. An occasional perversity may emerge from excitement connected to unconventional behavior, and in this 8th house there are possible obsessive and compulsive actions if emotions run rampant. Emotions can be almost disconnected from your personality, and these need greater integration or else a powerful mental orientation diverts this energy away and can also be emotionally self-denying.

If relationships start to assume coercive, restrictive and critical tendencies, then your inevitable response is a withdrawal from involvement; your need to follow inner messages and personal needs remain paramount. Part of this is sensitivity to your self-esteem, and there is a strong need for intimate affection; if this appears lacking, then a hurt reaction can be to find consolation with another lover. Emotional dispassion is a carefully erected facade rather than a reality, although emotional depths do not suit you either, and the touch of powerful emotions can seem disturbing and threatening. Several intimate relationships may be short-lived, briefly intense when sparks initially fly, but soon consumed by recognized personality differences.

Yet a search continues for a lasting, devoted partnership, where respect, tolerance, understanding, and shared commitments can prove empathic bonds, and love is integrated into a whole relationship which does not rely solely on fluctuating emotions. Sometimes being aware of your own sexual and emotional mutability makes you project similar feelings on to partners, and this magnifies a sense of insecurity in relationships which limits wholeheartedness. Partnership priorities may favor other levels than just sexual, and ease of friendship and enjoyment of mutual company can be equally enriching and valuable for you. Passions can be discovered through intellectual pursuits as well as through physical interaction.

Sun in Aquarius may increase unconventional, rebellious and erratic tendencies, and these become embodied in self-images; settling into relationships may take time and finding a suitable partner requires a clarity of complementary qualities that may not exist until you are older and more mature. Mercury in Aquarius intensifies needs for mental affinity and shared intellectualism, and the most important communication is exchanging thoughts, ideas, and talking together, and it is within that level that "interpenetration" is most fulfilling. Venus in Aquarius adopts idealistic overtones about partnerships, and often these and belief systems will shape intimacy; unconventional and futuristic relationships may evolve as joint creations. There can be a resonance between personal relationships and changes occurring in social attitudes to intimacy. Jupiter in Aquarius implies a relationship founded on common humanitarian and philosophical beliefs, and these may be the magnetic thread that attracts mutual attention and which provides the structure and purpose for partnership development.

PISCES

Sexuality and emotions open depths within your Pisces-influenced personality, and wild feelings can often "drown" an unprepared and unintegrated identity whenever your protective barriers dissolve. In this 8th house, your ego is expected to let go and surrender, and this can be with a lover or redirected as a mystical impulse. The siren-call toward a higher, more inclusive state of union beckons, and this is often experienced through intuition and empathy with a partner, dissolving separative isolation in a lover's arms. Imagination, romance, and perfectionism all contribute to a dream lover; finding someone to match this picture can be difficult, and often relationships are established by reference to mental and spiritual empathy prior to entering any emotional and sexual contact.

Heightened emotions, love, and sensitivity are Piscean qualities, although this does not always imply a corresponding awareness of others; often self-preoccupation with personal feelings and moods can decrease concern and attention of others. Your tendency toward self-sacrifice and martyrdom can imbalance partnerships, especially if vulnerability and dependency are exploited. You are adaptable, mutable, and easily impressed; powerful partners are likely to assume control over your submissive temperament, and compromise tends to be one way rather than by equal adjustments. Intense emotions flow out in a stream of perpetual giving to a partner, unless this natural offering has been twisted by previous, severe emotional batterings.

Imagination, fantasies, and escapism play important roles in intimacy, either as contributing to sexuality or as compensation for discontent. Romantic and spiritual expectations from sexuality are liable to be disappointed, and your disillusionment with mundane matters casts a gray cloak over your enjoyment of life. Self-images as a "victim of love" can assume masochistic resonances if preserved as an excuse for continuing unsatisfactory relationships. Your primary psychological impulse is to dissolve all barriers, experience empathy and communion with others, and to enter the unknown. This is possible through this 8th house, but the emotional anguish that may be exacted can be considerable even if most is self-created, and often descends into intimacy tainted by illusion, imagination, romantic dreams, escapism, and surrendered exploitation. Equally, however, intimacy can be an ideal route to contact the numinous through others, and passing this crisis of union can reveal much to the alert mind and heart.

Disentangling the complex web of "personalities" that dance across your consciousness, and learning how to discern the value of reality as distinct from fantasy and escapist imagination, can hold vital keys to a successful relationship. Resolving inner contradictions can introduce a clarity of purpose and perception that was previously unknown; when this happens, the strengths of the Pisces influence are more apparent.

Moon in Pisces accentuates latent psychism and intuition, and the personality becomes highly receptive to impressions from others and the environment; this can cause puzzlement when spoken words contradict feelings, and juggling subtle levels may complicate relationships unless there is genuine honesty of communication. Mercury in Pisces implies mental impressionability, and a partner may dominate by taking advantage of your indecision and irrational, changeable, and flexible thoughts and attitudes. A nebulous mind may be prone to vacillation and unable to concentrate will effectively. Venus in Pisces can be extremely submissive and pliant, a little too other-worldly and sensitive for an emotionally-draining world. Feeling reactions dominate all decisions, although if changeable bring confusion and loss of direction at every mutable shift. Tendencies to adapt to others may inadvertently create identity loss. Mars in Pisces suggests emotional instability, where passion, sensuality, and sexuality are exaggerated and invigorated to an uncomfortable degree. Loss of emotional control may be likely when provoked by heightened feelings, and obsessive and compulsive behavior may be revealed in emotional outbursts of frustrated desires and immature demands of a partner. Saturn in Pisces may adopt a self-sacrificial role as "dictated" by the demands of duty, obligation, and responsibility, where an emotional martyrdom can be enacted to the assumed approval of the social audience.

6 Raising The Dark Side— Repression and Taboo

THE DARK SIDE EXISTS in everyone, whether we choose to admit its presence or continue to deny and disown those parts of our nature which contradict an idealized self-image, or are considered unacceptable by fears that if openly displayed would be socially condemned. The dark side can become an inner swamp of rejection, fetid and defiled, slowly disgorging contaminating tentacles of self-disgust, hate, fear, paranoia, compulsion, obsession, greed, anger, aggression, guilt, and shame into the psyche, tainting us with a slowly virulent, degenerating poison unless we can discover a holistic and healing regenerative vision of ourselves.

Jung called this the *shadow* and previous occult teachings called it *the dweller or guardian of the threshold*, and in many forms and disguises the dark side has been embodied in myth, legend, and story as the dark twin or eternal adversary and tempter. During early childhood we commence creating our dark side as an inevitable byproduct of the socialization process, and this forms the ground attracting those dissociated fragments of self which we fail consciously to integrate. The bogyman of childhood fears is living inside us, and in a parallel action to locking the house door, we bolt inner doors to protect us from the shock of meeting our repudiated mirror-image.

The dark side grows from our interaction with others and with society, as represented by the concerns and experiences of the first seven natal houses. As a result of these encounters, we discover that our will is not supreme and that we cannot simply act as we please; our personality may provoke friction from parents and teachers, or we may quickly realize that friendliness and cooperation will bring adult approval and other benefits. Our personality and style of social expression is both molded by others and reshaped by ourselves to sculpt a socially acceptable mask. If we continue to rebel, and refuse to conform, then we are penalized in various ways. Yet through these inevitable changes which come from relating to the outer world, we may also discover self-knowledge and be aided in actualizing latent potential and talents. Social conditioning is an ambivalent process that can both support our development and simultaneously restrict and damage us.

Part of the 8th house psychological cleansing and regeneration comes by dealing with unresolved issues from previous relationships. In the context of repression, this includes early parental and social influences. Instinctive needs for survival and dependency are active in childhood, and these do not simply cease to exist in the psyche at maturity; indeed, these childish instincts and concerns often reemerge through unconscious projections into later adult relationships.

The primal fear of losing parental protection is replayed through possessively dependent fears of losing a lover and partner. Our fraught feelings and uncontrolled emotional outbursts during personality conflicts—and when relationships fail—are often childlike and immature, as we unconsciously equate our actual survival to the continuity of intimate love. Angered emotions, childhood spite, dramatic tantrums, and trauma are displayed in relationship breakdown as we "lose control" and repeat childlike attitudes, statements, and feelings. We can observe the mature, sophisticated personality being ripped away and replaced by an infantile personality that we had forgotten or buried deep within the psyche; yet it still exists and will reveal its presence in situations of crisis. The inner child still lives, and few of us will have not encountered its return through emotional stress.

Conditioning by parents, teachers, priests, and society is a major cause of self-denial and repression, as we soon discover that our freedom to act as we will is restricted and obstructed by others. We are taught to be conformist and conventional, modelled to become the contrived socially-cloned human of our specific culture and time. "Right behavior" guarantees social acceptance; anti-social behavior guarantees social disapproval, possible punishment, or alienated isolation. Social pleasures, advancement, and success are offered more freely to those who are not disruptive, and who do not challenge the status quo.

Our individuality and freedom becomes secondary in importance, either rejected by those in authority over us or self-repressed for fear of authoritarian anger and disapproval. We quickly discover how to be self-restrictive, to "button our lips" in suppression of genuine, honest, feelings, and to distinguish which parts of ourselves are "acceptable" and those which should be "hidden away." From the latent wholeness of birth comes the fragmenting and splitting of the psyche as our "angel and demon" are torn apart and separated within us; and for many, will never be reunited again.

Repression results partly from dependency needs on parents, employers, lovers, friends, religion, morality, politics, and social acceptance, and the conflicts that occur within these interactions. How we deal with these will determine our repressive inclinations and the degree of personality repression we consider necessary to ensure we are not rejected or abandoned.

Emotional pain is not encouraged to be openly revealed and often remains unacknowledged, gradually accumulating over time; few realize how this stored suffering can subtly destroy their lives. Many refuse to get in touch with their pain and allow emotions to be felt and released; this represses vital energies into the unconscious mind, where they can be transferred into psychological or physical symptoms which may create illness, nervous breakdowns, anger, aggression, compulsion, and obsession. Discovering how to regularly discharge emotions is necessary for inner health and also benefits physical well-being.

SOCIALIZATION AND TABOO

One of the major side effects of socialization is the emphasis placed on control; conditioning implies that allowing people to be actually free is socially dangerous—the specter of creating chaos and anarchy—and that behavior has to be regulated and directed along specific channels. This instills a fear of full personality expression, and our instinctive, spontaneous actions are manipulated by the ceaseless controls of parents, teachers, employers, religion, etc. This control becomes internalized to direct choice and actions, monitoring our inner life, and in many is eventually reduced by fear to a voice saying "no" to most inclinations, as a rejection of our nature and universe. Repression is always an excluding "no" which closes options, sensations, feelings, and thoughts—confining them to an infertile wasteland of the psyche.

This process is inevitable within a society dominated by a dualistic worldview and minimal understanding of the psyche's dynamics. In a cultural pursuit for technological progress and personal light, we can fail to comprehend the truth of Jung's assertion that though we may aim for perfection, our wholeness and completeness can only emerge when we also accept our imperfections, which involves a reconciliation with the dark side. Culturally, we lack a concept of wholeness, which individually and collectively allows the space for imbalance and division to dominate. A fragmented society is the inevitable collective reflection of millions of individuals who are psychologically fractured.

In the West, *taboo* directs attention to prohibited areas of life, those which are excluded from general exploration and investigation and culturally segregated; although taboo in the East can imply an area of sacred presence in life.

Collective social taboos emerge from a lack of understanding and integration; in a society displaying wholeness, there would be few taboos, the only ones would be matters crucial to planetary survival. The collective dark side taboo is a grouping of human tendencies, emotions, attitudes, beliefs, and actions that are considered socially unacceptable; yet the nature of taboo changes with periodic shifts of morality, attitude, belief, and fashion. Every social grouping tends to develop "taboo parameters" to which all members are expected to conform; these may even be trivial issues, but the consequences of crossing demarcation lines is group castigation and censure, with possible expulsion and isolation from social participation. This pattern was probably derived from early family and tribal cultures, where banishment from the supportive group invariably meant a lonely death.

Our instinct for belonging is still strong today, and while taboo injunctions may exert fascination, most avoid their allure by favoring the protection of group security and solidarity. Taboos develop from collective attitudes, and most social taboos are related to traditional and contemporary cultural repressions. The multiplied individual dark sides generate collective taboos which then overshadow individual choice and action like a vicious circle. My repressions become part of collective repressions which then continue to encourage and socially validate my repressions which reenergize the collective dark side—ad infinitum. Any who transform their own repressive nature and liberate their life may be forced into keeping their own counsel. They become "invisible," like the man of the Tao, or they are social "outsiders" whose presence can disturb the sleep and unconsciousness of those who stayed within the group.

Religion is often a source for many collective taboos. Christian beliefs pervade western culture, and despite the wisdom and high ideals of Christ, dangerous distortions have infiltrated these spiritual teachings—conceiving repressive social taboos. Sexuality has been affected by the negativity of early priests and saints teaching the division between spirit and matter, between the sacred and profane. The Church of the West dismissed other world religions as pagan and inferior, and disconnected human beings and divinity by asserting Jesus as the "only Son of God," and combined this with the Christian injunction to follow in his footsteps—a command that is destined to bring only failure, guilt and awareness of human weakness when compared with the incomparable perfection of Christ. From Judaism and Christianity we receive the concept of "original sin," condemning us and fragmenting our wholeness even before we were born, an attitude repudiating the sacredness of matter.

Lives become circumscribed by taboo barriers, and often we are not even aware of these limitations, so engrained are they in our psyche and worldview. Taboos are a stark "no" against something. The modern interest in occultism, magic, spiritual paths, wicca, astrology, paganism, and humanistic self-development is still tainted by taboo attitudes, which often attribute craziness, evil, and satanic beliefs to those involved. A collective fear shrinks away from the gnosis of self-realization, historically conditioned to perceive this as the preserve of priests alone, and which has attracted a taboo interdiction as "forbidden fruit."

The power of collective ignorance, avoidance, and repression seeks to restrict individual freedom to discover wholeness, recognizing that those who seriously pursue this path can escape from control and manipulation, and then attempt to wake others, too, by encouraging mass enlightenment. There are many recent examples of pressure placed on those with alternative beliefs and lifestyles from socially influential fundamentalist groups who continue to stoke cultural fears and repressions into renewed activity; after all, the main purpose of taboo is to perpetuate social control.

If we persist in allowing "no" to dominate our responses to the universe, then taboo repression will continue far into the future, because "no" is self-denying, and is a refusal of trust and relationship with life. Unfortunately this attitude is one that is most conditioned by social fears, and which takes deep root in people. If we can manage to transform our attitudes into a welcoming "yes" to the universe and ourselves, then taboo and repression can be dissolved to reveal the existence of a liberated and free state that we have lost or forgotten.

Many who search for spiritual light encounter great resistance when the dark side is activated—creating egotistical smoke screens—believing that black forces are attacking, or changing their spiritual practices as "such negativity must mean that this path is unsuitable for them." Some even drop their search and turn away in horror and dismay at what has been awakened. Novice meditators discover their "monkey mind," perpetually chattering and leaping here and there, conjuring a multitude of distracting images, memories, thoughts, feelings, and body sensations when they were expecting calm, tranquility and samadhic peace. All these experiences are reflections of our everyday state which we begin to realize for the first time. When searching for the light, the primary hurdle on every spiral level is the dark side in one of its many disguises; this is unavoidable yet still the illusion persists that an exploration of the underworld can be avoided. An alchemical image portrayed man as a tree, who, to maintain balance must have roots descending into the dark hell of the underworld, while the branches reach upward toward the spiritual heavens.

THE 8TH HOUSE DARK SIDE EXPERIENCE—THE UNDERWORLD DESCENT

The 8th house effectively commences a shift in human experiences. The first seven houses are more individual and personal in nature, while the 8th inaugurates a potential transition and alignment with collective and transcendental issues. The 8th house is where we bow in submission to something other or greater than ourselves. This may be to another person, a lover with whom we experience sexual and emotional union; to a more socially powerful individual or group of individuals, exerting authority and "power-over" us; to personal and collective repressed darkness, structuring society and our desires and motivations by a negative imprint; and to our fate, the innate pattern to which all life must conform and accept limitation. The shock of encountering these awakens us to realize that an egocentric perspective is insufficient and inadequate to comprehend and direct our lives; we are simply outnumbered, and this poses the problem of creating right relationship with others and of how we can live in a way that satisfies our needs and desires without causing suffering or exploitation.

The 8th house issues reflect an interface with life which animates a fundamental question to understand the meaning and purpose of our existence—the relationship of self and universe. This process will later shape the philosophy and religious impulse of the 9th house, and is continued in the 10th by social responsibility and constructive activity, in the 11th by identifying self with the collective group, and in the 12th by selfless service to humanity and planetary evolution.

As the 8th house beckons us toward the underworld for a healing regeneration, we are constantly close to a traumatic collision with the dark side of our unconscious and subconscious mind. The unconscious self wants to become both conscious and also stay unconscious, and will do so at the cost of great conflict and effort; we can be torn between longing for the light and fear of the light, knowing that either response will have great repercussions in our lives.

Light exposes the corners of the psyche and dispels illusions and self-deceptions. We become equally aware of our weaknesses, failings, and limitations, as our strengths, successes and potential, and the contrasts in our lives become increasingly apparent. Joy and pleasure are experienced more fully, but pain, discontent, and frustration may also be felt acutely. Increased awareness can shine throughout our psyche and life experience, and once the commitment to pursue the lighted path has been taken, the first challenge is waking to how demanding this journey will be and the scope of transformative regeneration that is required from us by a spiritual metamorphosis.

The 8th house—and by association, Pluto and Scorpio in the chart—becomes a repository of personal and collective darkness, as individual evasive repression of unacceptable parts of self is inexorably attracted beneath the surface into the hidden, unlit depths of the underworld, ostensibly removed from sight and attention. Here are born the "devils, monsters, evil demons and temptations" that plague humanity—the seed and fruit of our ignorance and self-dismemberment attitudes.

Primitive and primordial instincts are rejected by civilization, yet continue to live on behind closed psychic doors; we pretend that we have advanced despite the existence of primal lusts which still demand satiation and that war, starvation, oppression, and aggression are still rampant in the world, with torture, slavery, rape, murder and violence daily abusing people.

Our advance is partial, achievements have been mainly successful in technological progress and improving physical conditions; the further and perhaps more difficult advance is the transformation of human nature, through awareness and insight into the psyche's intricate patterns. If we can achieve this step, then we will be capable of truly regenerating our society and renewing planetary health. The collective dark side is visible in the world as an external reflection of the projected existence of billions of personal shadows. Only by maturing enough to accept our responsibility for contributing to the planetary dark side can we face the realization that "the forces of light and darkness, gods and demons are within us."[1]

In the 8th house, we are given an opportunity to meet our dark side and discover the wounds that sap the strength and vitality of life, both personally and collectively. In raising the dark side, we resurrect the ghosts of an unresolved

---

[1] Lama Govinda, cited by Tracy Marks in *Planetary Aspects* (Sebastapol, CA: CRCS, 1987), p. 64.

past which is partly our own and partly inherited through our parents who represent an ethnic tradition and cultural heritage. In contemplating a descent into the underworld, we are dealing not just with our own potential healing, but that of our society, too. Self and other are perpetually interlinked, and this insight is the essence of 8th house mysteries.

A symbolic image for this phase of the descending journey is the "wounded self," where, by admitting our wounds which need healing and integration, we prepare to stake all on an inward path to discover a unifying and redemptive treasure, trusting that we can reemerge reborn with a message of good news, hope, and optimism that a regenerative secret can be found. The "wounded self" is reborn as the "wounded healer," who returns with the mystery of self-healing to share with all who listen to the message. By healing ourselves and dissipating our share of the collective dark side, we may serve as a healing force for others. This is the task of the shaman and shamanka in the community, and one which all servers of the light are expected to perform. The healer can only heal through experiencing the common suffering that all endure; his or her knowledge comes from genuine personal crisis, and the transmission of this constitutes the wielding of regenerative power.

The 8th house is one of the psychic trinity of water houses—part of the triangle of soul—with the 4th and 12th houses, all of which deal with the past and offer possible descents for integration. The incentive for the quest is often a longing for emotional peace and security. Attaining liberating self-knowledge is an antidote for the feelings of nihilism, loss of meaning, purpose, direction, inner suffering, and existential anguish, so vividly depicted in Sartre's book *Nausea*[2] and explored by the group of existentialists which formed during the 1950s.

As the dark side slowly absorbs more of our vitality into its black hole the spark of life fades; boredom and dis-

---

[2] Jean-Paul Sartre, *Nausea* (New York: Norton, New Directions, 1959; London: Penguin, 1990).

interest deepen and a malaise of "Is this all life is…?" grows pervasive. As this dissatisfaction extends, a corresponding stirring of psychic residues of rejection and repression stimulates subliminal complexes and personality patterns to rise to the surface of consciousness. As these simultaneously begin rising, paradoxically the inner experience is of a descent, drawn down by the powerful source of the unconscious mind. Pressures and stress can be felt for a long period of time, often noted as intensified conflicts, clashing aims, motivations, and desires, producing a confused and uncomfortable psychological state.

Even though we may not realize our compulsive traits during this phase of inner turbulence, repressed energies and motivating desires are emerging for closer investigation and understanding. They can become more apparent in our lives, both as disruptive and disturbing feelings and obtruding within our relationships. Some feel an urge to be more private and reclusive during this period, struggling either to continue denying, controlling, and containing unintegrated aspects of their nature or to secure a degree of inner reconciliation and harmony. Some tend to make greater demands of partners and social relationships, releasing pressures through dominance and exploitation, or they devote compulsive effort to achieve compensatory ambitions and even act more ruthlessly. If latent obsessive tendencies exist, these, too, can be amplified and influence choice and actions.

We may be reminded of imprints of the past, especially stored pain, as memories are resurrected of those who have previously hurt us, all those rejections, humiliations, frustrated desires, adversaries, secret fears, insecurities, rage, and wounded fragments of self that have been disowned—all these can rise as if from the dead to confront us with their still-living presence.

Our self-centered reactions and resistance to relationship demands can expose cruel, destructive feelings and behavior, with urges to forcefully punish any who stand in our way, or who do not cooperate with our desires. Latent violence, lust, twisted passions, jealousy, greed, hate, anger, or revenge can be discharged as a poisonous overflowing from psychic depths. All the feelings that we have "swallowed" and repressed over the years can be regurgitated and relived. If this is not allowed, and we manage to arrest this process once more, then a greater damaging psychological contamination can develop, possibly leading to extreme neurotic, psychotic, schizophrenic and sociopathic illness. Reality can be increasingly distorted and misinterpreted. A lack of self-esteem and worth can project beliefs of universal impersonality, disinterest, and dispassion, deepening fears of fragility, vulnerability and insignificance in an uncaring world, and a feeling of isolated alienation intensifies the separatist mind even further.

As society evades dealing with the collective dark side, individuals have little understanding when this psychological cleansing process is active. Fears and threats of insanity register in most people's minds, and nervous breakdowns are common. Many misdirect their efforts to appease these inner demands and seek to establish emotional stability by reaffirming a preoccupation with satisfaction through money, sex, and power; they fail to understand that real peace occurs when these conflicts subside through a resolving self-insight, which heals insatiable yearnings and melts away compulsive desires.

Through this 8th house experience, we contact the psyche's need for periodic renewal, regeneration, and transformation which can reduce the inevitable repression that in varying degrees develops in everyone. This regenerative force is a transcendental power which our separatist mind sees operating as dualistic opposites, male-female, light-dark, pleasure-pain, high-low, spirit-matter; although insight reveals this to be an illusory effect and points instead to the holistic interplay that is actually happening. Our tendency toward a divisive black and white worldview of self and others becomes regressive and untenable, as this type of judgmental assessment can only create fragmentation and not unity. For inner healing to occur, the 8th house conveys the message that old, stagnant, and resistant psychological attitudes which are restricting the personality require elimination or rehabilitation prior to a new inner rebirth.

We have a simple choice. We either live with our wounds—infection slowly seeping from a disowned self—denying change and responsibility, and externally projecting our darkness to pollute the collective mind and then objecting at the world's painful distress. Or we acknowledge our need for healing and become committed to the transformative path, assuming responsibility to cleanse our own Augean Stables of accumulated decaying debris. We can reassemble defenses against admitting our darkness, hiding our compulsive, emotional secret self, or accept that repressive control is futile and self-defeating, and choose a way of refinement and self-reformation through introducing light to our dark side. Even the recognition that all desires, attachments, and needs require consciousness can encourage the transformation process, and may release imprisoned energies into positive and healing channels.

This is not a comfortable or pleasant process. We encounter parts of our nature that have been sadly and painfully ignored; our self-image is torn apart, our righteousness and superiority destroyed, and belief in our separate uniqueness is shattered when we reabsorb our shadow and dark side, and merge both light and darkness as one. Within this confusing process—accompanied by fear, anxiety, and panic—doors can open to reveal a higher self-perspective and new insights that usher in a permanent change in our relationship to others and life.

In our harrowing descent, we may experience a personal Hell, the consequence of ignorance and separation, which may be tasted as an eruption of inner bitter poisons, puncturing our egocentric dream and feeling like an internal psychological or physical burning, as primal forces are discharged. Like a phoenix, reborn in ashes and fire, so is the psyche renewed by the blazing heat of transformation, a crucible in which the alchemist's experiment turns personality lead into gold. We are purged, purified, consumed in this transmutation, as we let go of self-controls and surrender to the darkness of the psyche. Drowning in the deep reservoir of vital life, our response when offered the cup of self-created poison determines whether we will face death by continuing self-rejection or receive renewed life by self-acceptance. The bitter cup of sorrows can be the holy cup bearing the sweet elixir of change—the salve for wounds and pain.

The secret of integration is discovered when the separatist vision fades. Enduring the partial self's inner breakdown can lead to the breaking through of the holistic self. The path to spirit and light can be a labyrinthine passage through chaos, despair, and pain as we reenact a lifetime's defensive repressions—those abuses, rejections, humiliations, inhibitions, and the loss of power that has locked inner doors. Through outer catalysts we are forced to recollect forgotten traumas, often stimulated by sexual and emotional intimacy. We recollect encounters with authority, dependency on employers or belief-systems, or we remember parental disinterest and rejection of our childhood problems.

We may also rediscover the buried treasures of latent potential, still available for use when uncovered. By reconnecting to our power source, we reclaim autonomy, integrity, and authenticity. By being aware of how power is abused—manipulating others who are weaker and subservient—we can choose to redirect our power in ways that enable others to be empowered, we can encourage the rejection of manipulation and make a positive social contribution. We break free of compulsive and obsessive enslavements, and acquire a wiser, more tolerant attitude by comprehending our common humanity, where all share similar personality tendencies and face comparable difficulties. As the spirit of self-acceptance continues its revitalizing healing, inner pressures diminish and recede, leaving behind a sense of calm, quiet purpose.

DWELLER ON THE THRESHOLD

The occult and esoteric image for this redemptive and regenerative process is encountering the dweller on the threshold,
the dark barrier which prevents the release of spirit and inner
light. It can be useful to adopt this image during self-exploration, recognizing that the dweller is self-created; it is the residue
of an unintegrated, repressed past, formed by primal instincts,
inherited glamors and illusions, disowned aspects and the sum
total of separative thoughts, attitudes, values, beliefs, and ignorance. Collectively these build the obstructive thoughtform
of separatism which bars progress on the initiatory path,
and is composed of emotional and mental energies that hinder entrance through the "sacred portal of the inner temple."
Yet the dweller's barrier has a positive effect in that premature access to potent spiritual energies and inclusive awareness is prevented and prohibited until the seeker is ready.

As the underworld is a major path to the spirit, the 8th
house veils this guardian who protects the 8th gate mystery.
In *Glamour: A World Problem*, Alice Bailey states,

> The Dweller on the Threshold does not emerge out
> of the fog of illusion and glamour until the disciple
> is nearing the Gate of Life. Only when he can catch
> dim glimpses of the Portal of Initiation and an occa-
> sional flash of light from the Angel of the Presence,
> Who stands waiting beside that door, can he come
> to grips with the principle of *duality*, which is embod-
> ied for him in the Dweller and the Angel....You
> will stand in full awareness between these symbols
> of the pairs of opposites, with the Angel on the
> right and the Dweller on the left. May strength then
> be given to you to drive straight forward between
> these two opponents...and so may you enter into the

Presence where the two are seen as one, and naught
is known but life and deity.[3]

Between the polarity of angel-dweller and the confrontation with the principle of duality is the light of the
presence. Between the angel and dweller existing within
human nature is the cohesive, underlying presence, revealed
only through the transforming friction and conflict of apparent opposites. As the dweller faces the angel, the separate self
wanes and fades away as the inner contact is reestablished.
Esoterically, by merging the black and white lights the transcendent state is discovered. The axis of Taurus-Scorpio and
2nd-8th houses is redefined, and both opposites can profit from
their interaction. Taurean self-centered desire is transmuted
by Scorpionic spiritual aspiration, leading toward the eagle
phase, and Scorpio's experience of darkness becomes illumination in Taurus on the material level.

"The Dweller is one who stands before the gate of God,"
and this is only disclosed, "when the personality eagerly
enters into relation with the Angel, recognizes itself as the
Dweller...and begins the battle between the pairs of opposites and enters the tests of Scorpio.... These tests and trials
are ever self-initiated."[4] This esoteric symbolism of the testing of the spiritual aspirant reaffirms the prospective healing
of the dark side and the opportunity to awaken the regenerative process by uniting all aspects of our nature.

THE DARK SIDE OF 8TH HOUSE PLANETS

In our charts, the 8th house and natal Pluto and Scorpio
houses are areas of life where we can be purged of compulsive and inhibiting patterns, enabling personality rebirth

---

[3] Alice A. Bailey, *Glamour: A World Problem* (New York & London: Lucis Press, 1971),
pp. 39, 40.
[4] Alice A. Bailey, *Esoteric Astrology*. Vol. III of *A Treatise on the Seven Rays* (New
York & London: Lucis Press, 1971), p. 207.

within a context of holistic self-knowledge. In these areas of the chart, the impulse to destroy and renew is never far from awareness, and we may experience repetitive or periodic discontent in these spheres of life, whose only remedy is to change existing structures for the new to be born. This is the regenerative power of life, the ceaseless rebuilding and recreating of self and society in action. The 8th house natal planets, Pluto, and Scorpio are astrological points where we can both meet our old and future self, one held back by repressive old patterns, and one who we can become through transformation.

Any 8th house planets can signify potential for transformation and regeneration, often through their affinity with our dark side of disowned and taboo-connected psychic aspects. Working with an 8th house planet can uncover more treasure than anticipated, for their roots spread deep within the personality and can have unforeseen and surprising results. These planets may also indicate psychological inclinations toward particular types of repression, as if we find difficulty in handling these impulses correctly and prefer to avoid the challenge by denial. Alternatively, we may overemphasize and exaggerate these principles and functions in our lives, giving them an unequal share of personality power, and valuing their messages more than other planetary contributions.

The Pluto and Scorpio realm evokes a shadow-side of the personality, carrying the residue of unintegrated individual and collective "darkness." Arguably, darkness within the psyche may be an *a priori* presence from birth, a natural personality tendency, an impression received from the maternal unconscious or encoded within the parental genetic source. As we are a living interface between spirit and matter, there can be no permanent separation of light and dark; our suffering comes from trying to divide these forces, when we should be discovering how we can reconcile and unify them.

Planets suggest underlying principles and motivations existing within subconscious and unconscious levels that form the personality. In the 8th house, this indicates where collective fate and archetypal impulses intrude on the individual. Planets in this house can operate as a magnetic attractor for repressed and disowned energies, accumulating charged energies around a specific planetary principle. These planetary functions and characteristics can provide a key to understand and discharge a slowly expanding dark side within the personality. However, the difficulty of achieving this is that these planets are focal points for unconscious energies and archetypal patterns of behavior, and may prove elusive to clear perception. We may remain unaware of these planetary roles in our psyche and fail to consciously direct and use this creative power.

Astrologically, we point to an 8th house planet or planets, and state our need to become conscious of this principle and impulse, assimilate its message and discover how to integrate this into our psyche, so that it can function positively instead of binding us to the past by retaining repressed and disowned fragments of self. This planet may appear disguised as a subpersonality, trying to conduct our decisions by insistent instructions designed to either stop us from making certain choices or by pushing us into choices. We need to recognize that this planet has "intentions," and these include modifying our decision-making and experiences; the planet encourages us to "do something and to get somewhere." Whether this has negative overtones as a malevolent, tempting influence or positive ones as a guiding, benevolent influence depends on our reactions; self-acceptance liberates the energy of our dark side, while self-denial increases its virulent power. Once conscious, this planet can make great force available to a liberated personality, and will then operate as a highly energized and cohesive director in the psyche.

To "raise the dark side" we have to be transformed by exploring this planetary principle and 8th house issues. This requires investigating conditioning, instincts, repressions, disowned self, taboo-fears. It is only self-knowledge that can regenerate, heal, redeem, and redefine the self-society relationship and expiate the "ancestral sin and heresy of separateness." This quest directs us to closely examine this planetary reflection of our psyche, which is capable of renewing our life vision and providing a profound inner metanoia, a change of mind that equates to an unorthodox experience of the soul's dark night. Effort and sacrifice will be demanded before we can create a healing bridge between our fragmented selves, but in the 8th house this remains the only option available for a reunification and rebalancing to release light from darkness.

In trying to be conscious of this planetary principle and archetype manipulating our personality, we may feel pulled inward, detached from outer involvement; as we descend into the womb of the Earth Mother through Pluto's realm, we face the prospect of death or rebirth. This is symbolized in our experience of dissatisfaction, bondage, or restriction in important spheres of life, and exerts a requirement to withdraw any attachments and projections from external supports. Like Inanna, we willingly divest whatever prevents progress. In so doing, we realize how we have contributed to being "part of the problem," and if the trials are passed we can return as "part of the solution" to correct collective imbalances.

Our 8th house experiences may involve violating conscious moral codes, as part of shattering the conditioned, socialized self; this may occur as a deliberate rejection of consensus traditions, religious teachings, or by being "possessed" by powerful desires. Self-images are broken and others' opinions of us may be radically revised by our actions; we could be censured as amoral or immoral and face social disapproval and condemnation of our behavior. Yet in this friction and conflict a more autonomous self may gestate, as if we were publicly casting away an outworn personality skin.

Cultural repression is probably inevitable considering the impact of social imbalance; however, this need not continue and lives can be renewed by psychological healing. Reviewing several likely areas of inner fragmentation through planetary relationships may indicate principles that require attention and reconciliation, and in so doing begin to cleanse the dark side of the psyche. Inner change cannot occur until we consciously acknowledge the presence of conflicts and contradicting impulses, and transformation is not possible until we stop self-condemnation.

SQUARE AND OPPOSITION PLANETARY ASPECTS

Planetary aspects are channels of energy relationship between two planets, and symbolize a corresponding dynamic pattern in the psyche and personality matrix. The types of aspect especially associated with stressful tendencies are squares and oppositions, where a discordant interaction between two planets reflects innate psychological tensions. Squares and oppositions often indicate the presence of internalized conditioning and possible repressive inclinations, and may direct attention toward actual or latent personality fracture as a consequence of an inability to retain psychic unity or to integrate disparate needs and motivations. Due to their potentially restrictive influences on inner harmony and wholeness, squares and oppositions need attention and awareness, so that a healing adjustment can be taken which minimizes their stress-production and allows obstructed energy to be released for positive applications.

THE 8TH HOUSE SQUARE ASPECTS

The exact square is a 90° aspect, and an 8° orb is commonly allowed for its range of astrological influence. From the 8th house, squares are most often made to the 5th and 11th houses, and suggest a liability to experience interactive crises between these houses of life experience. The 8th house themes are added to by 5th house creativity, love affairs, pleasure seeking, speculation, and display of talents and ideas, and by 11th house identification with group ideals and social endeavors, communal creativity, and reformative activity.

The square is often experienced as two antagonistic and conflicting inner voices, feelings of being split, incomplete, confused by a need to reconcile contradictory tendencies that are apparently pulling in different directions and refusing to coexist. A frustrating and irritating tension results from these clashing parts of self which is unresolvable unless adjustment is achieved through greater self-awareness. Squares have a frictional quality as psychic disharmony rubs abrasively and causes internal discomfort. To ameliorate these conflicts, crises are generated that often force choices and decisions that produce important turning points in life and self-development. Squares can be connected to the experience of repetitive life problems which may be met as relationship failures, and will continue unless we learn lessons and new approaches to attitudes, expectations, and intimate behavior.

The square tends to draw psychological energies inward, forming stressful points which often imply the existence of subconscious protective barriers accumulating since childhood, and around which the personality has structured primary attitudes, values, and belief-systems. These defenses may act as psychological supports or "patches" over still raw and vulnerable wounds, preventing evidence of their living influence except through irrational and regressive reactions, often revealed when key buttons are pressed and habitual protective behavior patterns leap into automatic action.

Self-denial, disownment, and repressive controls are the building blocks of these defenses, hiding negativity and unresolved conflicts. Repression can come from parental, social, and self-image pressures, where low esteem, inadequacy, guilt, shame, inhibition, mistrust, and caution are unconsciously assembled to create a restrictive worldview. This may be marked by either acquiescence or struggles with external authority, and by personal desires colliding with consensus attitudes, with possible social rejection if people do not conform, posing problems of either self-denial or assertion against majority opinion.

Inadvertently, conditioned attitudes may erect unconscious barriers in our psyche that repetitively obstruct a consciously chosen path. The inner conflicts indicated by square aspects hint at lessons that cannot be avoided, inevitable crises that wait for our arrival during life. If we are to accomplish our potential, we have to deal with these, or pay the price in suffering and frustration when we ignore the challenge to progress. Squares are perceived as either stumbling blocks or building blocks in the psyche; our attitude to them determines whether they become impassable barriers of inertia or provide a momentum for advance and self-development.

If creatively and constructively approached, the square can be transformed into a source of motivation, producing impetus to initiate positive change. Instead of dissipating energy through ceaseless inner battles, a determined inner effort to resolve planetary-psychological disunion may ignite the fires of renewal. If reconciliation is achieved, the square becomes a channel for a transformative energy to diminish frustration and tension by increasing inner harmony, and redirecting liberating energies to attain personal aims. Obstacles can be overcome, and the square offers an opportunity to restructure the personality, equivalent to a rebirth of potential and renewal of life-direction.

In square aspects, planets remain in an agitated relationship unless we become aware as to how these principles operate within us. The tension between two planets can create periodic psychological upheaval, increasing the likelihood of nervous disorders, crisis-confrontations and undercurrents of fear, and anxiety disturbing stability. This friction between diverse impulses polarizes into two monologues with neither planet acknowledging or listening to the other. Both insist on their autonomy of aims, behavior, and primacy of need, rooted in individually defensive postures—refusing to cooperate, and to be synthesized.

The consequence of this inner adversarial stance is that mutual frustration, interference, and rejection develops, where both planets unconsciously challenge and block the intentions and contribution of the other planetary principle to psychic wholeness. It is often the slower-moving planet that restrains the faster-moving planet of the square, and dismisses or rejects that particular principle, distorting and diminishing its natural contribution; also, the applying aspect tends to be stronger than the separating aspect.

With squares, the psychological inclination is to either repress their uncomfortable activity by denying these energies, or to express them with excessive assertion. Both are imbalanced, posing problems of either a limiting inhibition or relieving friction by obsessive activity. Most individuals temporarily deal with squares by emphasizing one of the two planets, developing that principle exclusively to the detriment of the other planetary principle. This can have mixed results, although it is an imbalancing action. For some, this planetary emphasis can clarify direction and focus, offering an exit from an inner impasse, and enable concentrated energy to develop specific qualities, skills, and talents associated with the favored planet; through this, drive and motivation may be released, although this may have a compulsive power. Alternatively, the imbalance may imply the presence of latent obsessive complexes emerging from the unexpressed planetary principle, perhaps by attempting to dominate and possess the unconscious mind, subtly weaving its secret influence to regain control, or seeping energy into building the dark side personality.

If the square is between cardinal signs, then its influence is often felt as crises within home, family, love, or work, as if its dynamic energy emerges into external manifestation through the effect of individual attitudes in these spheres of relationship. The cardinal square type is desire-driven, stimulated by excitement and challenge, and demands satisfaction to reduce inner discomfort. We have to act in some way to diminish this tension, often provoking disruptive events by our actions until the square is resolved; we may become "our own worst enemy," a consequence of lacking self-awareness, impulsive and ill-considered actions, loss of moderation and perspective through selfish intent, and insufficient concern for others. Forethought, evaluation, cooperation, and compromise may be needed to adjust these tendencies.

The fixed square strengthens determination and willpower, focused on achieving desires and ambitions, and applying a stubborn persistence to gradually wear down obstacles. Power is directed to shatter frustrations, although clarity is required as to the nature of actual desires; creating suitable channels to express this slowly building energy is necessary for success. External controls and compromise are often rejected by autonomous impulses, and greater sensitivity to others' desires and needs may minimize any exaggerated self-centered preoccupation.

Mutable squares may have a restless, vacillating quality, where changeable desires and intentions may scatter energy into diverse interests and fluctuating application. A tendency to be overly adaptable and impressionable can displace a personality center, and an insecure and nervously active mind can be over-stimulated by the impact of ideas and relationship experiences. For stability, commitment and purpose are needed, and a diminution of external influences affecting personality equilibrium.

We need to explore squares from our 8th house and elsewhere in the natal chart, because these hold opportunities to discharge restrictive patterns and release energies that enable growth by breaking down obstacles in our way. The square demands that we take decisive actions and struggle to heal inner discomforts and frustrations; we are not meant to passively accede to them, but are expected to progress toward psychological wholeness by reorientating attitudes, and by how we select and experience these planetary principles operating through the personality. If we continue to suffer from an unresolved, abrasive inner state, then this is simply the inevitable outcome of ignorance; we are not fated to remain discontent, but evading effort will ensure that we will only create future dissatisfaction.

Issues that induce crisis and change from the 8th-5th-11th house squares can include: needs for leisure, relaxation and play; needs for creative expression; needs for romance and love affairs, emotional and sexual excitement; needs for intimate union; needs for a specific type of partner as a complementary personality; needs for children; needs to gamble, risk, act adventurously and speculatively; needs to belong to groups; needs to reform society and be committed to progressive social causes; needs for humanitarian ideals, attitudes, and actions; needs for friendships; needs for goal-setting, ambitions, and determining how aims can be fulfilled.

Possible ways to integrate these can include: participation in humanitarian pressure groups that are creatively committed to constructive social transformation; sharing with friends, partner, or groups any individual creative projects with social significance that are inspired and benefit from mutual encouragement; building productive and growth-promoting friendships, cultivating mutual assistance with similar-minded people; exploring romance and love, taking emotional risks in a search for intensity and union; choosing a partner who shares compatible social aims, beliefs, or creative commitments for mutual support and enthusiasm.

8TH HOUSE OPPOSITION ASPECTS

Carl Jung declared that, "unless the opposites are constellated and brought to consciousness, they can never be united."[5] This is the problem facing us with both squares and oppositions. The exact opposition is a 180° aspect, and an 8° orb is com-

---

[5] Carl G. Jung, cited in Tracy Marks, *Planetary Aspects* (Sebastapol, CA: CRCS, 1987), p. 163.

monly allowed for its range of astrological influence. From the 8th house, oppositions are most often made to the 2nd house, six signs apart.

Oppositions polarize two planetary principles that find problems in sharing common ground. Both principles and impulses remain distinct and separate, and the individual can have difficulties in coordination or establishing a complementary resonance between them. Tensions exist as both pull simultaneously, yet not together or in the same direction; messages contradict and choices juggle with two equally relevant but diverse perspectives. This psychological stress may result in extreme, inconsistent and contrary behavior, often externally projected in a struggle for balance played out within relationships.

The opposition's effect is more complex to determine than the square, as these are at work within the shifting interplay of self and other. Similar to the square, the individual may identify more strongly with one planet and tends to exclude, neglect, and undervalue the other one; or may swing like a pendulum between one planetary extreme to the other, feeling unsettled, confused, paralyzed and divided by stressful conflict. Both planets need recognition, and their strengths and virtues need equal respect and expression. If the balance between these two planets is disturbed, then stability is undermined. Like the square, the planets, signs, and houses involved indicate possible sources of imbalance, conflict and lack of integration; they require attention to restore a positive expression of psychological tendencies. Both challenging aspects offer the potential for increased awareness of planetary principles and corresponding psychological behavior patterns.

Exact and close oppositions connect signs that are natural polar opposites, implying that both need a mutual contribution of each others' energies and qualities for an effective joint performance. If integrated, both planets work together to benefit the whole psyche; each planetary function operates smoothly and without interference or distortion.

Some individuals recognize both planetary/psychological principles and needs, yet are unable to see how these can be productively united, and fall victim to indecision. There may be a fluctuating emphasis of changing planetary "controls" rather than both working together in harmony. One planet may be considered unacceptable, denied and disowned, seeing one as "good" and the other "bad." The neglected, undervalued planet is then forced into the unconscious by repressive controls, leaving the only option to declare its still existing presence through unconscious compulsive motives. Signs of compulsive behavior are often channeled through excessive demands made on others, perhaps the assertion of self-centered desires and willpower which interferes with relationship harmony by manipulative tendencies and exploiting situations for personal gain. Relationship stability and security is disturbed by separative action and inner discord.

With the opposition, the undervalued planet is often psychologically projected on to an external screen, usually reflected back to us by other people and by our worldview. This dissociated planetary principle is unrecognized as a fragment of our nature, and by projection we lose psychological unity; we are incomplete, something is lacking, pieces of the psychic jigsaw of identity have been displaced. These qualities, strengths, and principles are misperceived as personally lacking and present only in others or in the world. This often stimulates a search for meaning and wholeness to reclaim our fragmented self by reowning those unconsciously projected qualities.

The opposition phenomenon of projection is the psyche's way to create a mirror for self-observation, a context to realize our role in shaping reality. Experiencing this self-other relationship becomes a self-encounter; few are immune from this process of projection. We meet our disowned self reflected by others who "perform" this planetary role and function in our lives.

It is an astrological truism that the more we reject, obstruct, and deny inner tendencies, the more we unconsciously and magnetically attract these back into our lives through others. We may be drawn into relationships—intimate and social—where we contact people who display characteristics of our rejected opposition planet; this may activate an outer dispute or antagonistic exchange which repeats our failure to accept and integrate certain qualities. An outer "battle" may reenact an unresolved inner battle; our adversary may express these qualities in ways that counteract and collide with the overidentified planet of our opposition. Relationships affected by opposition projections may become forums for stressful conflict and personality impasses, as objectivity is lost by the possession of irrational and compulsive forces. The more that we deny this rejected planet, the more it appears in the outer world and through our relationships; we strengthen its secret life, and we may "become the thing we fight the most."

If there are several 8th house oppositions (or squares), these feelings of being pulled in different directions are amplified, and become even more crucial to resolve. These stresses may reduce effective action and delay decision-making, perhaps increasing vulnerability to others. Relationships are often where the stress is discharged and they become a source of impressionable manipulation; reluctance to make commitments may be observed, and a dependency bias on partners, or compromise to avoid conflict may also be symptomatic of evasion. You may rely on a partner to embody a displaced strength, quality, or principle for you.

Issues of independence, dependency, and interdependency may pose dilemmas in relationship projections, and the need is to awaken awareness of the self-other relationship. Personality qualities, contradictions, or complexes are exposed through intimate partnership, and we are faced with making those adjustments necessary for harmonious living and sharing. Objectivity and attention to others' needs are important for insight into opposition activity; we can withdraw projections superimposed on others, and in that process profound insights may occur as we discover how to reintegrate ourself, deepen intimate rapport and diminish separative attitudes.

The projected opposition planet may be the slower moving one, or one of the group which resonate closely with the unconscious mind—Moon, Mars, Uranus, Neptune, or Pluto; we may experience the discordant rupture of inner voices insisting how we should behave in distinction to how we want to behave. The other planets—Sun, Mercury, Venus, Jupiter, and Saturn—may attempt to impose their controls; yet each can mutually reinforce different planetary needs and may function most effectively by a seesaw alternate concentration on satisfying both planetary requirements. Until we are capable of giving alternate priority to each planet, by either consciously asserting each specific principle or devising a means to actively express each simultaneously, we will be liable to division, which can confuse purpose, divert energy, break down commitment and limit decisive action. We may endure swings of interest and motivation, as both planets seek to attract our attention.

The extremist bias of oppositions can be restrained by conscious regulation and use of the two planetary energies. We need to monitor how our oppositions are operating, and the degree to which we favor one and disengage the other. Neither planet should retain supremacy, and a reconciling balance can be established which naturally regulates their interaction. Neither is allowed to predominate or become antagonistic; they exist as a creative, interdependent balance, like the yin-yang within the Tao.

Resolving each natal opposition promotes awareness, releases imprisoned or misapplied energies, diminishes projections, and renews relationships, allowing increased understanding, and cooperative and creative compromise to assist harmonization. Decisiveness and directional clarity is improved, and more options and opportunities become available; additional personal strengths and qualities can emerge, and self-direction is possible. Consciousness expands to include greater personality complexity, contradiction, and ambiguity, introducing insight to create a meaningful synthesis of previously irreconcilable psychological tendencies. Inner harmony, and balance replaces contention once self-acceptance reclaims the disowned self. In this sense, working with oppositions and squares can help a spiritual integration to develop, one which resonates to the Tantric philosophy of inclusiveness and embracing the dark side.

The opposition directs attention to two areas of life that require balancing, adjustment, and synthesis. There can be feelings of antipathy to one of the two houses involved. In the 8th-2nd house axis, either may be favored by the individual, although the majority may feel more at ease with the social familiarity of 2nd house experiences rather than the more intense and complex 8th house concerns.

For some on spiritual and self-development paths, this polarity may be experienced in terms of "spirit or matter," inwardly attracted toward the 8th house mysteries and a corresponding distaste and disinterest in 2nd house materialism. However, the path of wholeness is to integrate both of these together, equally expressing each type of experience, and creating an interdependent relationship between them. This may be by a conscious decision to work with each independently and alternately, so that neither is denied and ignored, or by ideally developing a way to include both simultaneously, perhaps by discovering how to utilize money, resources, and possessions in ways that embody spiritual growth; more people in the human potential movement are now exploring ways to do this, some through business and right livelihood projects. The spiritualization of money attitudes are being redefined by the increasingly popular concepts of prosperity consciousness.

With the 8th-2nd house opposition, the issues that often induce crisis and change can include questions related to the following:

1) How we earn a satisfactory and sufficient income;

2) Our attitudes toward work, money, possessions, and purchasing desires;

3) How we determine our actual needs;

4) How we can creatively and productively utilize our talents and resources;

5) The degree of displaced self-identification with possessions and affluence;

6) Our emotional needs for financial security and survival fears;

7) How we utilize and share our joint income and possessions;

8) How money shapes our self-belief and self-esteem;

9) How joint finances can be used to assist others' needs and development;

10) How money can provide opportunities for rebirth.

Possible ways to integrate these issues can include:

1) Directing personal resources and talents into right livelihood projects—work that increases satisfaction and growth;

2) Assisting others to exploit latent talent and creativity;

3) Utilizing prosperity to increase opportunities for self-development;

4) Appreciating abundance, and exploring the paths of prosperity consciousness, restructuring value systems and beliefs about reality;

5) Using finance and loans for business ventures capable of expanding your growth and creativity;

6) Directing money toward self-development courses, and increasing leisure time to pursue study, meditation, psychotherapy to resolve inner conflicts;

7) Reconsidering your use of money in terms of world/ecological need;

8) Confronting death and the transiency of things for value-transformation;

9) Exploring the fact of universal interdependence and relationship.

MOTIVATING CHANGE THROUGH PAINFUL SELF-ENCOUNTER

Instead of viewing squares and oppositions negatively, shrinking away from their implicit lessons and frustrating interference, we can reperceive them as opportunities for growth and renewing change. They may pose painful questions and experiences for us, but this veils the regenerative prospect which they motivate us to seek, if only as an escape from stress. These aspects contain both "the problem and the solution," a hurdle and stepping stone; our attitude dictates whether we remain blocked or move onward.

Squares and oppositions challenge and provoke inner and outer crises, inciting us to examine our habitual behavior, attitudes, values, and worldview by pressures that are distressing, and disquieting; for some, these can ruin their lives or make increased suffering inevitable, yet awareness makes a resolution possible, breaking through unconscious, restricting personality patterns.

However, choosing change and wanting to grow requires determined and prolonged effort; transformation rarely occurs overnight, and the inertia of personality and society makes momentum difficult to achieve. The bright prospects and optimism of human potential techniques are extremely appealing, but similar to the spiritual quest, the testing first step becomes a difficult barrier. This is the conscious recognition and acceptance that, "I am discontent and dissatisfied; my life is not fulfilling, not properly working in all spheres of experience, and I feel incomplete, something is missing, and I lack meaning, direction and purpose. Isn't there more in life?" We have to admit the fact of our discomfort, and inner malaise; the search commences when we face this state and refuse to avoid its existence.

Self-evasion is no longer a tenable option. The feeling of a lost center grows more acute; our confusing, complex contradictions sound an inner cacophonous babel, and as our self-concealment strategies crumble, we stare into an empty void, apparently the source of our discontent.

What feelings spill out from this psychic darkness, the underworld of our repressions, disownment and rejections? We may feel lost, denuded of meaning and life direction, cast adrift in an uncaring universe, unable to grasp fulfillment. We may feel helpless, victim of others' decisions, manipulated by our dependencies, obsessions, and compulsions, possessed by addictions and desires that are never satisfied. We may suffer erratic, fluctuating emotions and moods that destabilize and interfere with relationships. We may futilely defend a loss of self-esteem and self-belief, divesting ourselves of potential and ability to change, seeing our future as one of continued failure. Physical vitality may be lowered, and health may be afflicted by dispiriting illness (including hypochondriac or psychosomatic symptoms). We may feel imprisoned by immovable barriers and limitations "imposed" by the world and by obligations to others; options diminish and alternatives fade through circumstances. We may become self-critical, whipping ourselves for our failure of "being human," condemning past actions and mistakes, and never forgiving ourselves. We may become self-condemnatory, rejecting and disowning parts, casting them into the darkness. We may feel trapped by our repetitive lifestyle, unable to break free of a self-created prison. Our relationships may fail to satisfy or collapse in disarray. Fears and anxieties may crowd out opportunities, narrowing life-experience. Inner and outer conflicts proliferate. We may compare our latent potential with our actual accomplishments and be shocked by the broad gap; we may have lost sight of our ambitions and goals. We may realize our failure in living our assumed values, ideals and principles, observing that we do not conform to them and only give lip-service to our beliefs.

The list can continue. This is the first encounter with the inner darkness, and for some, psychological "drowning" seems the only escape, yet others manage to transform this into an inspiration for radical change and releasing creative and regenerative energies. As full as the void is of "darkness" this is also the source of a transforming light. This descent into a psychic wasteland can renew lives, expanding perspective and understanding, providing new paths to manifest potential and enable self-healing. By redeeming and eliminating unsuitable behavior patterns and attitudes, a psychological rebirth can be experienced. Clarification of aims and desires can be rediscovered and a new self-image be created.

Important steps in this direction can be taken when we consciously deal with squares and oppositions in our natal charts. Actually attempting this can encourage great changes in our lives and personal wholeness, and should be undertaken by every astrologer who turns his work into a self-development path, rather than it remaining just an intellectual interpretative exercise. We need to synthesize, resolve, and constructively utilize the power of squares and oppositions in order to increase wholeness and harmonize the multiple inner voices of our planetary energies. In contemplating planetary aspects we can simultaneously examine our conditioning attitudes. By making a creative effort, we can reunite disparate parts of our psyche by working with the planetary reflections, especially reintegrating planets involved in squares and oppositions.

Each planet has positive and negative expressions (similar to signs and how we deal with the issues of each house), and most demonstrate a mixture of tendencies. Squares and oppositions suggest that these planets are out of synchronization; they may act compulsively, unconsciously and fail to function effectively—perhaps through lack of attention or rejection. Unintegrated planets always require bringing something back into line by a holistic perspective of the "multi-self" that planetary dynamics reveal.

Each planet needs its principle and strengths creatively and constructively expressed; each planet's needs must be met or else a nagging and interfering presence may ruin the contribution of our other planetary selves and distort psychological harmony. We need to listen carefully to each planet without criticism, judgment and condemnation, as each is a valuable part of our nature; none should be allowed to dominate, each needs to be integrated into the planetary group. If a planet is retrograde, then its expression and activity is likely to be more introverted and unconscious, and this should be taken into account when considering how best to evoke its higher potential.

Squares and oppositions attract key life experiences which—if we are alert—reflect important issues and realizations that we need to encounter; their inner incompleteness draws us into situations where we may become whole, even if this offers only painful recognition of a need for reconciliation. Through conflict the psyche attempts to awaken us to self-healing.

We need to consider each planet's ability for compatibility, its strengths and how it can purposefully cooperate with another planet. We need to evaluate planets, signs, and houses in natal relationship, and only when we positively express these energies are all voices content and productive, and activities truly satisfy. We may discover that the square and opposition planets resonate to their rulership of other houses, and that by association these may provide keys to resolving specific square/opposition issues. We may discover that any sextile, trine, or conjunction to square/opposition planets may also provide keys to their resolution, or are activated into greater effectiveness once we have creatively reconciled challenging aspects.

Space prohibits an in-depth look into specific square/opposition planetary aspects, but for wholeness we must take advantage of their potential, and raise our dark side into the light. Challenging aspects are a source to transform our lives, and what may start as an apparently irresolvable problem or psychological wound may metamorphosize into our greatest strength and achievement. This is the ageless task of the wounded healer; to confront our wounds and then heal them.

7 Planetary Guides and Inner Contacts

ONE OF THE LESS EXAMINED 8TH house associations is that of sensitivity and psychic gifts, with the potential reconnection to inclusive and spiritual levels of our being, perhaps through the mediation of "inner contacts." Astrological planets, signs, elements, and houses are symbolic representatives of our inner psyche; through working with these we may discover the holistic dimension.

For individuals whose 8th house is emphasized in their charts, a natural gravitation toward esoteric and psychological studies may be evident; certainly esoteric 8th house matters will be active in their psyche, but some with socially conditioned responses may choose to deny these. As esotericism remains an almost taboo subject, public attitudes display disquiet and unease, confused even more by fundamentalist Christian groups equating serious esoteric inquiry with Satanism; indeed, their adversarial worldview sees satanic practices as the root of all social evils. Those individuals who have an open mind toward esoteric exploration may seek emotional security through esoteric knowledge. By insight into the "spiritual laws of living" an inner peace may be attained, often by including a belief in reincarnational rebirth offering evolutionary progress over multiple lives. Contemporary psychology approaches this same need by the route of psychotherapeutic investigation of personality conditioning; both adhere to the Delphic injunction of "Know Thyself" at the entrance to the famous oracular temple.

This individual response to this 8th house opportunity to delve deeper into hidden realms indicates the degree of personal attraction to mysteries, taboos, and forbidden experiences; some are eager to taste the unknown, while others look away and retreat. This is a similar reaction to exploring 8th house issues for self-insight and with clients, and is not always welcomed or accepted.

It can be a strange, formidable journey through the gate of rebirth, and we may require support and assistance traveling through Pluto's kingdom and in returning to our world. To guide us on this rite of passage, we can evoke a planetary guide for a companion to walk with us.

Each planet is a living energy—a part of the psyche—and integral to our nature, connected to even deeper archetypes in the collective psyche. Ancient wisdom perceived the planets as gods and goddesses, and while we often dismiss this pantheistic doctrine, their power and influence is still intact and can be contactable. For those familiar with magical traditions, working with the astrological planet's energies can be combined with "the assumption of God-forms" often practiced in ritual magic; this can be extremely powerful and open psychic channels to archetypal forces and the overshadowing or temporary possession by specific gods or goddesses. Such experiments are for the trained ritual magician, operating in his or her carefully defined "universe" and with regard for contacting formulae and apt representative magical implements. Some feel uncomfortable with this type of approach and cannot conceive of various gods and goddesses existing in less tangible levels; often these are human attempts at identifying contacts and conveying energies which lie beyond normal human perception and yet can be experienced by sensitive attunement.

It is not my intention to examine the invocation-evocation of inner gods in the *Gate of Rebirth*; this is a specialist magical practice that requires careful handling and a firm grasp of self-insight and psychological dynamics. Any who explore their 8th house gate will invariably receive their own experience of this interaction in a less forced manner, simply through awakening attention to these issues in their life. However, each planetary god or goddess can reveal their nature and aspect of the rebirth mystery to the seeker; even one touch is sufficient to transform a life, because each 8th house planet promises renewal.

This house offers an opportunity for a mystical experience, contacting planes of reality that our five senses cannot ordinarily reach. An activated and integrated 8th house can increase prospects of communication with discarnate guides and entities. The modern interest in channeling is a sign of a collective reaction, especially during this period of Pluto in Scorpio (1984-1995, approximately) which animates 8th house affairs. We observe an abundance of current guides and channels endeavoring to educate their listeners; and we can only contemplate Jung's relevant comment that "the multiplicity of gods correspondeth to the multiplicity of man."[1] Indeed, Scorpio has been described as the symbolic gate through which Avatars are born, those mouthpieces of collective wisdom and evolutionary agents; increasingly the world is being flooded by them!

Planets in the 8th house can stimulate spiritual awakening through renewal and rebirth; the depth that this process will reach depends on individual response and cooperation. A powerful longing for emotional stability and inner healing may be resisted and denied, or may serve to motivate a genuine search. The 8th house polarity of self and other can easily function in terms of teacher-pupil, and any natal planet can assume a teaching role whenever approached with a spirit of sincere inquiry.

If there is a single 8th house planet, then the "teaching" received will concentrate on lessons related to that planetary quality and energy active in the personality and life-experiences. If there are several natal planets, then different lessons

---

[1] Carl G. Jung, cited in Margo Anand, *The Art of Sexual Ecstacy* (London: Aquarian Press, 1990), p. 239.

can be received, and these will span a broad range of possible insights, expressions, and applications. Any 8th house transiting planets can similarly be invited to share their lessons with us, not imposed on a passive personality, but as a dialogue and creative exchange. One interesting point is that due to 8th house sensitivity to more subtle energies and atmospheres, we have a heightened response to this planetary activity in ourselves, in others, and in our environmental atmosphere. We sense or "pick it up" more easily and have increased occasions to distinguish how it is functioning and affecting inner states and relationships; through attention, alone, we can learn a great deal.

SUBPERSONALITIES AND INNER CONTACTS

Contemporary psychological techniques find that working with *subpersonalities* can be rewarding and deepen understanding and integration. Psychosynthesis, gestalt, and transactional analysis explore personality by this approach. Connecting astrology to subpersonality inquiry produces evocative parallels, especially between planet and sign correlations to these "subjective characters," and a path of development could be built by aligning with planets via subpersonalities.

Each planet has a specific role and function in the psyche, contributing to the matrix of our lives. A planet assumes an identity and temperament reflective of its nature and quality, and can announce and exert its presence as one of the multi-selves existing within us. Planets can emerge as "the impulsive self," "the cautious self," "the planning self," "the future self," "the past self," and the path to wholeness needs to unite these and several others into a collaborative and cooperative group. For most people, the planetary subpersonalities are often felt as a feuding, disharmonious collection of conflicting impulses, fracturing personality cohesion by insisting on moving in disparate directions.

Subpersonalities may echo planetary aspects in their interaction; each can attempt to be autonomous, demanding that their needs are met; some are submissive to other, more assertive voices; some are disobedient, refusing group responsibility and control; others are willing to cooperate. We hear these diverse monologues emanating from different parts of our psyche as a continual background noise underlying thoughts and feelings. Some subpersonalities are shaped by previous times of crisis, forced out into "existence" by inner stress; perhaps as a release-valve, or as a quality or function needed at the time, an ability to endure, or for self-protection. Some are shaped by previous social conditioning, programs of reality, self-images and instructions of suitable behavior that run automatically like a manic tape-loop ceaselessly repeating in every similar situation.

We may observe these patterns in the unconscious repetition of certain types of experiences; we may continually select unsuitable lovers, creating inevitable emotional pain by our choices. We make similar mistakes until we listen to a teaching indicating a need to renew inappropriate old partner images. The divorce of parents during childhood may introduce a pattern which equates loss, pain, and rejection with love and marriage, and this may unconsciously operate during later adult relationships, ruining confidence and trust in a partner and introducing conflicting feelings into intimacy. In most cases of subpersonality identification an affinity to an astrological planet can be established. Through chart interpretations such personality patterns, themes or messages can be highlighted and perhaps identify possible subpersonality types; or, conversely, the combination of life stories can be later related to natal astrological patterns and specific planetary activity for additional therapeutic insight.

We can consider each planet as possessing positive contributions to our lives, seeing them as a friend or guide waiting to give us a special gift. No planet deliberately intends to harm us, even though their effects may sometimes be restrictive and harmful. Communication can be established by "dialogue" with planetary subpersonalities reflecting different parts of ourself—different needs, intentions, and desires. Each planet can act in either a positive, negative, or neutral manner, and they all strive for our conscious attention and expression.

The first step is to identify each sphere of planetary activity and function, by discerning prominent traits, attitudes, values, aims, interests, behavior, and worldview that have affinity to a specific planet. Our astrological knowledge should enable this recognition to be relatively easy. Then we observe how this planetary subpersonality is acting in our lives, and what type of message it is communicating; this is especially vital when the messages conveyed have negative and limiting repercussions, or prevent our progress and growth by the continued repetition of an old attitudinal pattern which is no longer apt and requires replacement or renewal.

In remembering the 8th house underworld descent, we can incorporate a suitable image for our theater of contact and inner psychodrama. We have already identified a planet with which we need dialogue, and as this will emerge from the unconscious mind, we can visualize a dark cave before us. Above the cave we can imaginatively project the glyph of the planetary subpersonality requested to contact us, and see this shining brightly as the subpersonality comes to the entrance. (Note: we are not descending into this cave, as this can stimulate darker images, uneasiness, feelings of fear, or loss of power.) We may have already determined a name-image for this subpersonality—the critic, the mystic, the priest, casanova, the devil, the rebel, the victim, the martyr, the tyrant, the optimist, the artist, the dreamer, the idealist, the frightened child, the explorer, the fool, the procrastinator—and we need to feel an emotional connection to this inner voice and part of ourself.

Visualize, feel, or sense the presence of this subpersonality at the cave entrance; this is the meeting place where dialogue can occur, a fusion of light and darkness where both feel safe. We need to ask what message this planetary subpersonality is trying to communicate, what it wants from us, what need we are ignoring to cause its agitation. It is essential to hear the subpersonality's point of view; if we continue rejecting its aid, then that source will contribute only problems and trouble. Similar to ourselves, subpersonalities can either evolve and be regenerated through integration, or degenerate down an involutionary arc through additional fragmentation. Their presence adds to interior richness, but if disunited, they can disperse personality stability; when we approach them with awareness and attentive respect, communication improves and unity is revived. Sometimes "unfreezing" a planetary subpersonality is necessary to unlock a planetary energy to contribute to our lives, and this can occur through regular internal dialogues; like people, subpersonalities do not enjoy being ignored.

We can deal with specific problems by this technique. First define a problem or area of lack. Decide which planet(s) is most likely to be creating or influencing this situation. Visualize the cave and wait for a sense of contact. Imagine the subpersonality name-image and thank it for coming, and for its contributing role and good intentions in your life. Ask what it is trying to accomplish now, what need it requires you to meet and how it wishes to be creatively expressed. State your appreciation of its endeavors and suggest a new task for this contact—a higher vision that requires a new contribution—and how this planet can benefit you by operating in a different way and releasing the old pattern. Agree to honor its needs more consistently in the future, in exchange for assistance to create your new vision and new self. Give thanks in anticipation of its future help. Sometimes experimenting with this process before sleep can be interesting and productive, for ideas, insights, and guidance can enter your consciousness through dreams, or during the next few days. For these techniques to be most effective, awareness must be maintained, or else subtle prompts may be missed.

There may be conflicts between the power of a past self (Moon or Saturn, for example) frustrating the aims of a future self (Jupiter or Uranus) where the problem is the transition from a limiting way of life into a more expansive adventure, much like the one faced by people when introduced to new age concepts and transformative attitudes! A dialogue between the two distinct subpersonalities is necessary, as neither is adequately communicating and collaborating. In this case, we may visualize inviting both to the cave meeting place, initially asking each to "present their case," and then having both there when explaining your own needs and intentions, requesting them to construct a compromise and work together to further your progress. The past self may realize that its messages of fear, anxiety, and caution are not simply protective now but are also inhibitive and regressive, and the future self may realize that the new lifestyle has to be introduced more slowly than an impulsive rush for change may prefer; together, both can evolve a way to ensure safe development and become supportive guides. Inner stability can increase as both past and future selves work in mutual understanding.

Another approach can be particularly useful when trying to resolve square and opposition aspects. We invite the two planets to the meeting place, and create a context for their dialogue. The first planet (our 8th house one) initially states its needs, desires, messages, feelings, wants, ambitions, and then the second planet does similarly. Then we ask the first planet to explain its response, perception, and point of view to the second planet's position, and then vice versa, the second commenting on the first planet's presentation. Then we request both to devise a way for greater cooperation, and understanding between them, and to diminish their conflict, because if continued neither can ever be fulfilled, and this friction is having detrimental effects in your life.

By such playful, imaginative, and educational visualization practices, we can gain considerable insight through internal psychodramas; planets and subpersonalities offer scope for varied creative endeavors, which can provide a basis for stories, music, art, and theater. In our alchemical path to transform ourselves, one reoccurring motif is always the quest to unify the opposites. We can develop a regular subpersonality contact, where we consult with each planet individually and then as a collective group for a "status report." Or we can highlight areas where we have felt unsettled—not fully integrated—and request greater activity by specific planets. We can integrate this with progressions, solar-lunar returns, transit activity, or we can approach a planetary subpersonality for dialogue when a transit takes it into a new house. This psychological educative game can have many permutations.

We can discover how to integrate "head" planets (Mercury, Saturn, Uranus) and "heart" planets (Moon, Venus, Neptune); or the assertive planets (Sun, Mars, Jupiter, Uranus) with the receptive, blending and compromising planets which may otherwise be overly dominated (Moon, Venus, Neptune). Balance and integration are the psyche's objectives. We may awaken our prosperity self through an 8th house-2nd house opposition or our idealist self through an 8th house-11th house square. Every planet and aspect can participate in a subpersonality dialogue if we choose.

Evoking the presence of Uranus as a subpersonality can be highly effective, as this is exalted in Scorpio. Uranus can release a charge of potent energy that initiates a death-rebirth process in our lives. Old restrictive and outworn forms that hinder progress are erased, and Uranus ensures that new opportunities become available through periodic change. Materialistic bonds are weakened, and a regenerative force stirs within the individual life. While this may appear initially destructive, it is really an evolutionary power and can be summoned when obstacles appear insuperable, although it may be wise to request that the touch of this Uranian contact and subpersonality is restricted to a specific area in need of change, or else the whole lifestyle may be suddenly uprooted.

For those skilled in meditation and visualization, astrology can provide many symbolic images for exploration and insight, and identifying each subpersonality can help to strip away the multiple masks of the self.

Planetary natal and transit positions can be referred to in Rudhyar's reformulated Sabian symbols for contemplative imagery.[2] Evaluating a natal chart by reference to these alone can provide food for thought, especially in the cross formed by the horizontal and vertical chart axis, and the images for each planetary position. If dealing with squares and oppositions, the symbol for their midpoint may suggest a possible route for reconciliation.

Alternative techniques capable of reflecting inner states are worth exploring, and can include tarot and qabalistic pathworking, which have numerous astrological correspondences; rune-readings; karma-cards—based on astrology; the Star + Gate system (which can elicit intuitional insight into personal issues) generate new perspectives, aid in decision-making, develop intuition and creativity, suggest better relationships, career expression, and assist achieving goals. The wide availability of subliminal self-help tapes and inner journeys are also helpful in transforming stuck psychological programs, and can be used in conjunction with subpersonality work; i.e., Sanaya Roman's *Becoming a World Server* or *Awakening the Prosperity Self*[3] can be combined with 8th-11th-2nd house square and opposition resolution.

So, instead of complaining about that baleful Saturn natal or transit aspect that's restricting your success and world recognition of your genius, why not set up an inner meeting and have a dialogue with Saturn, who only wants to be your planetary friend!

---

[2] Dane Rudhyar, *An Astrological Mandala: The Cycle of Transformation and its Symbolic Phases* (New York: Vintage Books, 1974).

[3] Sanaya Roman tapes: "Becoming a World Server," and "Awakening the Prosperity Self," are produced by LuminEssence Productions, P. O. Box 19117, Oakland, CA 94619.

8 The Initiation of Death— The Process of Renewal

DEATH. IT IS A STARK WORD, conjuring distressing and unpalatable images of finality, extinction, and loss; the climactic experience of life, and one waiting for our inevitable arrival since the moment of birth. The severing of the lifeline concludes the last action of our fate, and there is no avoiding the "grim reaper's scythe."

Reminders of death make us feel uncomfortable. Considering the implications of mortality and the passing of our lives—day by day, hour by hour—is a fact of life that is most often evaded, although as Jung states, "Death is psychologically as important as birth and, like it, is an integral part of life."[1] He continues: "Grounds for an unusually intense fear of death are nowadays not far to seek: they are obvious enough, the more so as all life that is senselessly wasted and misdirected means death too. This may account for the unnatural intensification of the fear of death in our time, when life has lost its deeper meaning for so many people...."[2]

For many, despite protestations of faith in religious beliefs of a blissful afterlife, Alice Bailey's summary of human reactions to death remains universally relevant. "Death to the average thinking man is a point of catastrophic crisis. It is the ending of all that has been loved, all that is familiar and to be desired; it is a crashing entrance into the unknown, into uncertainty and the abrupt conclusion of all plans and pro-

---

[1] Carl G. Jung, *Psychological Reflections* Bollingen Series, Vol. 31. (Princeton, NJ: Princeton University Press, 1970; London: Routledge & Kegan Paul, 1974), p. 324.
[2] Carl G. Jung, *Psychological Reflections*, p. 323.

jects. No matter how much true faith in the spiritual values may be present, no matter how clear the rationalizing of the mind may be anent immortality, no matter how conclusive the evidence of persistence and eternity, there still remains a questioning, a recognition of the possibility of complete finality and negation, and an end to all activity, of all heart reaction, of all thought, emotion, desire, aspiration, and the intentions which focus around the central core of man's being. The longing and determination to persist, and the sense of continuity still rest, even to the most determined believer, upon probability, upon an unstable foundation, and upon the testimony of others—who have never in reality returned to tell the truth."[3]

The preoccupation with death is rooted deep in humanity; it has been a fear and fascination that has motivated religious and esoteric inquiry for thousands of years. In our modern world of cultural exchange and interaction, we are not just limited to information about a single localized religious teaching on death; we can simply select several books and study the religious beliefs of various cultures spanning centuries of human thought, or visit ashrams, temples, shrines, monasteries, or take educative workshops to inform us of alternative religious beliefs.

If we wish, we can become converts to exotic, alien philosophies. As if arranged on a supermarket shelf, different religions and reputed afterlives are available for our choice. We can select the Islamic paradise, where followers of the Prophet can enjoy the pleasures of beautiful houris, wine, and gardens. We can pass on into the Christian heaven, a less active realm, but full of tranquility and angelic music. We can experience the stages of the Tibetan *bardo*, as the workings of the universal mind-created reality are sequentially revealed as we prepare to enter the light. We may enter the Valhalla

---

[3] Alice A. Bailey, *Esoteric Healing*. Vol. IV of *A Treatise on the Seven Rays* (New York & London: Lucis Press, 1972), p. 438.

of fallen warriors, perpetually reinvigorated each day for new feasting and fighting. We may rejoin the Great Spirit after performing the Ghost Dance and realize the truth of the shamanic vision-quest. We may review our life, in readiness for our next incarnation on the ever-spinning Hindu wheel of life, certain that we will make fewer mistakes, perhaps attain enlightenment and discharge bad karma the next time around. So efforts can be relaxed during this life. After all, there's plenty more to come, so why hurry when there's so much to enjoy and distract us in the world?

Each cultural set of religious beliefs shapes the afterlife of death in ways which reinforce beliefs in personality continuity. Despite humanity producing many detailed afterlife beliefs—which to rationalist perception are all equally bizarre and improbable—and mediumistic spiritualism claiming to transmit messages from the beyond which guarantee the existence of loved ones on other invisible planes, we still fear the departure from our body. Jung points to this human need to imagine continuity: "One should not be deterred by the rather silly objection that nobody knows whether these old universal ideas—God, immortality, freedom of the will, and so on—are 'true' or not. Truth is the wrong criterion here. One can only ask whether they are helpful or not, whether man is better off and feels his life more complete, more meaningful and more satisfactory with or without them."[4]

In this context, we choose whatever gives us inner support. If the thought of multiple lives is appealing, then reincarnation theories will be preferred; if the thought of eternal heaven attracts, then pick that one, and make sure your behavior secures admittance. If the thought of absolute extinction and annihilation is exciting, then an atheistic attitude is apt. If the thought of teenage virgins serving you in paradise can still stir a few desires, then the Islamic promise may be

---

[4] Carl G. Jung, *Psychological Reflections*, Bollingen Series, Vol. 31. (Princeton, NJ: Princeton University Press; London: Routledge & Kegan Paul, 1974), p. 326.

suitable. But beyond facetious comments lies a mystery that is extremely important in how we live our lives now; not in the future, or in the afterlife, or ten, or twenty lifetimes away.

DEATH—AN EXCUSE FOR SOCIAL CONTROLS

Death and rebirth concepts are fundamental to all religions and esoteric study. To compensate for fears of death here and now, the ritualized appeasement of gods and goddesses and the creation of other worlds beyond mundane appearance began to accumulate. Adherence to a specific religion was like the coin exchanged with Charon, the ferryman of the Styx, for passage into the next world; the threat of Christian excommunication was directed at any heretical questioning of the faith's tenets, and involved the Church casting any rejected individual into an outer darkness where no redemptive heaven would ever be found.

Through our fear of death, priesthood gained power over the human mind, substituting manipulative beliefs as a means of ensuring priestly influence and social controls. What has been lost through this cumulative conditioning process is the knowledge of renewal and resurrection during life, a wisdom removed from the masses and only finding sanctuary and vitality within nonconformist esoteric traditions existing on the fringes of society, traditions that have often been victimized and penalized for unconventional beliefs and practices.

One of the essential messages of the esoteric and human potential movement is that potential exists for positive and constructive renewal and rebirth in individual lives and society. If things are unsatisfactory and not working, then change them. It is a simple precept, yet one which is often resisted; the reason why is because acting in this way touches upon the application of "death" to outworn forms and structures. We then deliberately embrace questions of endings and new beginnings, transitions, and renewals, and fearfully recognize that to create a rebirth in any sphere of life requires the death of the old. We participate in a process that extends to universal dimensions, and if we learn how to successfully wield this energy in our own lives, we may also break free of those social controls based on fears of instability and insecurity.

Modern society continues its lemming-like rush because most people unconsciously live in conditioned ways, thus ensuring the retention of power by a minority elite whose concerns are less selfless or responsible than may be sensible or healthy for planetary progress. Those who are able and willing to transform their own lives are less receptive to social pressures, and are more likely to question existing collective assumptions; like most freethinkers in history, such minds are perceived as dissidents, disruptive troublemakers, or socially dangerous.

THE INDIVIDUAL AND MYSTICAL EXPERIENCE OF INNER TRANSITION

Culturally, we have lost those conceptual rituals associated with natural cycles of living change and transformation which induce understanding of universal processes, except within the materialist and consumer preoccupation with replacing outdated models. In imposing fixed order and control on our lives and society, we become simultaneously fearful of change uprooting stability and security. When this process of change occurs to us, either as an inner movement of psychological readjustment or by external decisions outside our volition, we see this as a threat to be opposed and resisted, rather than an auspicious sign offering positive growth and renewal. We tremble with fear that losing our repetitive personality programs will be death. Our trepidation is valid but our interpretation of the outcome is biased by ignorance and conditioning; a death of an old self is happening, and this is what the 8th house, Pluto, and Scorpio can inspire, but this is only the preparation for rebirth, not a final extinguishing of the flame.

We often panic when identity foundations are eroded from within, failing to recognize or understand what is happening or how to cooperate with this process in a positive and creative manner. We are too focused on the chill wind of impending death dissolving personality structures to welcome this as an opportunity for regeneration. We need to be reeducated again that resurrection comes from within, and as Jung remarks, "only that which can destroy itself is truly alive."[5]

There is more evidence for the validity of rebirth during life than there is for a cycle of sequential reincarnation. The 8th house, Pluto, and Scorpio concerns are with "death-rebirth" now, as an ongoing and liberating experience rather than only occurring at physical death. Self-development confers personal understanding of this psychological process; by the dying of the old and the birth of the new is discovered the passage toward the promised "life more abundantly." This involves the stripping away of illusions, self-deceptions, glamors, ignorance; a psychological divestment of all that we mistakenly identify as "our self." The process of rebirth is a progressive dissolution of limiting and distorting barriers, be this applied in lesser or greater "deaths" through the power of personal choice. Every sphere of life and self can be refined through this experience.

Stumbling into Pluto's domain, we can activate the rebirth process within the psyche; this is a part of the self that "seeks its own destruction," but only so that the ego (the center of separateness) also dies and is replaced by the Self. Jung notes that the "fear of self-sacrifice lurks deep in every ego, and this fear is often only the precariously controlled demand of the unconscious forces to burst out in full strength. No one who strives for selfhood (individuation) is spared this dangerous passage."[6]

[5] Carl G. Jung, *Psychological Reflections,* Bollingen Series, Vol. 31. (Princeton, NJ: Princeton University Press; London: Routledge & Kegan Paul, 1974), p. 329.

[6] Carl G. Jung, *Psychological Reflections,* Bollingen Series, Vol. 31. (Princeton, NJ: Princeton University Press; London: Routledge & Kegan Paul, 1974), p. 332.

For all aspirants, death in various masquerades periodically appears along the path, testing recognition and understanding. Physical death is a terminal release of everything; occult death is the ongoing release of the veils of Self. For all who wish to comprehend or transcend death, a crucial encounter is waiting. Lama Govinda said that "those who want to conquer the Lord of Death will have to meet him and to recognize him in the midst of life."[7] Augustine realized "it is only in the face of death that man's self is born."[8] Goethe's insight was that "so long as you do not die and rise again, you are a stranger to the dark earth."[9]

Through the 8th house, we contact the Plutonic function of the death-touch to all structures; our personality, body, and society cannot resist when old patterns of identity, behavior, attitudes, values, and beliefs no longer serve. We choose, however, whether our response to this "humane action" creates premature disintegration or rebirth. There is no escaping the psychological experience common to this; only our attitude can determine whether a psychological collapse or breakthrough is the likely result. A faith in rebirth may be a seed that allows us to rise from the underworld of depression or initiation, changed but intact. Jung contends that this belief, faith or intuition of rebirth "is an affirmation that must be counted among the primordial affirmations of mankind."[10] Indeed, it is a recreative power that all seekers of the light confirm by their own experiences.

The inner death is felt as a psychological fall into emptiness, as if identity foundations had suddenly subsided as a result of hidden erosion undermining the personality structure. Cohesion is lost and a sense of powerlessness and help-

---

[7] Lama Govinda, cited by Tracy Marks, *Planetary Aspects* (Sebastapol, CA: CRCS, 1987), p. 64.

[8] St. Augustine, cited by M. Montaigne, *The Complete Essays of Montaigne* (Stanford, CA: Stanford University Press, 1965), p. 63.

[9] Johann von Goethe, cited by Howard Sasportas, *The Twelve Houses* (London: Aquarian Press, 1985), p. 81.

[10] Carl G. Jung, *Psychological Reflections* Bollingen Series, Vol. 31. (Princeton, NJ: Princeton University Press; London: Routledge & Kegan Paul, 1974), p. 331.

lessness insinuates through the psyche. An internal void or abyss opens, and a sense of peering into bleak darkness assaults an inward gaze. Survival instincts are activated while sombre emotional depressions, loss of meaning and direction toll the ending of an outgrown self; our difficulty is that this is the only self we know and we are reluctant to let go. Anxieties and fears intensify as we confront the terror of an inner void that threatens to "swallow us." Our moorings to an existing reality are loosened without permission, and we face a meeting with death.

This convergence occurs at junctions or interfaces between inner and outer universes, a connection at a cathartic crossroads. Panic can force us further into an inner hell (whatever can shake us to our core); and in our despair, we feel suspended in this state forever, there seems to be no escape. Hell may only last for minutes, but the experience seems to last forever in a timeless space. This is the crucial part of the journey to rebirth; the paradox is that we have to accept this as our new reality before the journey can continue. The deepest depths of the psyche have to be dredged before an ascent and return is possible. Here we note parallels to Christ and the bitter cup, tasted in the garden of Gethsemane prior to his crucifixion and resurrection. For transformation and new life to be attained, surrender to the higher will has to shatter the separate and limited individuality; death, emptiness, inner darkness all demand acceptance. The last vestige of self has to be submitted in acknowledging that "Not my will but thine be done." This step is taken as the overwhelming desire to unite with something greater and beyond the self reaches its zenith; the personality reaches out in trust for the support of the unknown, seeking to reunite with the universal mystery.

Rebirth becomes a continual process within a renewed consciousness, where surrender has allowed a profound restructuring to occur and opened the entrance to a new, inclusive life path. The 8th house death reveals the fact that "a real initiation never ends," as this is just the start of a new process that incorporates perpetual renewal, and the abundant life promised by the drama of its exemplar.

It is interesting to note that all human states of consciousness which involve personality death come under the rulership of the 8th house; these include sexuality, drug use, ecstatic practices and religious trances. As the time is ripe for 8th house issues to be explored by modern society as a springboard for future progress, problems related to sexuality (values, morals, promiscuity, family structures, minority practices, AIDS, herpes, etc.) and widespread misuse of narcotic and social drugs (destroying individuals, communities, increasing crime, prostitution, addiction) can no longer be avoided. A potentially more constructive response has been the rapid expansion of trance-channeling (new age-style, pentecostal speaking in tongues, psychic mediums) offering predictions, guidance for living, and spiritual insights, although this can have mixed consequences. Dependency on channeled teachings may not be ultimately beneficial; there are dangers of charlatanism and financial exploitation of gullible people; the received teachings may be spurious and spiritually deceptive. As in all spiritual paths, discrimination is vitally necessary to avoid taking directions which lead into cul-de-sacs, or give the misleading impression of progress when the road is looping backwards!

Death and Esoteric Initiation

The 8th house allows us to contact the "initiation of death" during life in several ways. It is the House of Death, where restrictive patterns of psyche and form are broken down, prior to a transformative restructuring; personality can be reborn after outgrown egoic boundaries have been dismantled and purified by mystical crisis. In Mayan tradition, Scorpio was known as "the sign of the Death-God," and Pluto encourages plunging into the unknown through the gate of transition in search of "something more." By opening our psyche to these archetypal energies, we may encounter the most intense, primal experiences available to us, and the 8th house initiate is one who has undergone this path into the underworld, entered the tomb and returned reborn to share his or her message.

Scorpio is traditionally perceived as a regenerative, magical sign, associated with the secrets of birth-death-rebirth. Scorpio and Pluto are the zodiacal rulers of death and the dead, possessing knowledge of the raising from death, revealing how death is the entrance to a higher level of spirit. In esoteric teachings, Scorpio governs the arduous path of discipleship, which is a major turning point for humanity—or in an individual's life when the commitment is made to return to the spiritual father's house.

The testing symbolized by Scorpio involves the transfer from a self-centered consciousness into the universal Self, realizing union with all life. These trials involve regenerating physical, emotional, and mental attitudes and values that have been formed by the separative, dualistic consciousness.

The physical level is a test of "appetite," and requires a readjustment of habitual material desires, concentrating on the key issues of sexuality and money. The emotional level tests sensitivity to the outer world related to satisfying our needs and desires; negative emotions such as fear, hatred, anger, and greed require replacing by constructive, and creative emotional power. The mental level tests the exclusive mind, where intellectual barriers of pride, rationality, and logic can prove divisive, and an analytical perspective fragments the universe. Beliefs in mental superiority can lead to exploiting others by exerting "power-over" them. The false importance of the lower ego has to be substituted by the higher mind of unity and synthesis. Primarily, these tests relate to moving beyond personality dualism to become receptive to the spirit. Each adjustment made by this process marks an "inner-death" of the old personality pattern, and as each step onward is taken, the aspirant joins the company of "the living dead" as ancient initiates and adepts were once described—now most commonly attributed to zombie films!

The initiation of death is a core mystical, alchemical, spiritual, and occult event, the heart of the renewal process which can be ignited within ourselves. We may reenact the Phoenix mystery in lesser or greater deaths throughout our lives. We can live so intensely that one life experiences as much as the seven times seven lives of the fabled immortal bird; this power of creation-destruction-recreation lies within, waiting for release.

The experience of death in the underworld has many ancient symbolic, mythical, and religious parallels. The process of initiatory descent often culminated in enclosure within a tomb, sepulchre, crypt or chamber where darkness ruled and the world was far away. Some conjecture that secret chambers deep within pyramids were utilized for similar mystery practices; and the sacrificial entombments in barrows and mounds of the pagan sacred kings were designed to generate occult power and access to the "wisdom of ancestors."

The sepulchre of Christ is probably the most well-known in the West, in which his body was laid after crucifixion and from where he was mysteriously resurrected. The vault of Christian Rosenkreutz, the Master of the secret Rosicrucians is another significant, esoteric rebirth symbology. In Christian terms, resurrection was of the physical body and the redemption of creation; in Rosicrucian terms, the resurrection was of a secret body of knowledge and the redemption of those in ignorance. In both, the tomb represented the ending of life and the womb or cradle of a new beginning. The mystery is experienced only in the darkness, for there the light can shine most brightly and illumination comes when the spark of rebirth is kindled by the mystical death; only then can wholeness be discovered.

The signposts to these mysteries have been present for centuries, although the exact nature of the experience is always uniquely personal and woven from our own nature and being. Whether we descend into an ocean or a tomb we participate in the *Magnum Opus*, the Great Work, and the quest for the Philosopher's Stone. In alchemical terms, we are the source of our spiritual chemistry, we are the refining alembic and crucible in which the experiment to transmute matter is performed.

We become the phoenix, signifying the truth of Paracelsus' that "you should understand that alchemy is nothing but the art which makes the impure into the pure through fire."[11] What is this but the purgation by the underworld hellfires? Basilius Valentinus directs us in our explorations: "Visit the interior parts of the Earth; by rectification thou shalt find the Hidden Stone."[12] The Great Work that alchemists sought to achieve by transmuting the personality lead into the gold of spirit was the unification of above and below, the individual microcosm and the universal macrocosm; this is the essence of all spiritual paths.

The 8th house experience can reflect the threefold stages of the alchemical and archetypal pattern of death-rebirth. In the *nigredo*, the inner darkness is encountered; this includes the descent into the tomb, the dissolution and fragmentation of self as depicted by Christ, the sundering of Osiris by Set and the dismemberment of Orpheus and Dionysus. In the *albedo* comes the process of reintegration after the nigredo-death; this transforms, purifies, and reconciles by experiencing an inner healing reassembly. In the *rubedo* comes regeneration, resurrection, rebirth, and return with the treasure, the stone or elixir that has renewing potencies. The lost and forgotten primal unity has been recovered; the secret mystery of nature has been restored. And emerging from the Scorpio phase of nature's night, hibernation, and decay, comes the rebirth of vital, verdant new life at the turning of the cycle. In the underworld,

---

[11] Paracelsus, cited by Caitlin & John Matthews in *The Western Way*, Vol. 2 (London: Arkana, Viking Penguin, 1988), p. 199.

[12] Basilius Valentinus, cited by Alice Raphael, *Goethe and the Philosopher's Stone* (London: Routledge & Kegan Paul, 1965), p. 83.

the sacrifice of the individual life becomes the redemptive action which commences the universal life by the "initiation of death."

THE DEATH SIGNS

Esoterically, there are three "death signs" of the zodiac: the water signs of Cancer, Scorpio and Pisces, and the 4th, 8th and 12th houses respectively. Evolutionary growth and reincarnational beliefs portray various versions of these three phases of liberation, and suggest how advance is made over multiple lives. In Cancer, known as the gateway to collective humanity, the person is directed and influenced by the mass-mind, swayed by mass-emotions and reflects mass-consciousness. Progress is achieved by a slow struggle to undergo a "death" of previous bondage to the level of collective security and impression, and to emerge as a genuine individual who can stand apart from collective subservience.

The Cancer experience results in the Scorpio transition, where the individual confronts the nature and consequences of personal desires and their demands for material possessions, pleasure and form-life. The higher spiritual nature begins to stir, posing the challenge of response and orientation: which is more powerful, matter or spirit? Between the two poles the individual is torn, feeling attracted to both paths yet remaining undecided at an inner crossroads, enduring their crisis of doubt, hesitation, and dilemma until they resolve the conundrum of self-knowledge.

In Alice Bailey's *Esoteric Astrology* the death in Scorpio is occultly represented as the "...Ancient One dies by drowning. Such is the test. The waters envelop him and there is no escape. The fires of passion are then quenched. The life of desire ceases its appeal and to the bottom of the lake he now descends. Later he reascends to Earth where the white horse waits his coming." If the tests of Scorpio are successfully completed, and the "death" of form-attachment is undergone, the path continues to Pisces, where the final "death" of the dominant separative personality is experienced, when the power of matter is surrendered to the living spirit, releasing the imprisoned soul and liberating the hidden light, as implied in Christ's crucifixion and rebirth at the inauguration of the Piscean Age. "Death in Pisces via the energy of Pluto is transformation—a transformation so vital and so basic that the Ancient One is no longer seen. He sinks to the depths of the ocean of life, he descends into hell, but the gate of hell holds him not. He, the new and living One leaves below that which has held him down throughout the ages and rises from the depths into the heights, close to the throne of God."[13]

The inward path is not an escape from mundane demands, but is a willingness to fully embody existence in its wholeness and totality. Life is perceived as the axis of birth-death, where transformative change is simultaneously a death to the old and a rebirth of something new, a natural process operating in our reality and a constant flow of universal renewal.

"Death" is the companion of "life," and one whom we need to accept and befriend, as death is our entrance into a greater existence through superseding limited personality consciousness by the higher soul vision. Death is reperceived as a liberator, a force enabling us to break free of restrictive, crystallized ideas, beliefs, dogmas, frozen emotions, deadening routines, and constricting circumstances. Consciously, we can direct this energy at any unfulfilling area of our life, choose to change it and to declare, like Christ, that "Behold, I make all things new." The universe flows and is not fixed, except temporarily by our tendencies to control and restrict, so often directed by our needs for security and stability.

Transits and Opportunities for Renewal

Retreating from profound esoteric and mystical depths, we return to the mundane world, where this principle generally

---

[13] Alice A. Bailey, *Esoteric Astrology*, Vol. III of *A Treatise on the Seven Rays* (New York & London: Lucis Press, 1971), p. 214.

operates less dramatically within our choices, actions, and experiences. If we consider the element of the 8th house cuspal sign, or any secondary sign bridging the house, we may observe that we periodically meet the need for "death and renewal" on that particular elemental level.

An earth sign implies that our material and physical life will be the one most affected and which influences our conditioning attitudes. We may face disruptive experiences related to environmental stability, financial security, work, use of resources, material attitudes and values, conservatism, resistance to change, inertia, inflexibility, and possessiveness.

A fire sign suggests that issues of optimism, assertiveness, intuition, faith, imagination and creativity, idealism, passion, enterprise, ambition, and egoic independence may stimulate disruptive and regenerative changes.

A water sign indicates that emotional sensitivity, compassion, psychism, artistic and aesthetic perceptions, idealism, romance, perfectionism, self-deception, escapism, dreaming, and emotional manipulation of others may provoke renewal needs.

An air sign suggests a mental level rebirth, due to an active intelligence, intellect, curiosity, communication, and interaction with inspirational ideas. Renewal may come from the conflict of ideas, between conditioned personality attitudes and alternative ones from other cultures or types of perception.

We resonate most closely to one of these four levels of response; the level of affinity is where we are both strongest and most vulnerable, where we can "rise and descend," the point that can shake and awaken us and where death can strike us to our deepest center.

Evaluating planetary transit movements through this 8th house can alert us to possible opportunities for renewal which become available throughout our lives. Taking a positive and constructive attitude to the natural endings and beginnings of new life phases is a creative approach to adopt, and one that prevents a futile looking back to the past. The past is simply a foundation to build upon, not where we should now direct attention and energy toward repeating.

Transition comes in many disguises, and all life is a gradual movement and unfoldment of fate, those inner patterns slowly unraveling latent tendencies and potential. We live through the transitions from infancy to adolescence to adulthood; we marry and become parents and grandparents; we change careers, jobs, homes, relationships, interests, leisure pursuits, ambitions, dreams, and periodically close doors in our lives and unlock new ones. Life flows through transition movement, and each minor or major change is a little death, some so insignificant that we barely notice the passing, others making a radical impact and permanent impression on us, leaving us blessed or scarred in the process. The abundant life can only exist through renewing change; otherwise everything slowly becomes stagnant and lifeless. Attitude is the key to our response to "death and rebirth."

Within every life there are regular annual opportunities to cooperate with the 8th house's regenerative potency as the personal planets transit the natal chart. Whether we recognize these or make full use of the energies of renewal available to us is less certain, and many prefer to evade the challenges of creative change in favor of a more static and predictable lifestyle, where the known and familiar is considered as safe and secure. Yet establishing a repetitive, fixed life experience is often used as an excuse to avoid growth; personal attitudes, beliefs, values, and life-choices become molded into restrictive boundaries, marked by self-imposed defensive barriers against the threat of inner or outer change.

In contemporary society, the vision of periodic renewal and regeneration is still not fully accepted or integrated into collective attitudes. We have often lost touch with those psychologically necessary rites of passage where transition into new phases of inner awareness, potential, and growth are paralleled by shifts in outer activity and expression. The natural process of change is viewed with anxious suspicion as both society and individuals remain biased toward reactionary and conservative tendencies, looking backward instead of welcoming future opportunities and prospects for enhanced enjoyment, new experiences and invigorating progress. The unknown is tinged with unconscious fears and expectations that "it will be worse than what we have now," and resistances to renewal become inevitable when that mental attitude is prevalent.

This is often the dilemma that many feel when faced by life's choices, as the reluctance to release a firm grasp on the known and familiar reveals insufficient trust and faith in personal potential and the universe. As all who seek the inner paths know, this encounter is one that is repeatedly and regularly made when searching for the underlying spiritual reality or exploring themselves through meditation, magical ritual, and self-help psychotherapeutic techniques.

The fear that all of us undergo at every turn of the inner journey arises from our dim recognition that experiencing the mysteries of renewal will prove transformative in some unknown manner. We encounter phases of transition with alarm and hesitation, struggling to reerect protective and defensive shields, through inner reactions against even inevitable changes in life. We may reluctantly deal with the process of adjusting to aging and the encroachment of eventual death, as each year fades into personal history and memory—the collapse of professional ambitions, careers, businesses—the failure of a marriage, as the bright light of love becomes extinguished in the ashes of acrimony and pain—the struggle of raising a family, the maturation and departure of children to pursue their own lives—the puncturing of our dream-bubbles, those desires for an ideal life, torn and tattered on the sharp rocks of life—all of these may be part of the process.

Few of us escape some type of radical and transformative experience which leaves its wounding mark from that day onward. Fears of the unknown may be natural, but the challenge is to confront them, acknowledge their presence and message, and then refuse to bow down before them in surrender; if we do that, we forfeit our lives and freedom, options become constrained and fewer, and we slowly begin living in a severely restricted and imprisoning environment, as fearful attitudes diminish our decision-making and close many doors to life. Over time, if we follow this defensive path, fears erode our vitality, disempowering and turning us into a brittle psychological shell, where any powerful gust from life can disturb a fragile inner balance and crack our defenses wide open. We may believe that we have created an invulnerable lifestyle, but like Archilles' heel, the weak spot will attract the arrow of potential renewal when the time is right, and until it painfully strikes there will be little forewarning.

One important contribution of astrology is the analysis of phases of change in people's lives, through transits and progressions related to their natal charts. The imminence of transits that signify opportunities for individual renewal and regeneration can be noted, with insights provided into the likely nature of changes occurring as symbolized by the planets and houses involved. By applying astrology, we can identify the underlying patterns, purposes and directions that planetary influences represent to an individual. We can note those life areas where opportunities are currently or soon presented, those lessons that may require greater understanding, the meaning of crises and challenges, and the channels to release a renewing potential to improve the quality of life. Through astrological insight, support can be given during periods of decision-making and through turning points, by providing a "light illuminating the way through confusion and darkness."

When planets transit the 8th house, demands for renewal and rebirth are activated. These may be prompts to follow through existing and recognized needs for changes, either inwardly or in the outer world, or they may bring to consciousness less acceptable or repressed needs which have been ignored—yet which require a healing integration into the psyche and lifestyle. Inevitably, we are confronted with the command to change in some way; this may be of varying individual significance as to eventual transformative repercussions, but how we respond to this command is the

key issue. We can continue to reestablish resistance to unful-
filled needs, rejecting insistent messages as long as possible,
or we may listen carefully and modify attitudes or situations
so that inner needs are honored. Persisting in rejection we may
discover that outer circumstances develop which will eventually force us to confront our resistances, perhaps through
our lifestyle collapsing in disarray.

The planetary principles of our inner psyche do not control us, they pose questions of response, perpetually challenging
us to pursue our highest path possible; they encourage and
attempt to guide us, if we are receptive to their shaping
touch. When we ignore their influence and inspiration, the
consequences that result are our own creation.

In considering the messages of transiting 8th house planets, awareness may be needed in respect of each individual's "planetary sensitivity" and inner responsiveness. Most
people are especially receptive or attuned to particular planetary principles whose presence in their natal chart and by
transiting movement has significant effects on their lives.
Actually establishing what these key planets are may come
from noting certain natal factors; a planet in the 1st house, the
ruler of the 1st house, a planet conjunct the Ascendant, ruler
of the Sun sign or a highly aspected planet. Discussion with
clients focused on their responsiveness to specific planetary
principles can help to define a "key planet," whose influence
may carry a greater significance in both the client's inner
and outer life; this planet may be felt or intuited as a distinct
presence, revealed through acknowledged needs or evaded
through repressions, depending on how the individual deals
with planetary messages. When this planet (or planets) passes
through specific houses or makes a transiting aspect the
effects are more marked and personally important, so a focus
on the implications can be creatively constructive as opportunities for renewal can be taken.

In some charts, the outer planets Pluto and Neptune
may never actually transit the 8th house, and some may

never experience Uranus either; this depends on the natal positions relative to this house, and in Pluto's case, the variable time spent in each sign. Planetary influences tend to be impersonal, shaping experiences and posing the challenge of choosing particular life paths and accepting the consequences of personal decisions and judgments. Planetary activity is reflected by changing inner attitudes and outer situations. This may be a slow, subtle rearrangement or sudden events that uproot the existing worldview and lifestyle. The influence may last over the whole transit duration through the 8th house, or may be condensed into a short period overflowing with transformative crises and experiences.

Always the question persists: what is your response? What is your choice? At a crossroads, alternative paths co-exist, presenting both opportunity and confusion; taking the right road ultimately relies on our degree of self-knowledge and our ability to hear those deepest messages. Life is woven by small and large choices; and none more so than facing the crossroads of the 8th house mysteries which can regenerate our lives. But only if we recognize and choose that path.

Looking at specific planetary transits through the 8th house may help us to be aware of opportunities. Do we insert this key into the lock, turn it, and pass through the eighth gate? Or do we turn away, content in our familiar world and fervently wishing that nothing will ever disturb us? We answer that privately in our inner sanctuary, and our lives reveal the answer.

TRANSITING SUN

The Sun transits each sign and house every thirty days, and will remain in the 8th house for one month, offering a reasonable period to annually contact the mysteries of this house. The Sun symbolizes human psychological dualism, reflecting both the separate ego and the veiled, indwelling Self, and represents the evolutionary path between the individual and the universal, our unique solar path to wholeness and integration that lies at the heart of all religions and inner quests.

The Sun motivates us toward our progressive destiny and individual unfoldment by an innate need for meaning, and direction in life, a path that requires us to manifest our potential as fully as possible. This transit offers an opportunity for a deep reconnection to a more inclusive center of our spiritual being. Touching this can be regenerative, breathing new, vigorous higher life into us, renewing and investing us with a released spiritual nature, and enabling progress on our solar path which perpetually searches to become more of ourselves, by achieving aims and attaining the unifying and transforming holistic vision.

During the Sun's passage through your 8th house, you may experience a need to move beyond all existing social and self-imposed boundaries, restrictions, and barriers, in an attempt to break free of any feelings of imprisonment. You feel inspired to eradicate constraints, desiring some form of expansion that calms and satisfies this inner impulse. Whether consciously recognized or not, the search is to discover a higher, inclusive state of union and to leave behind the isolated, separative nature; yet this cannot be achieved immediately, and the path proceeds by taking one step at a time. You may feel a state of dissatisfaction, disruption, disenchantment, and agitation, where an undefined inner pressure strives for release. Unconscious and disowned needs may spur compulsive actions, failing to recognize your deepest motivations and displaying an ambivalent reaction to experiences, unsure of what you are actually looking for. Your reactions may veer between extremes, wanting to taste every experience as deeply as possible or being inclined to withdraw from contact and evade life, by retreating into privacy and seclusion.

Relationships may prove a source of contention, especially within intimacy which may take on greater intensity yet be liable to emotional confusion and arguments. Your emotions

appear volatile and unpredictable, you may be "touchy, vulnerable, and aggressively provocative," possibly unconsciously looking to provoke relationship battles as an excuse
to expel emotional pressures and inner conflicts. Perhaps
through painful experiences come the opportunity of renewal,
if you recognize the need for transformation and apply a
genuine effort at constructive, creative change. Sexuality and
your image as a sexual being may be valuably explored,
although again your reactions may prove contradictory, either
wholeheartedly embracing this facet of your nature and surrendering to intensity on every level, or by resisting heightened feelings and senses.

Whether the 8th house mysteries open to you or not
may depend on how you handle the challenge of fear; your
wiser choice is to relax and surrender to the moment, and be
willing to change whatever is unsuitable and restrictive in your
life, enabling forward steps to be taken. Fears of responding
to the expansionary impulse will prove self-limiting and
generate additional feelings of dissatisfaction, posing those
questions of your aims, purpose and life-direction even more
uncomfortably. The need is for self-insight, to pursue your inner
demand for life-meaning and answers, and this transit suggests one route is through discovering the light within religious, spiritual, magical, and self-transformative paths.

TRANSITING MOON

The Moon transits each sign and house within a four week
period, and will remain in the 8th house for approximately
two days, and although it will return thirteen times a year,
the Moon's influence will often have less dynamic effect than
other planets. The Moon is concerned with individual creation
of rhythmic habits in life, both in predictable personal attitudes, values, and routines and in the organizing of daily life,
and can often resist forced changes in these patterns. The Moon

principle reflects needs for stability and security, favoring conformism to social beliefs, resulting in instinctive, repetitive reactions arising from subconscious predispositions and conditioned personality reflexes. Automatic responses develop within every level of our being, physical, emotional, and mental, shaping our lives and often establishing defensive shields to protect our vulnerability. The sense of relatedness lies in the Moon's province, and emotions and feelings are affected by our lunar affinity.

Passing through the 8th house, the Moon reconnects you to primal energies which may be experienced as stressful inner pressures and feelings of accumulated tension with an emotional volatility which may be quickly agitated and irrationally provoked. Your subconscious and unconscious mind is attracted to "rise" by the Moon's magnetism, and this can feel uncomfortable and disturbing, depending on if you repress and disown fragments of yourself. The opportunity presented is to purify emotions and instincts, by acknowledging and accepting them as they emerge from inner depths. If they erupt through experiences of intensity, passion, and relationship conflict—which is likely at this time—then attention is required for self-healing once the phase is completed. These pressures demand release, and may spill over into relationship arguments and crises, bypassing normal relationship patterns and are usually emotionally derived.

You may need to observe if you are acting in a compulsive or obsessive manner, when irrational behavior results from temporarily uncontrolled emotions, as if a river suddenly overflows its banks. Searching for release, you may demand greater emotional satisfaction through sexual and sensual demands, and your feelings will be highly vulnerable and sensitized; an off-hand comment or minor rejection could be exaggerated by you into a major crisis, resulting in the relationship being reassessed, renewed, or even destroyed. You may experience perceptions into others' hidden feelings, attitudes, and motivations, or psychically sense atmospheres. One lesson which you may realize is a need to modify your relationship behavior, so that greater harmony can be reached with others. The occult worlds, psychic development, and spiritual growth may also become more attractive at this time, especially as you experience and recognize the necessity for greater self-understanding through psychological insight.

TRANSITING NORTH AND SOUTH NODE

The North Node of the Moon will spend approximately eighteen months passing through the 8th house, and offers a renewing insight into how progress can be made toward achieving the vision of our future self, which is symbolized by the nodal natal sign and house. (Obviously the South Node will be going through the 2nd house at the same time.) This is commonly interpreted as the pole of the nodal axis which is attuned to universal progressive, evolutionary, and spiritual energies, and individually represents the opportunity for *becoming* or a higher level of *being*, as a result of actualizing the potential of inner unfoldment. The North Node may symbolize a personal dream of what we hope to become, an idealized vision that magnetically attracts our efforts and aspirations to attain. This operates as a voice from our destined future self, providing hints and guidance as to the path we should travel to maximize potential and to liberate our unrealized self. The North Node transiting cycle moves in the reverse direction than the other planets, from the 12th house to the 11th and eventually to the 1st house more than eighteen years later.

The 8th house challenge and renewal opportunity involves the need to express a new creativity that has been discovered during your previous eighteen month transit through the 9th house. The nature of this will be related to your experience of the North Node activating your higher mind, attitudes, and values, awakening new ideas and ideals; perhaps a vision of your future options may be sensed. However, inspiring dreams alone are insufficient for progress, and they demand that your creative spirit is applied within the tests of daily life, so that your ability for creative renewal by releasing potential becomes real and not just latent. By anchoring ideas and aims in the mundane world, you can discover the nature of your creative process and how applicable, effective and appropriate it really is; this is the trial of all ideas, where they are exposed to the scrutiny of the world and public attention. You may feel inclined to leave them as intentions, or resist the effort of manifesting them, but this does not lead to progress, and creativity becomes dispersed through lack of tangible expression.

You need to be wary of the attraction to simply indulge in great creative and idealistic dreams; a realistic appraisal of your talents and potential is necessary, as the greater the dream the less chance there is of you achieving its manifestation, and the exertion of even beginning may appear daunting. The South Node resistances active in your psyche may attempt to persuade you to continue dreaming, which dissipates energy and provides excuses to escape from inner creative demands.

A personal rebirth can occur through reliance and trust in your higher promptings and judgment, and progress and application can be generated through steps taken to actualize your vision. It may need realizing that whether your efforts become fully successful or not, the underlying valuable message is discovering how self-discipline is important to achievement and completion of aims. Understanding this lesson alone can give much satisfaction and the means to confidently take future progressive steps. Memories of past failures should be dismissed, and not allowed to interfere, as this is a new phase and opportunity for success, and the choice is yours to decide to take full advantage. The creative inspiration will be founded on the 9th house experiences and probably include correspondences to the themes, interests, and characteristics of that house's natal sign, while the 8th house sign indicates how you can manifest this inspiration.

There may be an attraction toward reliance on group or peer associations—at work or in social settings—but this may be best avoided as a temptation to dependency may diminish your freedom to creatively exploit the new directions offered by independent thought. Your challenge is to stand as a unique individual and release your creative light; if you allow yourself to be absorbed within a group or cause at this phase, you may be choosing an escape route from inner demands for a rebirth through creative expression, perhaps by fears of being judged by others, and a lack of self-belief and confidence.

TRANSITING MERCURY

Mercury transits the twelve houses once a year, and may stay in the 8th house for a period of between two weeks and a month, depending on its retrograde cycle relative to this house. Mercury is the planet of active intelligence and the lower mind, where the influence of individual thought processes result in choices, decisions, aims, planning, and communication—especially by applying logic, analysis, and rationality to issues and challenges.

As Mercury enters its annual sojourn in the 8th house, you may experience a diminution of confidence in the value of a rational worldview. Stirrings within your unconscious mind—which are less recognized by Mercury—may be creating "heavy hints" that the depths of the psyche are not controlled, constrained, or understood by intellect alone. Self-analysis transcends the value of logic, and your contradictory nature may become exposed to make you realize that there is more than your philosophy presently includes.

Your world may feel less stable, secure, and certain, perhaps sensing that your understanding is more superficial than you have believed. Events may reflect this or rationality prove ineffective in all situations. Your emotions may be powerfully agitated, especially if the realms of deep feelings and sexuality are the "message-bearers." The dimensions of life that offer opportunity and renewal through deep experiences are awakened, and sex, death, taboos, and intensity may become more attractive, demanding greater attention.

Curiosity and needs to explore and discover new life-directions may be activated, as the hidden realms of the underworld tempt you with promises of secrets and mysteries. Investigation and research may be your favored approach, trying to retain a cool, detached spirit of inquiry when probing areas of life which can generate others' passions and raise objections to crossing taboo boundary lines. Perception can suddenly transcend superficiality and register undercurrents in people and situations, opening a psychic sensitivity to inspire a reassessment of your worldview.

Spiritual and occult paths may be more appealing and interesting at this time, and awareness needed to register when life-messages are being given to you. You may feel less communicative than usual, preferring to veil your own secrets while wanting to see and expose those of others, as if pursuing a voyeuristic compulsion. A rebirth of mind views can occur, breaking down any tendency toward fixedness, and becoming more receptive to the paradoxes and subtleties of existence, starting with your own complex nature and learning greater tolerance of others. Resist any temptations to assert intellectual supremacy as a disguise for inner needs for "power-over" others, or at least recognize and understand this trait.

TRANSITING VENUS

Similar to Mercury, Venus transits the horoscope once every year, spending approximately one month annually in the 8th house, offering an opportunity to reconnect to a renewing union through individual emotional and social responses, relationships, and by expressing a creative and artistic impulse. Union implies an intimate interrelationship, and this is the key mystery of the Venus energy, posing challenges of how we react and deal with this deep need within the psyche. We may shy away from the need to share, merge in intimacy, and surrender to our whole nature and to the universal life, or we may willingly open ourselves to the bliss that an attuned mind, heart, and body can experience when aligned with our higher Self.

During this phase, you may search for greater intensity in sexual relationships, family interaction, friendships, and socializing, responding to your need for contact, sharing and the free exchange of energies. Your path toward the mysteries of renewal lies in close interaction with others, and any solitary withdrawal is avoidance at present. Your concerns are to establish right relations between yourself and others, to create satisfying, meaningful, and mutually beneficial exchanges, introducing beauty, harmony, and insight into the value of "treasures" that you can give to intimates and also receive in return.

Your sexual and love life may be highlighted, and you feel or experience greater passion and seductive powers; magnetically, you may attract others more easily. The energy of union is a powerful impulse, and love may be more easily evoked. Feeling opened to others, you may be more relaxed and less defensive, with self-imposed inhibitions cast away, allowing deeper intimate experiences that can contain a transformative charge only realized later. Sexual encounters may have elements of entrapment and manipulation, so be attentive as to any undercurrents that are hidden from sight. The urge to explore "mysteries" tends to dominate, and this can range between desiring to probe the mysteries of someone who attracts you, to more esoteric interests; their connection is "curious desire," and pursuing this beckoning finger may create several adventures, or confront you with depths that were not anticipated.

Aesthetic needs for beauty and harmony will be important, possibly resulting in a renewal of your domestic environment, appearance or lifestyle in an attempt to attain your perfect image. Finances, business, and partnerships can be favored at present, and issues of inheritance, joint possessions, or marriage may demand awareness.

TRANSITING MARS

Mars takes twenty months to transit the twelve houses, and will remain in the 8th house for approximately eight weeks annually, complicated by retrograde movements, and provides a renewal opportunity of how we outwardly direct our energies, to reassess or reaffirm our direction and to ensure progressive, constructive, and positive steps toward our aims. If we are failing to make our mark on the world, or dissipating energies in futile unproductive actions, Mars offers a chance to discover new approaches in each specific area of life. It is our responsibility whether we use this or ignore renewal options; our choice will become clear through our later experiences and degree of life-satisfaction.

Responsibility and wise action are two requirements to express Mars at this time, and especially so when relating to others. You may feel shaken by an upsurge of primal passions, sexual needs, aggression, agitated emotions, and impulses for either confrontation or "power-over" others. Mars can indicate a volatile energy, and you may have some difficulties in directing this.

Trigger points for conflict may be with intimate partners and issues of joint finances and resources, perhaps sparked by your need to dominate and control. With uneasy feelings barely controlled, you may unconsciously project disowned anger and aggression at those close by, failing to recognize that it is your own repressed energies and lack of integration which you are really reacting against. Your fragmented self can cause stress and tension, and wounds which need healing are misinterpreted and misdirected as feelings of anger apparently provoked by others. The sexual arena may become a surrogate sphere of contest, struggling for control and power as a means of defining self-assertion and identity. Alternatively, failure to assert Martian power is misdirected toward blaming others for the unwise choices that you have made.

Sometimes guilt impinges from your unconscious mind, creating an ambivalent and contradictory set of inner attitudes and responses. Certainly the need to confront those darker desires and emotions that are present may initiate a new perception of self, as acknowledgement is given to those less positive expressions of lust, envy, jealousy, greed, and self-ish, exploitative desires. These energies may require a cleans-ing of your inner Augean Stables of the collective debris of unhealthy, unintegrated, and negative personality tendencies.

Occult worlds, psychic and psychological exploration, and regenerative mysteries may all appear extra fascinating at pre-sent, so take full advantage of the opened inner door to the hidden universe, and pursue intentions to investigate these more deeply even after this transit has passed into the 9th house search for life-meaning. Mars can enjoy a raw, primordial wildness, and none is more demanding than entering the inner "wildways."

Personal values may be tested, and the crusading Martian spirit may be summoned by circumstances that demand a com-mitment to your beliefs and ideals, challenging your honor, integrity and virtue, through demonstrating your principles rather than paying only lip-service, and forgetting them when expediency rules. Resist temptations to impose and con-vert others to agree with your worldview; allow them free-dom to develop their own, and even if everyone in the world followed your precepts, it still does not mean that you are right!

Joint business ventures may appeal, demanding your coop-eration and initiating power, but ensure that these schemes are financially feasible and viable before committing yourself. Your combative spirit may feel ready to take on the world, but even that does not guarantee success.

TRANSITING JUPITER

Transiting Jupiter symbolizes renewal opportunities through personal growth, and the expansive ability to release potential during life. There is an aspirational quality to Jupiter's effects, stimulated by a restless striving for more in life, where an innate trust in universal beneficence can become a gateway to rebirth as the individual's optimistic faith enables a transformative opening to receive a higher wisdom. While intellect is involved in this process, the step is toward accessing a higher level of mind, one that is more intuitively aligned, and self-centered preoccupations can be transmuted by integrating inclusive attitudes and values, which serve as guiding principles and embody Jupiter's wisdom. An affinity to the Jupiter energy and its ray of hope can awaken personal power through a renewing resurgence of confidence, self-belief and conviction. Jupiter has an approximately twelve-year transit through the houses, and on average will remain in the 8th house for one year.

This phase will confront you with the consequences of your choices and actions during the previous year, when Jupiter transited the 7th house. Relationships and partnerships will provide the major focus for these, and you may face the experience of relative success or failure of your efforts. Renewal can come from employing a realistic clarity to relationship expectations; the presence of illusions and glamors may be starkly revealed within intimacy, social relationships, or business partnerships. You are challenged to observe how valid and appropriate your expectations actually are, or to accept that they have been unrealistic and extreme. Opportunities exist for either new growth and expansion of your outer relationships, or for the cessation and death of those which are proving unsuitable; evaluating these requires clarity, insight and a pragmatic realism, and Jupiter mediated through 8th house concerns reflects the need for progressive change rather than evasion.

Yet growth may not come easily; if your choices have been made through inadequate self-knowledge, then there may be difficulties in the practical working out of intentions and purposes, especially within partnership efficiency as harmonious relations become harder to achieve than anticipated. If this occurs, look at the nature and quality of your contribution to the situation; perhaps through a change in self-expression you could improve and renew the relationship in those problematic areas. If your dreams and expectations are revealed to have been unrealistic and unworkable, then this fact requires acceptance, and you may need to experience the cessation of hopes, carefully extricate yourself from the situation, note the lessons involved and prepare to walk onward, a little wiser into the future. Something of value can be extracted from every situation, even if pain, disillusionment, and disappointment is unavoidable.

Conflict with socially conventional attitudes and beliefs may occur, both from others and reflected as internal contradictory messages. You may be inwardly pressured to become more assertive and to display your unique nature, breaking free of the mold of conventionality, which may provoke opposition and a lack of understanding from others. Issues may challenge you to defy a social convention, attitude, belief, or worldview, meeting the trial of either compliance to social conformity or asserting personal power and independent views. If this stand is taken consciously, and is not just a contrary reaction against external pressures, then a renewing inner growth can occur, even at the cost of a "death" to an old life pattern. While it may not be apparent, underlying issues during this phase may be quite crucial in determining your success now and in the future, especially in the determination to be yourself and to be realistic in relationships.

If you allow the pull of others' desires, attitudes, values, and worldview to influence your choices and decisions, perhaps through unconscious conformity to conventional social behavior, then you are likely to lose direction. The path forward has to come from within, unraveled as you move onward by self-development, and following your own light. If you consciously choose to move in socially influenced directions, then fine; but if you follow them without self-inquiry and thought and without seriously determining if they are suitable for you, then you may be sowing seeds of future problems. Inevitably, some degree of social conformism is necessary, but on the path to your holistic self, this adaptation should be made without compromising your unique identity and purpose.

TRANSITING SATURN

A complete Saturn transit through the twelve houses takes approximately twenty-nine years to complete, and Saturn will remain in the 8th house for two-and-a-half years. Saturn has a reputation of being an uncompromising teacher, imposing restrictions, constraints, obligations, and responsibilities on individual freedoms and options, pending either an integration of certain key attitudes and values, or the acceptance and learning of important life lessons before the way forward is reopened.

Saturn's role is to bring order into individual and collective life, a form of organization, building a foundation for the safe development of later progress; Saturn tends to prevent boundaries and barriers being broken until the time to move beyond defenses has been reached. Time and patience are saturnine lessons, especially where ambitions and dreams are stirring, possibly creating preconditions before their attainment and satisfaction, testing the will and perseverance to achieve them. Tangible ambitions and material results are Saturn's preferred aims for individual social contribution. The realms of work, duty, and responsibility are often the channels to sense Saturn's presence, demanding internal order and self-discipline as prerequisites to success. Saturn's limitations are only a temporary imprisonment; some may be released as soon as transformative inner changes are made in attitude and value, others when it is safe to do so. Caution, stability, and security are Saturn's needs, which result in an ordered, organizing universal energy that none can evade.

Where Saturn is positioned can be a sphere of restriction, challenging you to discover a way through, and during the process undergo an experience of renewal. Obstacles persist while essential changes are avoided or unrecognized as necessary; sometimes a shift in perspective may be adequate to move forward, other times a more radical transformation may be required. Through adversity and encountering outer and inner resistances, the spirit may be strengthened and deeper qualities positively evoked; Saturn's impassive control and order is not meant to pose an insuperable hurdle, but demands genuine development to transcend, as renewal is not given away for free.

During this transit, the spheres of finance, sexuality, emotions, mind, and spirituality may be emphasized. The opportunity is for this to become a period of rebirth and radical change in one or more of these spheres. You may have to release certain existing attitudes, values, beliefs, desires, attachments— either due to the impact of circumstances, or by personal choice. A sense of "endings" may necessitate inevitable changes. Feelings of unease are likely, yet defining this sensation can be difficult, as outer life may remain the same; yet an inner process is happening, magnetically drawing your attention to these areas of life, prompting you to review the nature of your ambitions and desires to determine their current validity.

Inner messages—which may also be mirrored by outer events and people—challenge you to look closely at the essentials of your life, to reevaluate your controlling attitudes, instead of just automatically and unconsciously repeating previously established habit-patterns. One stimulant to self-inquiry may be the impact of realizing mortality, which can spontaneously arise by deep changes in the psyche, an awareness of your own aging, health problems, or by the death of someone you know. When close to the shadow of death, fear and self-protection can be one response, or a determination to live life to the fullest may be another. As death is inevitable, dealing with its reality can often stimulate lasting changes in attitudes and beliefs, and this encounter is valuable to developing a richer and more mature perspective, although it is your choice how you respond to this.

Sexuality and intimate self-expression may awaken you to a new dimension of life, perhaps by realizing the importance of sexual energies in relationships and the potential transformative impact of this potent force on yourself and others. You can emerge from this phase in "the house of sex" with a greater understanding of your sexual nature and identity, possibly integrating this more effectively. Yet how Saturn deals with the issues of sexuality varies considerably. The availability of a sexual partner may be lost, and lessons can occur through a period of sexual frustration and celibacy, suggesting a need to rechannel sexual energies within your nature and via other routes. Alternatively, you may enter a period of intensified sexual activity and exploration, discovering new intense depths with a permanent partner or with several lovers. You may choose to withdraw from an intimate relationship that is failing to fulfill, freeing you to enter a new one, or to experiment more freely. Your insight into sexuality and its renewal potential may simply come through a deeper loving experience and heart involvement with another.

Occultism and spiritual concerns may also awaken as an inner shifting flux questions many of your established life patterns, beliefs, and attitudes. Saturn may partake of the undermining 8th house energies linked to Scorpio and Pluto, designed to force change upon any who are resistant. Even outer circumstances may be transformed if the need is great enough. Much depends on how entrenched your defensive patterns are, and what degree of "shock" may be needed to shake them apart. One positive way of using this transit is to accept that attitudes and values are not fixed, but should be responsive to changing inner and outer needs, and are secondary to fulfilling your higher path. Experiences will reveal how apt these remain in daily life, and if your attempts to express them are proving unsatisfactory, indicate that these require transforming. Listen intently to the prompting inner whispers, as following these could save much time, discomfort, and suffering.

TRANSITING URANUS

Uranus marks sudden, unusual, and unpredictable changes, acting as a shock to the established order, in both the personality and lifestyle. Uranus can be disturbing and disruptive, bringing one phase to a surprising end, while simultaneously opening a door to a new path where prospects exist to discover renewal and new growth. When stagnation is too restrictive, suffocating the spirit and the release of innate potential, then Uranus can come like a whirlwind of chaos, sweeping barriers away, like a divine reaction against allowing human needs for the stable security of the ordinary and mundane to gain total power. Uranus demands reform and revolution, creating a space for new revitalizing insights into reality.

Uranus' individual effects are to heighten needs for independence, freedom, non-conformity, and unconventional behavior and interests, where the constraints of order fall victim to the need to shatter any feelings and situations of imprisonment. Uranus is the first of the transpersonal planets, those extremely potent inner forces and archetypal principles whose touch is regenerative, and whose impact cannot be denied. Uranus takes eighty-four years to transit the houses, and will remain effective in the 8th house for approximately seven years. Often its impact may be especially visible when Uranus has just entered a new house, and its intention to shake things can then be most apparent.

The 8th house Uranus transit can become a test of how you respond to change and renewal, especially in terms of realizing how your attitudes to this shape eventual life-consequences. Try to observe how your recent reactions to unavoidable externally imposed changes and self-chosen redirections may have had beneficial results, providing new avenues of exploration and discovery, new interests and pleasures, and revealing the positive fruits of cooperating with the energy of renewal. Or, you may observe that your resistances and preference toward the fixed and familiar lifestyle have diminished your commitment and flexibility, and you have tried to oppose the rearrangement of matters, temporarily dissipating renewal. Despite attempts to raise shields against Uranus, change will inevitably come through some source, and noone can resist forever as Uranus can shatter any defenses.

Uranus influences you to create new perspectives toward those powerful primal energies active within sexuality, emotional passion, the hidden depths of life and the mysteries of death. Fascination and curiosity may be heightened, and a new attraction toward investigating these themes may develop, either as a need to become free of instinctual drives through greater understanding and detachment, or as a need to probe deeper, to experience and experiment with more commitment. Sexuality could become a greater preoccupation, perhaps through a partner who opens you to a more intense dimension of sexual activity, or as a determination to redirect this power into other channels, perhaps toward an idealistic creativity. Emotions can become a battlefield, and relationships may either suddenly and shockingly end, or new ones burst into life.

Dreams, wishes and ideals now demand practical demonstration in your life; the value of time spent in thought has passed, and these are to be tested in the crucible of daily life to reveal their true quality. The opportunity is to live your most important dreams and ideals, discovering whether these are comforting self-illusions that you indulge in merely as mindplay, or are truly inspirational and creative, being committed to allow them to reshape your life now. Through application you discover if these can become real, by making efforts to transform yourself and lifestyle accordingly. As many painfully discover, practicing beliefs and ideals can be extremely difficult in the world, and most tend to quickly compromise for the sake of expediency. This can eventually lead to only giv-

ing lip-service to ideals, and generate inner confusion, conflicts and a feeling of failure. Uranus can inspire an idealistic vision which sets a goal, encouraging you to aim toward
it; through this process, you can move beyond many current
limitations, make real lasting growth and release latent potential. Be alert to the vision-hints that can flow from Uranus'
activity during this phase.

One constant companion of idealism is disillusionment;
your encounter with "death" may involve experiencing the
collapse of cherished dreams, ideals, and beliefs, or being challenged by the outer world for your particular views. This can
be a painful process, stimulating much self-inquiry if your ideals
fail to stand the test of reality, yet equally they can be the source
for renewal. Perhaps a reevaluation may ensure that some
progress can be reached even if the goals are sensibly pitched
at a lower level of expectancy; sometimes the mountain cannot be scaled by a direct ascent, a more circuitous route may
be wiser, and each step forward provides hope and encouragement. Ideals need shaping, too, until they can be effective,
and Uranus can excite visions that may be beyond your present capacity to achieve, and with failure comes the loss of
positivity.

Adaptation may be necessary to pursue your path, which
will include your interaction with others, either within intense
intimate experiences or participating in collective activity
hoping to contribute to constructive social changes. The
breadth of relationship is a hidden theme to this transit which
needs deeper exploration. One consequence of this renewal
phase is your possible emergence as a "channel for change,"
where apart from recreating your own nature, you can serve
also as a transmitter of radical, constructive, socially regenerative energies; but this depends on the degree to which you
allow your own transformation to proceed.

TRANSITING NEPTUNE

Neptune takes some 168 years to transit all houses and signs,
and remains for approximately fourteen years in each house.

The natal house position of Neptune relative to the 8th house will determine if you will experience this transit during your life, as in most cases Neptune will only pass through six transited houses. Neptune is the visionary dreamer of the planetary gods, an inspirational presence evoking idealism, dreams, fantasies, creative imagination, heightened sensitivity, and aspirations to achieve a personal vision-quest; how real this may be on the mundane level is a permanent question-mark attached to Neptunian influence. Interwoven with inspiration is also illusion and glamor, where Neptune's effects are often subtle, elusive, undefinable, yet profound, and feelings of anxiety, fear, and needs for withdrawn seclusion may be prominent. Neptune stirs the depths of the unconscious mind, and awakens sensitivity to the hidden worlds, which can be uncomfortable and disturbing, especially when a phase of inner psychological dissolution is also happening.

Neptune's passage into the 8th house provokes extremely powerful primal forces innate within your psyche. Sexuality, death and rebirth are essential in the natural cycle, which requires from you a new perspective toward the polarized energy of existence, as sexual activity generates both life and death within form. Sex and death often carry a taboo quality in Western society, and many feel deep unease with these in their own nature and social interaction, whenever self-acceptance and integration is not total. Experiences may occur that oppose you directly with these issues and question your attitudes and responses. A need for greater awareness is likely, or a reassessment of how existing attitudes influence your choices in life; for instance, an inability to fully accept the changing process of life and a reluctance to face your inevitable physical decline may result in a lifestyle of control and security emphasis, diminishing options and freedoms.

Neptune aims for freedom from limiting boundaries, and is a force that animates the mystical quest for non-separation and realized unity. Imprisonment in form and restrictive attitudes is liable to be touched by Neptune, so that renewal comes when fixed behavioral patterns slowly but permanently dissolve. One of the favored channels for this in the

8th house is through sexual union and merging with a lover which dissolves personality barriers, if only temporarily, or allows a new self-experience by the transformative power of love. The impulse for heightened sensations and feelings can be released in moments of losing sexual control, a passionate abandonment to the ecstatic intensity of the moment. Yet the peaks of orgasmic sexual pleasure also involve a complex set of reactions, and your whole personality becomes affected by loving interaction.

Alternative responses to Neptunian influence may occur; these range from an intensified preoccupation with sex—perhaps by discovering new depths and pleasures with a new partner, or reawakening existing intimate relationships. Multiple partners may appeal for a time, or sexual confusion may dominate, as anxieties and a reevaluation of your sexual identity may be required. Sexual impulses may be internally redirected, especially if influenced by a spiritual quest, as certain traditions hold ideals of sexual transcendence. Exploring your sexual nature is necessary for integration into your whole being; this needs a genuine embrace rather than inner distancing away from these instinctive urges and needs, and pushing away your sexual self as if it is almost another being. Neptune suggests the prospect to allow this energy to flow, turning life into an exquisitely sensual experience, and indicating how sexuality can open doors to register the refining and transformative potency of union and surrender.

Relationships are liable to fall victim to Neptune's confusing and deluding effects, and emotions swept by powerful currents as tranquil inner seas are broken by storms. If you hold unrealistic expectations or are superimposing projections onto partners, families and friends, you may discover that your demands for their conformity to these are rejected or challenged. Renewal can come through withdrawing expectations and projections which are interfering with any relationship.

Neptune's encounter with death implies a coming to terms with the inevitable climax of your life, the cessation of dreams. Contemplating this can result in radical changes to how you choose to live, as attitudes, values and priorities are rearranged. Living by "How long is your life? As long as your next breath," can encourage attention to enjoy the moment, and to live in ways that maximize life-appreciation as much as possible. If your lifestyle has unsatisfactory elements, then opportunities are present to revoke self-inhibiting barriers, and choose to create a more fulfilling life.

Life includes many minor phases of "endings and beginnings," of small deaths during life which offer rebirth and potential new directions, and the path to experience the abundant life sees death as the gate to liberation. Confronting "death" may seem somber and disturbing, yet can intensify a life, stripping away inessentials and the tragic wasting of time. Alternatively, fears of this process can lead to reimposed inner and outer barriers, in a futile attempt at self-protection from the natural flow of existence. Reactions against change can create depressions and repressions, or tendencies to escape into the fool's paradise of oblivion through addictions to drug and alcohol abuse, or other forms of self and life-evasion. These are no answers, and escape only proves to be self-consuming, a collapse into greater suffering.

Finances, too, may prove problematic unless consciously and carefully handled with due caution. A tendency to be misled, deceived, or to fall prey to uncertain personal values may leave you over-gullible. Realism and communication are required to evaluate schemes properly, and business schemes need alert attention, or else one "death" may be your own financial stability.

TRANSITING PLUTO

Pluto's transits through the houses and signs takes over 245 years, and has varying periods in each house and sign of between twelve and thirty-one years. The natal position of Pluto will determine if an individual will ever experience this transit, and many will not. Pluto is the planet of regeneration, and passing through its own 8th house will be at its most potent.

Pluto is a planet of culmination, marking a transition between the known and the unknown by the phase of meta-morphosis and memorable transformations that change lives. Pluto transits often include periods of inner pressure, where previously repressed or disowned aspects of the psyche rise to the surface of consciousness, providing an opportunity to redeem an unintegrated shadow-self. We need to examine the motivating compulsions of our dark side when meeting Pluto, or the reflection of our unredeemed self can prove too hard to bear. Pluto demands that we purge ourselves of unhealthy repressions, bringing inner darkness into the light for purification and understanding, and to reintegrate our frag-mented selves into a new unity. If we respond positively to Pluto's message, instead of resistant avoidance which can pro-voke the consequence of additional suffering, we may discover and reaffirm our personal power and potential, and make full use of Pluto's constructive, transformative energy.

Inner and outer relationships characterize this Pluto transit, and greater clarity and care is required as powerful stirrings deep within your psyche are liable to prove dis-turbing and unsettling at this time. In particular, under-standing your sexual and aggressive drives is important, as you may have tendencies to mix these with compulsive needs for control and "power-over" others, both for self-satisfaction, aggrandizement and as a release of an over-flowing inner reser-voir of energies. You may become increasingly preoccupied with these means of assertion, or alternatively, feel frustrated by a lack of them, a loss of sexual expression, and a failure to assert your power sufficiently. Learning how to use your libinal energies in a more creative and constructive manner may be a Pluto message to you at present. You can either empower or disempower yourself by your inner attitudes and reactions to these primal forces.

Relationships will be ripe for reevaluation, and you may need to ensure that they contain renewal energies, and remain important, relevant and "living exchanges" between partners, family, and friends as distinct from a superficial contact still persisting by past momentum. Try not to look just from your own perspective, needs, and desires, but also creatively imagine and include your partner's needs, to guarantee mutual relationship benefit. A renewal of self-expression may also help, especially to avoid any accusations of exploitation and dominance. Relationship intensity will be heightened, and power struggles can become more prevalent if both partners strive for supremacy, so attention may be valuably directed to minimize unproductive conflicts that arise purely from personality disharmony.

Pluto's regenerative qualities may result in a disturbing period undermining your life-foundations. The degree to which this may occur will depend on your hidden need for transformative change, and can happen independently of your choice and volition; what may need realizing is that this is the consequence of your own actions, choices, attitudes, and values. You have sown the seeds of your future reality, consciously or unconsciously. Yet this may prove the stimulus for a rebirth in your life, making new directions inevitable and unavoidable. Observe closely what lessons and implications of a changing situation are revealing to you, and look honestly at how your choices have sown seeds of divisive conflict, especially if the focus of this change is within intimate relationships. Perhaps adjustments may be sufficient to reestablish a new balance, but remaining in a fixed, resistant posture will only encourage Pluto to initiate an even more profound weakening of foundations.

Business interests and money matters may be prominent and increased opportunities can come to your attention. Care is needed to avoid over-enthusiasm and optimism for this route of renewal, and ethics and integrity should not be abandoned in the pursuit of quick riches. Pluto's lessons are subtler than that, and preferably your direction should include socially responsible practices. Money may become an issue of contention, either within family budgets or with business partners, so ensure that clear communication clarifies and resolves disagreements, or else a financial breakdown and rearrangement may be one negative result of change.

Occult and hidden spheres of life can intrigue, and it is an apt time to deepen self-scrutiny and especially investigate those unconscious compulsive patterns which secretly direct your behavior and form those attitudes and values which shape your life. Open more to personal transformation paths which are available, and you may discover that a great rebirth can happen, as you find new ways emerge from important self-insights which can be currently accessed. Change will rarely come overnight and will need time to permeate you, until, like the phoenix, you can reemerge with a new self-vision of your nature and potential, and be ready to follow a new direction.

9 The Wounded Healer

NO ONE PASSES THROUGH LIFE unscathed. Whether our wounds originate from the world and others, or by hidden inner conflicts locked away in a secret secluded battlefield of the psyche, unwanted crisis and change is inevitable. For renewal and the flow of life-energies, the old has to be released, either willingly or by imposed events beyond our control. We may resent and resist this natural process stirring us from our sleep of inertia and automatic life; we may still invest emotional and mental attachments to whatever we are moving beyond; we may obstruct change and risk an even more painful future crisis. But eventually we have to cease our retentive hold on the familiar, eliminate whatever is outworn and restrictive; we simply have to let go.

Depending on our attitudes, change may be a distressing or liberating experience as we dimly sense something new growing in our depths. Similar to physical gestation, this can be a long, internal, and private process, and we may be uncertain as to what is actually happening. As with childbirth, resistance is futile and relaxation minimizes the pain, although rejection of change can result in psychological equivalents to miscarriage, abortion, and stillbirth.

Rebirth is a central motif in planetary myths, legends, and religions. Its universality signals that this is a shared archetypal pattern present in human personality foundations. The "twice-born" attest to the experience of rebirth, but for the majority this is still only a faith and hope. Rebirth is an antidote to the limitations, stagnation, and malaise of life that afflicts so many who lack meaning and purpose. The contemporary res-

urrection of self-development quests in Western society only
scratches the surface of human need; visions of planetary and
individual rebirth are now becoming more prevalent and
insistent.

Something new is on its way to being born. Rebirth,
renewal, rejuvenation, regeneration, and healing self and
society are now cultural priorities in every sphere of life. We
are poised at an evolutionary crossroads, faced by realizing
our planetary *responsibility and creative power*; we can destroy
ourselves and the Earth by our attitudes, values, decisions,
and separative actions or we can transform these by a holistic vision, healing our wounds, and set in motion a planetary
resurrection and give birth to a new cultural worldview. We
are responsible and we possess the creative, magical wand
of power; humanity confronts the consequences of freewill
and the fruits of either conscious or unconscious decision-making. Ignorance is no longer an acceptable excuse.

One of the key 8th house lessons is that independence
expressed by a separative mind needs transforming into conscious interdependence; nations are now facing this transition within economics and politics, and individuals need to
discover integration into "group life," the awareness of shared
responsibility and unity that will characterize the future
Aquarian society. All we see now is the struggle of the early
stages of this transition—conflict, confusion, and darkness is
more apparent, interspersed with increasing glimmers of
hope, progress and optimism.

The function of Pluto is as a transformer, eliminating whatever has outlived its positive use by withdrawing living
energies, so this produces a gradual decline, decay, and disintegration—death. Pluto then initiates the renewing of the
universal cycle, when the dark depths are transmuted into life-
liberating light, and transition is taken to the next level. All
inhibitions to new growth are broken, and cultural and psychological structures are rebuilt in a more suitable form by
the energies released on this path of descent-ascent-return.
In the underworld of social and personal disintegration, the

devils of our own making are met, those consequences of our choices—our unredeemed and unintegrated nature.

The poet Rainer Maria Rilke once said, "if my devils are to leave me, I am afraid my angels will take flight as well,"[1] but this is a misunderstanding of wholeness and the real effect of Plutonic ministrations. In the underworld transformation, devils are reborn as angels, wounds are healed and the apparent extinction of the light in darkness is revealed to be an illusion as light blazes forth renewed on its return. The purification of negativity reignites the inner light in the redemptive experience known by mystics, occultists, yogis, alchemists, and gnostics.

In entering the underworld of the eighth gate, we discover the location of powers that are life-giving, renewing, and healing. Admittance includes acknowledging our wounds, failures, weaknesses, fears, resentments, angers, passions, desires, compulsions, secrets, guilt, shame, rigidity—all the ways that we can sting and poison ourselves and others. We admit our participation in the human condition, sharing the inner struggles that all experience and misinterpret as personally unique; egoic separation crumbles at this disclosure, and by accepting our oneness with humanity, wholeness can be born. The wounded healer may then emerge, able to assist others to confront their devils by the light of understanding, tolerance, and knowledge. The final step is a leap of trust and faith into the abyss, a letting go to a natural universal process.

As Blavatsky's *Secret Doctrine* states: "Pluto is a deity with the attributes of the serpent. He is a healer, a giver of health, spiritual, physical and of enlightenment."[2] Yet his cloak of darkness and fierce intensity frighten those unable to see behind the stoic, impassive mask. We can evoke Pluto's power in all areas of life: often we meet him without recognition as his influ-

---

[1] Rainer Maria Rilke, cited by Howard Sasportas, *The Twelve Houses* (London: Aquarian Press, 1985), p. 76.

[2] H.P. Blavatsky, *Secret Doctrine*, Vol. II (Pasadena, CA: Theosophical University Press, 170), p. 26.

ence permeates all 8th house issues. As the invisible presence
of death he waits, innate in all existence; he hides deep within
our wounds, a healing presence requiring awakening; he
slides into our emotional and sexual relationships, source of
many encounters with emotional pain and rebirth; he is the
force available to renew attitudes, values, worldviews, ideologies, the liberator of stagnation and inertia, the power
that guarantees either evolution or destruction.

The alchemists relate the tale of an old, barren king
unable to rule as he has lost his sacred ability to create new
life. His kingdom has become a wasteland, his people are dying,
and decay and infertility afflicts his world. The life-energies
no longer flow in renewal. Inertia has deposed his authority.
His option is to perform the sacred marriage to a close relative—a union of two energies connected to the same source—
and to meet his destined partner, he must descend into the
depths of the earth (or sea) to consummate his union. At the
ecstatic climax the King dies, torn to pieces and devoured in
the darkness. The Queen of the underworld is now impreg-
nated, and at the end of gestation, the king is reborn as a vir-
ile youth. New life flows through him and the kingdom's fertility
is restored; the new cycle progresses until at last, the king is
old, weary, and once more has to descend for renewal.

This process is one that we recognize as the seed of
renewal; somewhere in our life we are the barren king sur-
veying a wasteland. In the Grail myths, the king is Amfortas,
stricken by a genital wound, symbolic of his inability to seed
new life, and illustrates the misuse of his Scorpio power
through falling victim to temptation. His healing came from
the touch of Parsifal's spear made holy by his transformative
trials.

Scorpio introduces us to the way of the disciple, the
warrior who gains strength and healing by embracing the dark
side of himself and humanity. His conversion comes from his
intense unyielding nature, dedicated to fulfilling his purpose and destiny. Scorpio's challenge is to attain self-sover-

eignty, to consciously direct his fate and to rule his stars by mastering his scorpion-self and soaring on eagle wings to see the greater vision from the higher elevation. The purgatory of inner division stirs him to return in repentance like the Prodigal Son, crossing the battleground of separateness until insight awakens unifying and healing energies. From his higher altitude, new attitudes, values, and intentions form. He claims his spiritual legacy and opens his storehouse of hidden powers, previously invisible to all who were impure and profane. Returning with his treasure, his work now commences.

The 8th house should never be lightly dismissed or considered superficially; it is a gate of transformation available to everyone willing to follow the road to rebirth. Each one of us can become healers. We start with ourselves, salving our wounds in the underworld's fountain of life. We can then share our good fortune with others, helping society to heal its divisions and laying the foundations for a planetary rebirth. After all, astrology has not survived as an ancient teaching for centuries, only to be limited to trivial daily newspaper predictions; it is part of the great world wisdom tradition and can perform a much greater role in the *Magnum Opus*. In entering *The Gate of Rebirth*, every man and woman can discover his or her own mystery. The initiate's way is a solitary experience, even when there are many others sharing the same journey. We have to light our own light in the darkness; no one can do this for us. In how we choose to live our lives, individually and collectively, lies the response to this. The 8th house teaching is inner and outer right relationships. Choose wisely.

BIBLIOGRAPHY

Anand, Margo, *The Art of Sexual Ecstacy*. London: Aquarian Press, 1990.

Bailey, Alice, *Glamour: A World Problem*. New York and London: Lucis Press, 1971.

————. *The Labours of Hercules*. New York and London: Lucis Press, 1977.

————. *A Treatise on the Seven Rays*, 5 Volumes. New York and London: Lucis Press, 1971.

Blavatsky, H. P., *Isis Unveiled*, Vol. 1. Pasadena, CA: Theosophical University Press, 1972.

————. *Secret Doctrine*, Vol. 1. Pasadena, CA: Theosophical University Press, 1970.

Campbell, Joseph, *Hero with a Thousand Faces*. Princeton, NJ: Princeton University Press, 1990; London: Paladin, 1988.

Ferguson, Marilyn, *The Aquarian Conspiracy*. Los Angeles: J.P. Tarcher, 1981; London: Paladin, 1982.

Frankel, Viktor, *Man's Search for Meaning*. New York: Pocket Books, 1984; London: Hodder, 1987.

Haich, Elisabeth, *Sexual Energy and Yoga*. Santa Fe, NM: Aurora Press, 1982.

Hillman, James, *The Dream and the Underworld*. New York: Harper & Row, 1979.

James, Henry, *The Varieties of Religious Experience*. New York: Longmans, 1935.

Jung, Carl G., *Man and His Symbols*. New York: Dell, 1968; London: Picador, 1978.

―――. *Psychological Reflections*. Bollingen Series, Vol. 31. Princeton, NJ: Princeton University Press, 1970; London: Routledge & Kegan Paul, 1974.

Marks, Tracy, *Planetary Aspects*. Sebastapol, CA: CRCS, 1987.

Matthews, Caitlin & John, *The Western Way*, Vol. 2. London: Arkana, Viking Penguin, 1988.

Meyer, Michael, *A Handbook for the Humanistic Astrologer*. New York: Anchor Press, Doubleday, 1974.

Milton, John, *The Poems of John Milton*. New York and London: Oxford University Press, 1958.

Montaigne, M., *The Complete Essays of Montaigne*. Stanford, CA: Stanford University Press, 1965.

100 Great Books. John Canning, ed. London: Souvenir Press, 1974.

Raphael, Alice, *Goethe and the Philosopher's Stone*. London: Routledge & Kegan Paul, 1965.

Rubin, Jerry, *Growing (Up) at 37*. New York: M. Evans, 1976.

Rudhyar, Dane, *An Astrological Mandala: The Cycle of Transformation and its Symbolic Phases*. New York: Vintage Books, 1974.

―――. *The Astrological Houses*. New York: Doubleday, 1972.

―――. *The Astrology of Personality*. Santa Fe, NM: Aurora Press, 1991.

Sartre, Jean-Paul, *Nausea*. New York: Norton, New Directions, 1959; London: Penguin, 1990.

Sasportas, Howard, *The Twelve Houses*. London: Aquarian Press, 1985.

INDEX